The Impact of the Holocaust in America

The Jewish Role in American Life

An Annual Review

The Impact of the Holocaust in America

The Jewish Role in American Life

An Annual Review

Volume 6

Bruce Zuckerman, *Editor*
Zev Garber, *Guest Editor*
Jeremy Schoenberg, *Associate Editor*
Lisa Ansell, *Associate Editor*

Published by the Purdue University Press for
the USC Casden Institute for the Study of the
Jewish Role in American Life

© 2008 by the
University of Southern California
Casden Institute for the
Study of the Jewish Role in American Life.
All rights reserved.

Production Editor, Marilyn Lundberg

Cover photo:
Students—including Holocaust survivors—in an English language class pledge allegiance to the flag.
United States Holocaust Memorial Museum,
Courtesy of Hilda Wiener Rattner

ISBN 978-1-55753-534-4
ISSN 1934-7529

Published by Purdue University Press
West Lafayette, Indiana
www.thepress.purdue.edu
pupress@purdue.edu

Printed in the United States of America.

For subscription information,
call 1-800-247-6553

Contents

FOREWORD — vii

Beth Cohen — 1
From Case File to Testimony: Reconstructing Survivors' First Years in America

Michael Berenbaum — 31
in collaboration with Martin Goldman, Linda Hurwitz, Rositta Kenigsberg, Dale Daniels, Barbara Appelbaum, Noreen Brand and Miriam Klein Kassenoff
Survivors as Teachers

Steven Windmueller — 63
A Jewish Perspective on the Global Economic Revolution in a Post-Holocaust World

Richard Libowitz — 81
Bringing the Holocaust to America

Lawrence Baron — 103
Imagining the Shoah in American Third Generation Cinema

Peter J. Haas and Lee W. Haas — 119
Thou Shalt Teach It to Thy Children: What American Jewish Children's Literature Teaches about the Holocaust

Steven Leonard Jacobs — 139
The Impact of the Shoah on Jewish-Christian Relations

Marvin A. Sweeney — 159
Post-Shoah Theology and Jewish Biblical Interpretation in America

Zev Garber — 191
A Citadel Fitly Constructed: Philo-Semitism and the Making of an American Holocaust Conference

Marc A. Krell — 219
Association for Jewish Studies Conference, 2006: A Response

ABOUT THE CONTRIBUTORS — 225

ABOUT THE USC CASDEN INSTITUTE — 229

Foreword

In past volumes of the Casden *Annual Review*, the annual publication of the Casden Institute for the Study of the Jewish Role in American Life, the editors have always tried to cast as wide a net as possible. For example, in our immediately preceding volume (Volume 5), we published articles considering politics, values, art and image, education, and demographics as they impact upon Jewish culture in America and especially in the American west. Thus, the previous volumes of the *Annual Review* have always had a tendency to be both eclectic and comprehensive—with their aim being to consider a broad gamut of subjects relevant to the main concerns of the Casden Institute.

With this volume (Volume 6) we have decided to take a different editorial tack: to focus instead on a single topic and to present articles that largely consider aspects of this topic alone. The topic we have chosen is one that, on the one hand, may seem highly familiar, since it is a well-traveled and well-considered area of interest in Jewish studies; indeed arguably *the topic* in modern Jewish thought: the Holocaust or Shoah. On the other hand, our aim in this volume is to consider the Shoah from a perspective that has been largely unexplored in the literature and, not only that, is particularly appropriate to the Casden Institute's area of interest: namely, the impact of the Holocaust *in America*.

In order to pursue this topic in the most effective manner, I have invited Zev Garber, my long time friend, colleague and collaborator on numerous projects, to serve as guest editor for this volume. Zev has always shown an exceptional ability to put academic projects together in a number of scholarly areas relevant to Jewish studies with a creativity that is tempered with the best editorial judgment. I was confident that, with Zev in charge, we would bring into the *Annual Review* an interesting mix of articles that would allow us to explore this less familiar aspect of Shoah studies and make it come alive for us. As you will see, as you read the articles we present here, he has more than fulfilled this expectation.

Zev used the occasion of this volume to convene a special session at the Annual Conference of the Association for Jewish Studies on December 17–19, 2006 in San Diego, bringing together a group of outstanding scholars to present papers on the impact of the Shoah in America. The Casden Institute was proud to serve as a sponsor for this special session, which, by any measure, was a great success. Most of the articles that constitute Volume 6 of the *Annual Review* were originally read at this scholarly meeting. We have also included a short response to three of the studies that was given at the meeting by one of the participants. In many respects we have been able to follow the eclectic tendencies typical of earlier volumes while still maintaining a focus on our basic theme. Thus, articles herein consider topics such as the immigrant experience in coming to America after the trauma of the Holocaust; how the Shoah has shaped more recent interpretation of the Hebrew Bible; the role that survivors have fulfilled in educating American youth not only about the Holocaust itself, but also about how values—especially in regard to tolerance—can and must be shaped by eye-witness testimony on the Shoah; the impact of Holocaust in film, especially in "third-generation" cinema; the issues and difficulties of presenting the Shoah in children's literature; the dialogue between Christians and Jews, especially in America, and how that dialogue has been constructively influenced and shaped by the Holocaust; the way in which Jewish business activities have altered in the post-World War II environment and in the aftermath of the Holocaust, and how the lessons of the Shoah have facilitated the change from nationalist to global economy; how the image and awareness of the Holocaust developed in the American media. Yet for all the range that these articles encompass, throughout them all runs a common theme: that the Holocaust has indelibly marked almost every aspect of American culture. Indeed, we cannot think of America, American ideals and values, America's role in the world today and the future of America in an increasingly dangerous world, without recognizing that the Shoah casts a long shadow across all these concerns and serves as one of the primary points of horrific historical reference by which we, as Americans, must measure ourselves.

In any effort such as the Casden Institute's *Annual Review*, there are many people who have made this volume possible. Zev Garber and I, in our roles as editors, are grateful to them all. First among these is Alan Casden himself, who always keeps a close eye on the work we do on this volume, not only to insure that it maintains the highest standards of academic excellence, but that the articles are also relevant and understandable to readers beyond the scholarly community who care about Jewish culture in America. I also want to single out Ruth Ziegler, whose enthusiastic support of the Casden Institute has made so many aspects of our work possible, including this volume. She is the Casden Institute's best friend. We have also received solid support from the

Foreword

USC administration, especially the University's President, Steven B. Sample, the Provost, C. L. Max Nikias, and the Dean of the College of Letters, Arts & Sciences, Howard Gillman. Susan Wilcox, Director of Development for College Advancement, has been the one to whom I have often turned when I have an idea that needs careful thought and consideration. I can always rely upon her for a frank opinion and a telling insight, without which this volume would be much the poorer. Lisa Ansell, who came in over the last year as the new Associate Director of the Casden Institute, has devoted many, many hours to the careful reading of the articles in Volume 6. Her comments and edits have been invaluable—as indeed she has proven invaluable in shaping all aspects of the Casden Institute's development over the last year and a half. Marilyn Lundberg, my colleague in so many endeavors, has done her usual polished job on all aspects of the production of Volume 6.

Finally, I reserve the last word for the former Assistant Director of the Casden Institute, Jeremy Schoenberg. Jeremy, as the saying goes, was "kicked upstairs" last year and now works in the Provost's office at USC. But before he left the Casden Institute, he devoted invaluable time and energy to the editing of most every article that appears in Volume 6. His careful editorial work laid the foundation for this volume, and I will be grateful to him not only for this, but also for the many times he has aided me (and still continues to aid me) in fostering the growth of the Casden Institute. To him I would like to dedicate this volume.

Bruce Zuckerman, *Myron and Marian Casden Director*

From Case File to Testimony: Reconstructing Survivors' First Years in America

By Beth Cohen

INTRODUCTION

From 1946 through 1954, 140,000 refugees of the remnant of European Jewry settled in the United States.[1] Their numbers were surprisingly few. Eventually, however, they would be transformed from "refugees" to "Holocaust Survivors," and their impact on American life would be profound and far-reaching. Holocaust memorial museums would be built. Television programs and films would bring images of the Shoah to a wide audience. Video-testimony projects would document witnesses' accounts, and their stories would serve as moral compasses, pointing us in the direction of a more just and humane world.

But it was not always so. Immediately after World War II, the United States with its restrictive immigration laws—unchanged since the 1920s—and fixed quotas did not welcome these refugees. The United States government, while professing sympathy for the plight of displaced persons ("DPs," as they were called), hoped that they would go to Palestine.[2] Many American Jews for seemingly ideological reasons thought likewise. However, when Britain failed to lift the "White Paper," the Jewish quota for Palestine that limited the number of visas to Jews to 1,500 per month,[3] President Harry S. Truman issued a directive in December 1945 that allowed 39,681 war refugees to enter the United States. These refugees included 28,000 Jews. Eventually, Congress passed the first Displaced Persons Act in 1948, which permitted entry for 205,000 DPs of all nationalities and religions (Dinnerstein 38–71; Wyman 135–36; Genizi 29).

This legislation enabled the majority of those Jewish DPs destined for America to reach this country in the immediate postwar period.

From 1946 on, the media regularly captured the arrival of the newcomers in optimistic, emotional terms. This was due in part to the nation's upbeat postwar mood. Journalists also worked to counteract lingering antisemitic and nativist sentiments by evoking sympathy towards the rescued victims of Hitlerism. Typical was one *New York Times* reporter who described a Jewish DP's first moments on American soil. As he "stepped on the gangplank under a gray afternoon sky, a free man on the last bridge to the country of his choosing, and walked on to the bunting-draped pier at Canal Street, he gripped his son's shoulder and his face streamed with tears of happiness. He kept murmuring in Yiddish: 'We are here . . . Now I believe we are here' " (Samuels, "DP Chief Arrives in Land of Choice").

Arrival was one hurdle for these Jewish refugees; facing the future in a new country was quite another: "How would they fit into American life?" wrote the same journalist about the newcomers' concerns. "What would their contribution be? Above all, would Americans accept them—into their homes, their communities, and their hearts?" (Samuels, "DP's in America" 12). The author was pleased to state that the newcomers' fears were completely unfounded; help was forthcoming, and their adjustment was quite simply "miraculous" (Samuels, "DP's in America" 12).

Other accounts similarly emphasized the speed with which the Jewish refugees became model citizens and blended easily into the fabric of American life. One such story described a group of seven outstanding students who were receiving high school diplomas. A nineteen-year-old in the group "spoke of his hopes for a career as a chemical engineer. His cheer," noted the author, "seemed genuine; his ambition blotted out the horrors of concentration camps" (Kaplan 6). These descriptions portrayed America as the land of redemption, emphasizing challenges overcome, stellar academic success, and social acceptance.

If we were to look only at these media accounts, especially given the public perception of survivors today, we would have the impression that survivors' paths toward their new lives in America were smooth, their reception by the society warm and welcoming. But was this the actual experience for those who lived it? In fact, survivors often tell a different, more complex and troubling story.[4] In oral histories and interviews, they speak of the excruciatingly difficult period of adjustment, sometimes extending for years. They recall their outright rejection by American Jews and even by their own relatives. They remember the message they received in no uncertain terms: forget about the past, keep

From Case File to Testimony 3

quiet about horrific wartime experiences and just move forward. It is this gap in perceptions that interests me and has provoked me to raise some of the very same questions posed by the *New York Times* journalist about survivors of the Shoah of nearly sixty years ago: How did they *really* fit into American life? Above all, how did Americans *actually* accept them—into their homes, their communities, and their hearts? To this one can add: Who helped them? What kind of assistance did they receive? How did the survivors perceive the nature of the help they were offered?

That survivors settled in almost every one of the United States would seem to suggest that they were widely accepted and supported,[5] but statistics, like the media accounts, tell only a partial story. What I wondered was what truly lay beneath the so commonly depicted shimmering images of hopeful new Americans? As I searched agency records, listened to and conducted oral histories, and scrutinized contemporary media accounts, my goal took shape: to return to the time before DPs had been turned into "Survivors" with a capital "S" in the eyes of the public, to peel away the outer layers of media hyperbole and sentimentality and capture that period in a more historically authentic way.

Fortunately, just as I began my research I happened upon a collection of case files written by social workers at the Jewish Family and Children's Services in Denver, Colorado. These reports included the majority of survivors who settled in Denver during the years 1946–54. When I realized that such records existed for Denver, I set out to learn if the same was true for New York. Nearly sixty percent of survivors settled in New York City, and their perspectives would be key to my analysis. Further research revealed that the New York Association for New Americans (NYANA), a Jewish agency created in 1949 to work with refugees in New York City, still exists today. Did they have early survivor case files and might I use them? I asked NYANA and am grateful for their positive response to both my questions.

Thus far I have analyzed over 350 case files, which have become the starting point of my study. Unmediated by time or by our current iconic perception of survivors, they provide a clearer window into the world of refugees, DPs, *greeners* (the Yiddish expression for newcomers) in the immediate aftermath of the Holocaust and depict a universe that is parallel to, but vastly different from, the unfailingly upbeat images that appeared in the contemporary media. In addition to the case files, I analyzed agency documents, conducted scores of interviews, and scrutinized video testimonies made by survivors as well as agency workers. These tools helped throw a bright light on the years 1946–54, which enabled me to pull apart and then resynthesize the multiple strands of a more complex and darker story.

Survivors' first years in the United States is the focus of this paper, and my aim is to outline some of my key findings from my study. As I have endeavored to reconstruct this period, I have also grappled with issues evoked by these unique materials. I will, therefore, also explore the usefulness of this evidence, comparing period records, such as case files, with oral histories recorded some fifty years later.

JEWISH POSTWAR REFUGEE AGENCIES

While the case files give an inside view of the daily treatment of the refugees, they must be understood in the greater context of Jewish communal assistance to the newcomers. The Jewish community's commitment to helping its own is deeply ingrained, which was apparent in its institutional postwar response to the DPs. This was especially so when it became increasingly clear that Great Britain was not going to readily permit unrestricted immigration to Palestine. America, whether the Zionists liked it or not, would have to become a viable option. In order to encourage Truman to increase the number of DPs allowed to enter the country, Jewish leaders committed themselves to supporting their European brethren once they arrived in the United States, and Jewish organizations even provided affidavits to those who had no American relatives to sponsor them. Until then, it had fallen to the immigrant's family to see that the newcomer would not become a public charge. Now the greater Jewish community decided to help shoulder this burden.[6]

Jewish leaders created a new agency to fulfill this mission. On August 1, 1946, the National Refugee Service merged with the National Council of Jewish Women's Service to Foreign Born to create the United Service for New Americans (USNA).[7] While—intentionally—there was nothing in its name to suggest it, USNA was strictly a Jewish agency funded by the United Jewish Appeal. Its goal was to work with the Joint Distribution Committee in Europe and with local cooperating Jewish communal agencies around the United States, such as the Jewish Family and Children Services in Denver, to facilitate the resettlement of refugees throughout the nation.

USNA encompassed a substantial bureaucracy, including a board of directors, an executive assistant director and numerous departments staffed by an army of workers. In 1946, as Truman's directive brought the first survivors to America, the machinery of the new organization was poised for action. The agency was divided into two branches of service: national and local. Its national arm included the following departments: Migration Services, Location Services, Corporate Affidavit Reporting Unit, Naturalization and Americanization Service, Port and Dock Department, National Reception Center, National Settlement Services, and European Jewish Children's Aid (EJCA). Its local division for refugees in New York and Long Island included Family Services, Religious Functionary Division (RFD), Vocational Service Department, and Business and Loan Services Division. USNA was thus a multi-service agency that supervised every aspect of resettlement, from port and dock reception to naturalization advice.

While scenes of emotional reunions between long-lost families were often showcased in the press, many DPs had no one to greet them when they disembarked in America. Molly and Heinz Sandelowski arrived in New York in late November 1947. They were among the quota of German Jews to benefit from the Truman Directive.[8] Molly remembered the first moments after she, her husband, and baby daughter disembarked: "We were outside on the pier with our baggage. We were very lonely because so many had friends or relatives who greeted them. We were sitting there with nobody to meet us" (Sandelowsky). This job fell to USNA's Port and Dock Department. Agency staff, and volunteers delivered those who were going elsewhere to their connecting trains, while those staying in New York went to designated reception centers.

Although the stay at a reception center was temporary, refugees could remain there for weeks, even months, while they searched for housing in New York's tight postwar housing market. Although the centers were more often scenes of confusion and chaos rather than models of orderliness, USNA's publicity department frequently used these centers as showcases enlisted to inform the public about the newcomers. In 1947, for example, USNA sponsored a Thanksgiving dinner at one shelter, and staff instructed children to dress in Thanksgiving garb. A photo capturing the moment appeared with the headline "Modern-day Pilgrims Happy" in the *New York Daily Sun* (Faulk). The subtitle of the article, "Beginning of Americanization of D.P.'s [sic] in Local Shelters Finds All Thankful," set the tone for the popular image of the DPs as well on their way to becoming "ordinary Americans."

Newly ensconced in the reception centers, the immigrants met with caseworkers from the Family Service Department (FSD), but the FSD was initially ill-prepared to handle even the small number of DPs allowed into the United States by the Truman Directive. In its first year of existence, the FSD's relief load grew from forty-eight to three thousand families, and the agency soon found that it could not keep up (White 211). At a time when immediate help was crucial, refugees usually had to wait from five to six weeks for initial contact with USNA (White 79). Disappointed, some refugees made their own plans because they felt that they could not rely on the agency.

USNA realized that it needed to respond to this challenge quickly. By the end of 1947, the staff grew to more than six hundred, including 173 working for the national program and 229 aiding those in New York (this disparity reflects the greater numbers of DPs staying in the city), and the clerical staff to support this expanding bureaucracy jumped to 203. The budget ballooned as well, from approximately a third of a million dollars per month in early 1947 to almost one million dollars per month by the year's end (White 79). With a total budget for 1947 of $9,153,500, USNA could boast that it was the second largest voluntary social service agency in the country, topped only by the Red Cross.

By 1948, USNA recognized a simmering tension: it could no longer function as both a national and local agency, as the majority of newcomers wished to—and did—settle in New York City. To address this problem, USNA created the New York Association for New Americans in 1949. As with USNA, the Family Service Department was its largest division and the source of many of the case files in this analysis. Its caseworkers assessed the newcomers' needs and met with them until they were self-supporting. Based on my analysis of the files, it is clear that the agency's social workers had tremendous control and influence over the refugees' lives. They referred the DPs to the Vocational Service Department, to doctors, and to the Religious Functionary Department; they also determined the amount and extent of relief in each given instance.

What becomes immediately clear from my research is the agency and its sub-agencies' focus on employment. The main goal was to help DPs find employment as quickly as possible and enable them to join the ranks of productive American citizens. By its own accounts, USNA and its affiliates believed they were doing an exceptional job. USNA President A. Rosenberg called it "an era of magnificent achievement" (4). An article in the *New York Times* in September 1952 quoted from a recent USNA report: "More than three-quarters of the Jewish refugees who arrived in this country on the first displaced persons ship after World War II have become American citizens and almost all are leading happy and productive lives." It went on to note that "within three months after arrival 89 per cent [sic] of the employable newcomers had jobs although not every one [sic] was able to find employment at his highest skill level or in his profession" ("U.S. Citizenship" 9).

From Case File to Testimony 7

The agency's assistance, however, was not the only reason for DPs' success in gaining employment. Another less sympathetic possibility underlies the results. While Vocational Service Departments, both in New York and elsewhere, were extensive and included vocational counseling, job-finding services, educational counseling to assess applicants' abilities, and supervision of training plans, their services were not unlimited. Several months after thousands of DPs began to arrive in New York City, NYANA revised its mandate. While previously the NYANA had promised to help to DPs for up to five years, it trimmed back this commitment by initiating its "8-4" policy, which limited agency assistance to just one year. That meant that DPs had to seek work using whatever resources they could find outside of these more official channels.

THE CASE FILES
Contrary to media reports and USNA's declarations of success, the case files illustrate a less than salutary picture of agency assistance and, along with it, a less than happy vision of refugees' adjustment in the aftermath of the Holocaust. Mr. and Mrs. G, twenty-nine and twenty-three years old, respectively, arrived in New York City on April 26, 1949, with their twenty-month-old twin boys. Sponsored by Mr. G's brother-in-law, they turned to NYANA for help when their relative could or would no longer assist them. The family needed funds for an apartment, clothing and furniture. In addition, there were medical bills: the twins had urinary tract infections that required a doctor's attention. The agency worker who met with the family believed that Mr. G felt burdened by his current situation; nevertheless, she noted, "He gave the impression, however, that he was able to take hold and follow through with help from the agency" (Case File 320-49).

For the next year, the G family met with representatives from NYANA, who documented their frequent meetings in the case files. These notes chronicle Mr. G's attempts to find work—at any unskilled job—and the constant rejections of his applications for employment. NYANA's Vocational Service Department's help was also enlisted to no avail. The VSD counselor noted that Mr. G "had very poor qualifications at that time." Perhaps his unprepossessing appearance was a disadvantage, too. The caseworker wrote: "He is a very slight man who wears glasses and always wears a hat. He has a small stubble which indicates that he does not shave closely. Mr. G has a very very meek appearance and a very meek way of speaking" (Case File 320-49).

Mr. G explained to his social worker that he tried to find a spot at a fruit store but the employer had no place for him. The agency felt he was not making "a real effort on his part." Finally, Mr. G secured work at a laundry but was too weak to handle the rigors of the work, and, as result, the establishment let him go. An undershirt factory in Brooklyn next employed him; but it was a poor season, and he was soon laid off. Mr. G then found a position cutting and delivering chickens at a kosher butchershop in Brooklyn, but the shop owner pronounced him too slow for the job. In the meantime, the twins were beset with constant health issues. Finally, three weeks after Mr. G began working as a delivery boy, he returned to NYANA to report that business was not good and that they also had to let him go. By then, it was mid-January and the clock was ticking. In another four months, under the "8-4" policy, NYANA would terminate its aid to the family. Mr. G suggested that his wife, who was an experienced seamstress, find work, and the caseworker agreed that this was a feasible plan. Mrs. G would seek employment, and in her stead Mr. G would care for the babies at home. Several weeks later, however, Mrs. G was hospitalized with heart problems and a hand infection. She was unable to work, and Mr. G was unable to look for employment because of the children. Things began looking up slightly a few weeks later when Mr. G found a training job in machine diamond cutting: After twelve weeks of training, he would earn a minimum salary as a diamond cutter. Although the VSD was skeptical, Mr. G was excited about the future potential of the training, and the VSD approved the continuation of Mr. G's subsistence allowance through the end of the training period. Eventually, Mr. G completed the apprenticeship and began earning twenty dollars per week.[9] On May 25, 1950, NYANA terminated financial aid to the G family as its "8-4" policy mandated. Mr. G expressed concern over his meager income, and the caseworker explained about welfare and the Brownsville branch of the Department of Welfare where Mr. G might report. After that, as far as the NYANA was concerned, the G family was on its own.

In another example, the H family arrived in New York City in June 1949, just two months after Mr. and Mrs. G. Like the adult members of the G family, Mr. H agonized over finding work within the limits of NYANA's "8-4" policy. He was a forty-eight-year-old widower with three teenage children: two sons, nineteen and fifteen, and a seventeen-year-old daughter. A shoemaker by trade, he had worked for a short time after arriving but lost his job during the slack season.

Mr. H approached NYANA when he was laid off and his sister-in-law, the refugees' sponsor, could no longer help the H family. She told the caseworker that "she had been supporting the H family for about 10 weeks and that she had absolutely reached the end of her resources . . . she has 3 children of her own to support and her husband is a clothing operator and works on a piece basis" (Case File 323-49). Mr. H wanted nothing more than to work and support his family on his own. He confided to the caseworker that "at one time in his life he had earned a good deal of money and had been able to take care of his family satisfactory [sic]. It was hard for him now not to give the children the things they need, and to see them in want and in need of so much" (Case File 323-49).

Try as he might, Mr. H could not find steady work. Like Mr. and Mrs. G, he was beset by various illnesses, which necessitated frequent visits to the doctor's office. Even when he regained his health, there were simply no jobs to be had for a nearly fifty-year-old immigrant who had few skills and spoke little English. The economic climate, too, played a role. The garment industry in New York was slow to recover after the war, and this affected Mr. H and many other DPs who were drawn to and had connections in the trade.

Since choices were few, Mr. H decided that his eighteen-year-old son must abandon plans to attend school and, instead, become the family's chief breadwinner. It pained the father to push his son to search for work, but he believed the family simply had no other choice. Unfortunately, the young man, who had studied auto mechanics, had no better luck than his father in securing employment. As the winter season descended, Mr. H appeared in NYANA's office with a request for warm clothing for his two youngest children. The caseworker noted, "Both children were very poorly clad wearing nothing but thin jackets and looked quite shabby" (Case File 323-49, Nov. 28, 1949). When asked if their sponsor, Mr. H's sister-in-law, might be of help in locating clothing, he commented that "the children have very little contact with their aunt because they are so busy with school activities, and the relationship there has not been very good." The sponsor's children, their American cousins, "have not been very kind to the H children" (Case File 323-49, Nov. 28, 1949).

Shortly before the end of his first year in America, Mr. H met with his caseworker to discuss "the family's movement towards independence in relation to their ending with the agency" (Case File 323-49, Nov. 28, 1949). Neither Mr. H nor his son was employed, but they would continue their efforts and the younger children would also seek summer jobs. The daughter was prepared to forego her return to high school in the fall, if she found work in the meantime. Still, they were concerned about the consequences if none were employed by the time they received their final relief check from NYANA. Again, the advice was the same as that given to the G family. They were directed to their district office of the Department of Welfare, and their relationship with NYANA was terminated.

In the situations of Mr. and Mrs. G and Mr. H and their respective children, we do not know what transpired after their cases were closed. Did they manage to find some kind, *any* kind, of work or did they turn to welfare once the Jewish agency and their relatives could no longer assist them? We do not know and can only imagine what lay ahead for them as they struggled to find a place for themselves in America.

While the NYANA files rarely report beyond the first year in the United States, they are a rich source of information about survivors' beginnings in this country. The circumstances of the G and H families are not unique. Rather, they exemplify recurring patterns and themes throughout the hundreds of files I scrutinized, highlighting several thorny questions: How can we reconcile the stories in the files with those in the postwar media? What do we learn about mismatched expectations, between the agencies and the refugees and between the refugees and the relatives who sponsored them? Were illness and despair, rather than strength and renewal, prevalent among survivors? Were these newcomers perceived as typical immigrants by the professionals charged with their care, or did the agencies see any of the aftereffects of the Holocaust on them?

As I probed these individual histories, a mosaic of survivors' postwar experience began to take shape—and the pattern was far from rosy. Granted, there were instances of those who fit the desired narrative of resilience, who found work quickly and had no need of assistance from either the Jewish agencies or from their relatives. For many, however, the economic path was bumpy, the emotional terrain treacherous, and the help they received disappointing.

Comforting as it would be to accept uncritically the cheerful stories that were highlighted on the radio and in the newspapers, the reception of European refugees by both the Jewish communal agencies and their American families ran the gamut—from solid support to outright rejection. Yes, there were those citizens who met their kin at the dock and gave them a place to sleep and food to eat. But the opposite extreme is also in evidence. While others supplied affidavits assuring one and all that they would offer proper custodial care to their immigrating relatives, they, nonetheless, relinquished responsibility even while their relatives were en route to the United States (Case File Report, Box 9, File 1943). The overall pattern that emerges from the files, however, shows that relatives were willing to offer limited help to DPs at first, but that support often dried up after some weeks. NYANA's and the Denver JFCS's records are full of such examples. Consider, for example, the B family of three, who "arrived in this country on June 6, 1949. They spent a short time with their relative and affiant, Mr. V, who was only able to provide housing for them for a short time"

(Case File 306-49 8), or the sponsor who told the NYANA worker "his help to the G family is very limited . . . as far as financial assistance was concerned there was none she could give" (Case File 320-49 5), or the relative who could no longer help because "her financial situation was very bad" (Case File 323-49 1).

Financial help was one expectation, and emotional support another. Newcomers, by and large, accepted the fact that, despite sponsors' promises, they could not count on the financial backing of their relatives. When it came to emotional support or lack of it, however, the refugees voiced their feelings unequivocally. Mr. T, reported one social worker, "made it pretty clear from the beginning that he was still smarting from the experience he had with his relatives during the eight week period he had stayed there. . . . They had promised that he would be able to remain with them until housing was available, and now they were telling him that he had to leave" (Case File 327-49 1). One young couple spoke of their disappointment when they were not invited to their relative's Passover Seder (Case File 361-50). A young woman remembered her wealthy uncle, who sponsored her but did not ask her, a lone newcomer, to his home until months after her arrival. Another woman recalled, with bitterness and bewilderment nearly fifty years later, the actions of her American family. Not only did the relatives fail to meet the woman and her family at the port, but they had deliberately avoided the meeting by heading off for a vacation in Florida several days before the refugees arrived. Upon their return from Florida, they expressed dismay that the newcomers were still expecting to see them and still expecting help (RG 50_549, 02*00).

Refugees may have expected help from family in order to get established in their first job, but often this assistance, too, did not materialize. As a result, survivors turned to the refugee agencies and their Vocational Services Departments along with other programs. What becomes absolutely clear from the case files is the centrality of employment to the agencies' goals. The agencies' primary agenda was to put the newcomers to work, since securing employment and financial independence was the yardstick by which the DPs were deemed successful. Try as they might, however, scores of newcomers could not find employment. Fighting the economic climate together with NYANA's one-year time limit proved to be a challenging combination. Added to this was the stunning number of cases in which illness (perhaps in as many as sixty percent, according to the files) was present, which wreaked havoc on both the agencies' goals and the individuals' hopes for the future.

What was the agencies' general perception of the newcomers? The types of services offered—limited financial assistance, vocational counseling, and

English lessons—suggest a fairly conventional attitude. That is, the agencies saw the DPs as typical immigrants and were very nearly blind to another dimension, the aftereffects of their Holocaust experiences. In scrutinizing the files, this absence of recognition of the connection to the recent past is glaring, as time after time the refugees make their needs pitifully apparent. One woman told her caseworker that she "suffers severe dizziness, heart palpitation, high blood pressure and a variety of anxieties" (RG 50_549, 02*00). She went further, describing how she "wakes in the middle of the night screaming and although she does not remember exactly what the dream was all about, she does know that she has very bad dreams and nightmare [sic]" (Case File 322-49). Her traumatic experiences plagued her waking life, as well. She feared the dark and subways and "occasionally, she suddenly gets the idea that they are about to be deported and worries about that for days at a time," her social worker noted (Case File 322-49). While she was most eager to work, her nightmares kept her awake for hours, and she had difficulty rousing herself in the morning (Case File 322-49). Others revealed a variety of symptoms. "Mr. H," wrote his social worker, "has been feeling ill. He said that in the past he had suffered from a stomach condition and this bothered him again now" (Case File 322-49, Sept. 21, 1949). But added to this was something new: "At the present time," continued the report, "he is suffering from constriction of the chest which makes it difficult for him to breathe and he feels choked up all the time." Mr. B simply stated two months after his arrival in August 1949 that he "is very nervous and upset since he is in the United States and has not been feeling well" (Case File 306-49).

    Mr. E, twenty-six years old, reported that he suffered from frequent headaches and stomach upsets, but a check-up "failed to disclose any specific ailment," and the prescribed medication did nothing to alleviate the pain (Case File 312-49). As he tried to find relief from his headaches, he also searched for employment to no avail. On a visit to the E family's lodgings, the social worker described their place as clean but "a typical slum apartment" (Case File 312-49, May 18, 1950). Mrs. E had just given birth to a third child and hardly had enough to feed her family. The young mother was desperate, and the year of NYANA's assistance was drawing to a close. Mrs. E told her caseworker "that the best thing for her would be to commit suicide" (Case File 312-49, May 18, 1950). As far as we know, Mrs. E did not end her life, but the weight of her situation and how it affected her is clear. Moreover, she is not the only Holocaust survivor to have contemplated or attempted suicide during the first years in America. One woman in Denver slashed her throat and wrists but survived, because, she believed, God wanted her to care for her only child (Case File Report, Box 9, File 1943). The case files and oral histories contain other examples of those who thought about, attempted, and, tragically, succeeded in ending their lives. Again, these voices shatter the optimistic images promulgated in the contemporary media, where no such reports are noted. The case files and testimonies contain many examples that challenge today's conventional image of the triumphant survivor, which the postwar press promoted. While it may be painful to acknowledge these battles that survivors fought after arriving in America, this is nonetheless essential, if we are to grasp in an authentic fashion, the experiences of survivors during this period.

In the course of my research, I occasionally discovered interagency communications that revealed long-term agency relationships with refugees extending beyond NYANA's one-year limit. Mrs. F and her thirteen-year-old son Herman (pseudonym), for example, immigrated to the United States in late 1949 and settled in Denver. Four years later, Herman decided to move to New York, and his mother followed him. In May 1951, the director of NYANA's Family Service Department wrote to Dr. Alfred Neumann, executive director of Jewish Family and Children's Services (JFCS), Denver, stating that Herman "became actively psychotic" and was admitted to a state mental hospital (Fitzdale). The FSD director continued: "Mrs. F is also in ill health and pending clarification of her medical status, is unable to work. In general," she added, "we anticipate this family will require our help on a long term basis" (Fitzdale). Included in the correspondence is their American relatives' statement that they were not in a position to assist the F family "in any way, shape or manner" (Mr. G).

The story of the F family was one of the few examples that documented an ongoing relationship between NYANA and newcomers. Since it was a rarity, I thought it important to turn elsewhere to supplement my findings and determine any patterns or conclusions. Because the JFCS in Denver had no "8-4" policy, I focused in particular on their records.

The JFCS's staff worked with refugees as part of their regular caseload, but there was no strict mandate for terminating service to their clients. Although the staff discussed the length of time of assistance with USNA and generally did not extend aid beyond one year, they continued to dispense help for a longer period when a case warranted it. Studying those refugees who had long-term relationships with these agencies offers a fuller picture of what the NYANA files already strongly hint at. For example, the JFCS worked with Mr. B and his family for six years (Case File Report, Box 9, File 1766B 4). Mr. B arrived in Denver after he was diagnosed with tuberculosis.[10] While he was at a sanitarium (the Jewish Consumptive Relief Society), he met a young woman, another DP, and they became lovers. When the woman became pregnant, the two married but then decided that they did not want to keep the baby. The husband was taking a training course, and his bride wanted to support him, which she did not feel she could do successfully while caring for a baby.

Despite her glowing descriptions of Jewish family life in Europe before the war, Mrs. B insisted on putting the baby up for adoption. However, the couple did change their minds after Mrs. B gave birth. She stated to her case worker that "she never dreamed that she would actually be able to come through a pregnancy and bear a live healthy child as she had done" (Case File Report, Box 9, File 1766B 4). Still, Mrs. B's change of heart was short-lived. When Mr. B refused to give up his training in order to support his new family, Mrs. B panicked and again asked the agency to place the baby boy with a family, stating that "she wished both she and the baby were dead" (Case File Report, Box 9, File 1766B 4). The JFCS obliged and the baby was placed with a foster family, but six months later, the parents decided to have their son come back to live with them. Unfortunately, they did not live happily ever after.

The B family was reunited, but each member functioned poorly: Mrs. B suffered from a serious heart condition as a result of her concentration camp experience; Mr. B collapsed at work because of his compromised health condition; as a result he had trouble holding onto a job. As for the boy, he was diagnosed with kidney disease; and, on top of that, mother and child were injured in an automobile accident. The couple's marriage was affected, and after three years, Mrs. B returned to relatives in Hartford while Mr. B remained in Denver. Seven months after his wife's departure, Mr. B reported that he wanted to leave Denver, although his destination was undecided. He disliked the weather in Connecticut and considered going to California, but he finally decided to join his wife and son. After nearly six years, the case in Denver was closed, and what became of this family is unknown (Case File Report, Box 9, File 1766B 4). What is clear, however, is that eight years after these refugees arrived, the Holocaust was still very much impacting their lives.

There were other instances in which families were actually torn apart due, in part, to the actions of the agencies involved—not because the agencies actually sought the dissolution of the families but because they perceived that there was no other choice or way to support the families' needs. Mr. and Mrs. D, for example, turned to the JFCS when Chaim (pseudonym), their twelve-year-old son, ran away from Denver (Case File Report, I-065 record group).

He managed to get as far as New York, where he was found staying at a public welfare shelter. Chaim's father told the social worker about "the difficulty which he has had in Europe and in adjusting in this country and was able to say that he was impatient with the boy because of his own nervousness and unhappiness" (Case File Report, I-065 record group). He further noted that surviving the war in hiding had been brutal, and the murder of their daughter even more devastating; after one and a half years in the United States, the family's struggles were hardly over.

For a short time after his return to the family, Chaim was a model of good behavior, attending both school and appointments with his social worker assiduously. Once again, however, the story did not end there. When the youth began to withdraw from his parents and began to stay away from home—sometimes overnight—the couple returned to the agency for guidance. This time a psychological evaluation was initiated. Chaim "is neither psychotic or neurotic," the psychiatrist wrote, "but . . . this is a simple behavior and [sic] disorder" (Case File Report, I-065 record group). The parents were at their wits' end. Simple, orthodox people who spoke little English, they seemed adrift in their new home and puzzled over the agency's explanation of their son's hostile behavior. The agency did suggest a solution: give the JFCS custody of the boy, after which he would be sent to Bellefaire, a detention center in Cleveland (Case File Report, I-065 record group). The parents agreed, but the decision was taken with great reluctance. "Having survived, which in itself to them constitutes a miracle," the social worker reported, "it seems particularly tragic to them now that they have to be separated when an opportunity finally presents itself for them to live together normally as a family" (Case File Report, I-065 record group). Chaim spent nearly three years at Bellefaire; the reports about his progress there and his visits home were mixed. He finally returned to live with his parents in 1953 and planned to finish high school. Whether or not he did is an open question: the parents refused to continue working with the JFCS, and the case was closed (Case File Report, I-065 record group).

That the D family's wartime experiences had a profound impact on their lives in America seems obvious, yet what happened during the Holocaust seems to have had little bearing on the agency's approach to them. One children's worker did appear to recognize the aftereffects of the trauma that the D family had endured and responded with sensitivity, but unfortunately her contact with Chaim was brief. This, at least, shows that such an approach could potentially yield positive results.[11]

These examples, like it or not, point to a harsh reality that survivors had to face after the war. They reveal struggles and heartaches rather than a consistent picture of triumphs and successes. They fill in the gaps between the optimism displayed publicly and the reality of life for postwar immigrants who were also survivors of genocide. They highlight the conflicts, the mismatched expectations and the disappointments, as survivors, burdened by a traumatic past, stumbled forward towards an uncertain future.

What lay ahead for survivors is no longer unknown. Thanks to the plethora of oral history and video testimony projects, it is now possible to learn more about survivors' postwar experiences in their own words. This, too, is illuminating. Later video recordings allow us to understand better a survivor's early years in the context of a lifetime. Having differing oral history formats stimulates us to compare sources, such as the early case files and later video testimonies, and to explore the value of each for historians. Various methodologies also permit us to explore the evolving historiography of recording survivors' oral histories and raise questions about the effective application of these oral histories for reconstructing survivors' early years in the United States.

The case files I analyzed were invaluable to this reconstruction. From the examples I have given, it is clear that they conjure up a vivid picture, away from the public eye, of the newcomers' first experiences in the United States. Through the prism of day-to-day interactions between the newcomers and those who were officially supposed to help them, a much more nuanced picture is revealed. These unedited and uncensored reports transcend their original intent, and become, instead, a paper excavation. The case files transport us back to the 1940s and 1950s and force us to see survivors as DPs, refugees, and newcomers. In the process of piecing together another life in America, all of the cracks and disagreements, illnesses, vulnerabilities, hardships, and successes are glaringly and unsparingly documented. The files display the subjective and selective viewpoints of the case workers, the information included or omitted left to the discretion of the recorder and determined by the time he/she invested, his/her personality, and agency standards. All of these elements are there (or not there) in one form or another. Because I wanted, in particular, to focus on the grey areas, nuances of attitude, perception, and sensitivity that are key to the story, the case workers' unconscious subjectivity served this study well. However, one must be exceedingly careful to place these records in proper context. What might seem agonizingly heartless and insensitive when viewed through a twenty-first century lens appears to have been the norm sixty years earlier. That is why it is essential not only to explore the broader historical context of twentieth century social work as I did through contemporary mental health journals but also to be mindful of recurring themes through careful analysis of hundreds of files. Had I only seen a few, their validity as "ordinary" examples could rightly be called into question. But through the study of many, I have been able to establish patterns that ultimately have coalesced into a portrait more fragile than the public image of resilience and strength typically presented.

At times, the case files reveal a great deal by implication—by what they *do not* say. For example, they do not directly address the refugees' Holocaust experiences, a silence that speaks volumes about the social workers' and the public's attitude towards hearing about the then recent destruction of European Jewry. The emphasis on "moving on" for survivors was clearly the standard expectation, but any effort to do so was necessarily handicapped by the burden of Holocaust memory. The shadow of the Shoah was so obviously present in the newcomers' lives yet glaringly absent, by and large, in the explicit agenda of the social workers. They did not choose to make connections between survivors' illnesses and recent experiences nor did they encourage survivors to speak about them. Their goal was to move refugees off relief and into the work force. If their clients brought up their wartime experiences, agency workers downplayed or dismissed them. Social workers described those who insisted on talking about such things as "neurotic" or "obsessed with their past." The dominant attitude always emphasized the need not only to move forward but also to forget.

As my research progressed, I realized that I would have to draw upon other sources such as oral histories and video testimonies to confirm my conclusions. How did more recent narratives of survivors triumphantly returning to life mesh with the stunning number of those consumed by illness and despair? Did these issues fade with time? Was America as deaf to survivors' needs as the files suggested? How did their experiences as newcomers bear upon the commonly held notion that survivors refused to talk about their experiences until much, much later in their lives? The process of examining both early files and later survivor interviews and testimonies answers some of these questions and also reveals a great deal about the postwar relationship of America to the Holocaust. In the search for sources to broaden and deepen my study, this broader issue was given sharper relief as well.

If this deafness towards survivors characterized mid-twentieth century America, a crusade to preserve eyewitness accounts describes the end of the century. As the murder of European Jewry became sanctified as "the Holocaust," and refugees were transformed into "survivors,"[12] interest in recording their stories before it was too late came to be recognized as essential. By the late 1980s, national Holocaust centers dotted the American landscape, and inevitably there were also local initiatives to document eyewitness accounts of survivors within smaller more distinct communities.[13]

Yaffa Eliach,[14] survivor and professor at Brooklyn College, and her colleagues in New York were among the first to begin recording survivors' stories in the early 1970s (Gurewitsch).[15] They interpreted "oral history" literally. The term defined both the audio-taped format and the content of this effort, whose founders believed there were gaps in written documentation that could only be filled in on the basis of individual eyewitness accounts (Eliach and Gurewitsch 67). Specific survivors were identified with this purpose in mind. The intent of the interview was to elicit a factually accurate oral history, as densely detailed as possible. That this mode of inquiry was termed "oral history" as compared to later designations of "video testimony" is key to understanding the historiography of recording survivors' experiences. In the early oral history projects, the term reflects the philosophy of the day: the basic assumption was that the material gathered could and would serve as a reliable source of history, recorded by trained historians, transcribed, and subject to intense cross-referencing and verification of facts. If any aspect of the tape did not meet the rigorous standards, it was deemed worthless and then discounted and discarded (Johnson and Strom 288).

The early oral history efforts focused on specific wartime experiences and, to a lesser degree, prewar experiences. This is important, too, because it highlights what was considered central and what was deemed less important for the documentation of the Holocaust in the early 1970s. Holocaust studies, in general, and oral histories, in particular, were new and had yet to gain wide legitimacy. Certainly, the reception of survivors in America was largely outside the focus of scholars at that time. In contrast, these earlier efforts can serve as a baseline that allow us to track how the recording of survivor testimony subsequently evolved into something quite different.

In 1978, a group in New Haven launched the Holocaust Survivors' Film Project.[16] By 1981, the project had collected two hundred testimonies, the tapes of which launched the Fortunoff Video Archives for Holocaust Testimonies at Yale in 1982. Its aim was "the collection and preservation for educational use of eyewitness accounts of the Holocaust" (Hartman xxv). The Yale model was a complete departure from the methodology of the earlier audio interviews. "Instead of statistics and data," noted Yale professor and archive founder Geoffrey Hartman, "the testimonies provide living portraits and are the nearest we will come to the actual experiences and thoughts of eyewitnesses" (xxvi). The new approach, developed with the input of Hartman and other survivors, was founded on the use of an unstructured interview. The interviewers (they used two) were trained to remain passively in the background. Their role was to facilitate but not to lead, allowing the survivor to shape and drive the interview. No longer did the historian dictate the framework and scope of the interview for the purpose of supplementing the historical record. Rather, the voice of the survivor took precedence.

Just as this approach was cutting-edge, so was the technology. Survivor-driven narratives were preserved on videotape, in a studio, and this gave new status to the survivor. Now, the visual element became a key part of the record, and body language became an integral aspect of the testimony: facial expressions, tears, sighs, and other body language, and silences were registered and shared with the audience. This soon set the standard for oral history projects.

As public interest in the Holocaust and its survivors exploded in the 1980s, so did the number of video testimony projects. All over the United States, from San Francisco to Providence, Rhode Island, Holocaust centers sprang up and inevitably grassroots oral history followed, designed to preserve the stories of survivors in their communities.[17] Some local initiatives trained their interviewers, while others turned to established projects such as Yale's for guidance.[18] Often the recording of testimonies was a community effort, in which individual, local institutions relied on volunteer interviewers.

One of these local initiatives of the 1980s was located in the Cleveland, Ohio, branch of the National Council of Jewish Women (NCJW), which videotaped willing survivors in that city.[19] This collection added to my study by providing a locale outside of New York and Denver in which to further explore survivors' perceptions of their first years in America. Understanding this period was not critical to Cleveland's project or others at that time, and the attention paid to the survivors' postwar life varied. Still, these interviews captured the beginning of survivors' reflections on their post-Shoah lives. To be sure, some interviewers concluded abruptly at liberation, while others encouraged a happy ending, urging the survivors to focus on their children and grandchildren, even if the survivor did not seem so inclined. Yet the viewing of many of these testimonies could still allow a researcher to recognize patterns of experience. Especially because the interviews did not emphasize postwar life, what the survivor felt was important enough to mention bespoke its significance.

Many of the experiences recorded by the Cleveland group resonated with those in the case files. The recollections of Mr. B, a Czech survivor, provide one example of the kind of welcome survivors received in their new communities. In 1984, thirty-five years after Mr. B arrived in Cleveland, he remembered that he "had a pretty rough time. I came with two dollars in my pocket." "Did you get help?" the interviewer asked. A flash of emotion flickered across Mr. B's face and disappeared. "I didn't get much help from the Jewish community," he recalled. People told him, "If you have it so hard, why don't you go back to Czechoslovakia" (RG-50.091*198). Another man responded to a similar query. "You asked the question, and I must be honest," he stated. His aunt sponsored him but "she had some girl for me to marry and was unhappy that I came with my fiancée. Because of that," he believed, "she didn't help me much" (RG-50.091*0005). One woman declared that she never wanted any charity or help. Nevertheless, she stayed briefly with her American relatives who sponsored her. On her first day in Ohio, the newcomer described the memory of her cousin dropping her off downtown, saying, " 'This is Cleveland'. That," the survivor declared, "was the end of the family relationship." These are a few of many oral histories that speak to the chilliness with which survivors were received by their American relatives and sponsors. Were there others who described warmth and hospitality? Definitely. One woman spoke about a man who helped her husband find a job and "was like a father to them" (RG-50.091*19, Tape 3). As with the NYANA files, there was a range in the quality of receptions, from genuine acts of caring to outright rejection. This video material enriched and confirmed my findings from the early postwar case file material.

 The guided interview format of the NCJW Cleveland effort, which followed a questionnaire, guaranteed that most interviewees would answer the same questions and produced structured interviews with chronological narratives. The majority of NCJW interviewers stayed a rigid course, which, at times, served my research well because it gave consistency to the interviews. At the end of the testimony, for example, interviewers were trained to ask how the Holocaust affected the survivor's life. There were those who spoke about their life's accomplishments with justifiable pride. For others, however, the answers were hardly upbeat, sometimes leaving the interviewer at a loss for words. One woman commented "Everything: mentally, physically . . . I mean I'm strong but . . . I have nightmares at night . . . it's terrible . . . I cannot go to sleep without a sleeping pill. And if I wouldn't take a sleeping pill," she continued, "I couldn't sleep." Nervously twisting her hands, she added, "I used to be on four Valium a day for over ten years" (RG-50.091*0019). One Auschwitz survivor talked about the struggle to regain her health in the United States. "I went from doctor to doctor," she recalled, because "from nerves I was choking—anything I ate I choked on" (RG-50.091*0004). One child survivor recalled her mother's battles with depression after they settled in Cleveland. "She didn't care about herself anymore," her daughter remembered. The doctors, she believed, did not know how to treat her mother's symptoms, which included palpitations and angina. They prescribed pills for depression as her health deteriorated. Her daughter was distraught and bewildered by her mother's downward spiral. "And I couldn't understand it." She remembered wondering, "why this was happening to her, why she couldn't fight the way she used to, why she couldn't dress the way she used to and be beautiful the way she used to." Instead, she stated, her mother "just resigned herself" (RG-50.091*0073). Again, these sources reinforce similar sentiments in the case files that belie the optimistic postwar narrative of resilience. Some spoke of broken lives; others described the ongoing effect of the Holocaust as they moved unsteadily forward in America. Certainly there are examples of smooth progress, too. As Lawrence Langer has argued in his analyses of Holocaust testimonies, we must unflinchingly confront the less than triumphant examples, rather than focus solely on a redemptive message, if we are to arrive at an authentic, more realistic and nuanced understanding of the postwar experience.

My analysis has also benefited from two other testimony projects that have allowed me to broaden and deepen my study. One is the United States Holocaust Memorial Museum's Postwar Testimony Collection and the other is the Survivors of the Shoah Visual History Foundation (now the USC Shoah Foundation Institute for Visual History and Education).[20] Steven Spielberg created the latter after making the film *Schindler's List* in 1994, the goal being to videotape survivors around the globe while there was still time to do so. It remains the most ambitious effort to collect survivor testimonies to date and, initially, the most controversial, particularly in the academic world, where some scholars looked suspiciously at an oral history project they feared would be tainted by Hollywood. As scholarly debate raged, the foundation pushed ahead and consulted with historians, oral historians, psychologists, and survivors. Regional offices were established in major cities in America, Canada, Europe, and elsewhere to coordinate interviews. The project attracted widespread interest and garnered an army of volunteer interviewers (all of whom were required to attend a three-day training session) and videographers. The results are impressive. The collection now comprises nearly 52,000 interviews from all over the world, including the United States, Europe, the former Soviet Union, and Israel, and is becoming progressively more accessible to researchers and educators as no other testimonies have ever been before.[21]

Unlike other such projects, the Shoah Foundation expressly trained its interviewers to devote twenty-five percent of the interview to life before the war, fifty percent to the Holocaust years, and twenty-five percent to what followed thereafter.[22] This was an important turning point in the evolution of eyewitness testimony, since it places the Holocaust in the context of a survivor's life span. It also, once again, reflects our society's perception of survivors and their accounts: these are "testimonies" rather than simply oral histories.

Of course, I have been particularly interested in what the final quarter of the Shoah Foundation interviews might reveal. Some, indeed, reverberated with my earlier findings. In one testimony, for example, a survivor of Auschwitz recalled her period of adjustment after settling in a town in South Carolina. Externally, her life appeared to be going well. She had three healthy children, a husband who was working and a home. Yet every day brought fresh reminders of her murdered family. One afternoon in the early 1950s, her husband invited some friends over for a visit. As the group sat talking, she slipped away to the bathroom and contemplated suicide—the woman wanted to slash her wrists. She did not do so, but realized she needed professional help and turned to a psychiatrist whom, she believed, significantly helped her (Interview 43565, 3:18:05).[23]

Another man spoke about his beginnings in America in 1947. He described, with bitterness, how "his people," American Jews, did not want to have anything to do with him and his wife after they settled in Providence, Rhode Island.[24] He suffered throughout his life from migraines and nightmares, but also managed to make a living and raise a beloved daughter. These accounts and others like them echo the struggles expressed earlier in the case files. Yet they go further because we see them in the context of an entire life—a life recreated after the Holocaust. This permits us to see accomplishments, some modest some spectacular, as well as the battles many continued to endure.

While some survivors spoke with candor, others were reluctant to have uncomfortable aspects of their lives scrutinized or preserved. For example, when I volunteered as an interviewer for the Shoah Foundation, several survivors confided, off the record, that they could not speak frankly or publicly about their American relatives. This is understandably sticky territory. While they were wounded by the treatment they received, nonetheless, they did not want these experiences recorded for posterity. Others did not want to appear ungrateful, especially now that they were invited to participate in the important task of telling their story.

Many participants in the Shoah Foundation's project viewed their testimonies primarily as their legacy to their children, grandchildren, and generations to come. In fact, many children of survivors encouraged their parents to tell their story for the family and for the future. This idea of testimony as legacy is reinforced by the solicitation of a message from the survivor at the end of the interview as the survivor's family members gather together to add their comments. Ending the interview in this way serves one of the project's appropriate purposes, that of undisputedly depicting 'Am Yisrael Chai (the Jewish people live on); still, this does not always encourage a frank appraisal of postwar life.

Testimonies that cover an entire life span, however, also raise another question. A survivor softening or suppressing details of the postwar years may speak to the passage of time, the quietude and perspective of old age, and the arrival of grandchildren rather than any conscious effort to efface earlier experiences. Or it may simply reflect that, in the retelling of Holocaust years, which is in fact the central piece of the interview, the postwar years have a diminished role. Nevertheless, while recognizing the irreplaceable value of these testimonies, a historian must still be conscious of the agenda and the inherent strengths and weaknesses of this—or any—oral history project in evaluating its testimonies' usefulness.

One project that expressly concentrates on the Holocaust's aftermath is the Postwar Testimonies Collection at the United States Holocaust Memorial Museum (USHMM).[25] Recorded as follow-up to the museum's Holocaust oral history project, these testimonies highlights survivors' lives in America after the war and are a fertile source of information about this period. Again, inspecting many interviews brings certain patterns to prominence and has allowed me to compare both theme and structure across sources. In contrast to other projects from the 1990s, this one utilized audiotapes only, which have then been transcribed. Working from the printed page is clearly a different experience than viewing video testimonies. As in earlier oral histories, the words are central. What is said is more important than how—or even who—is saying it. This methodology may also speak to the relative importance attached to the subject matter: Holocaust testimonies would seem to require video but postwar accounts can be handled in a more circumscribed fashion.

One theme that originates in the case files and reverberates through the USHMM's postwar collection is how much survivors needed to speak about the Holocaust, even in its immediate aftermath. Few Americans, however, were prepared to listen. One man remembered that before his mother was sent to Belzec (a death camp in Poland), she admonished him to "tell the whole world what the German murderers did to us!" Because of this, he stated: "I started to tell, even in the beginning people didn't want to listen. But I spoke, and they thought I have an obsession. Some people didn't like it. Later, twenty years later, people started to realize and they listened. . . . But I started to speak the first minute I left Poland, and I told the stories. And people thought that it is something wrong with me" (RG 50_549, 03*0004).

Quite a few others confirmed both their desire to speak and the icy response they received. Some attributed this to a lack of understanding; others recalled a response of disbelief. A survivor of seven concentration and labor camps recollected that after the war "some of them didn't believe. Others say well, what's the big deal, a lot of people had trouble, Irish and Dutch, why I had to make a blow up about it" (RG 50_549, 02*0070). Another woman resented it when people asked, "Why didn't you fight back?" (RG 50_549, 02*0117). One man noted that the Holocaust "was a taboo subject. They didn't want to know, they didn't want to face it," he explained (RG 50, 233*0073). One woman simply stated: "They never were interested" (RG 50_549, 02*0026, 33).

On the other hand, some were not ready to speak. Said one man about his American relatives, "They did not want to know too much, and I was not ready to reveal myself. I, I didn't feel like exposing myself" (RG 50_549, 02*0064). Still, when many did in fact try to speak, they found that the outside world did not really want to listen. Beginning in the early case files and continuing through several oral history collections, over and over survivors shatter the myth of their postwar silence.

CONCLUSION

The gap between the optimistic public images of refugees and the accounts I discovered in the postwar case files of the Jewish communal agencies prompted this study. Using a range of sources to reconstruct the postwar experience of survivors' early years in America, I found that a complex picture emerges. It divulges a range of experiences that challenge the notion of a resilient return to life and highlight many unsteady journeys fraught with a myriad of challenges.

In order to explore this mosaic of experience further, I also studied hundreds of orals histories from the 1980s through the 1990s. This enabled me to follow the trajectory of survivors' lives and test my earlier findings. It also permitted me to compare the usefulness of these sources in light of the historiography of oral history from the 1970s through our day.

Oral histories—such as those from Cleveland, the USC Shoah Foundation for Visual History and the USHMM Postwar Collection—immeasurably enriched my analysis of survivors' postwar experiences and confirm my findings. There are, however, drawbacks to using such sources, as well. All oral history and video testimony projects have their own missions and goals, which become evident in all of the recordings I examined. Combined with other factors, such as the nature and degree of interviewer training, interviewer style, and survivor eloquence and candor, these recorded interviews have all yielded a spectrum of useful results that nonetheless need to be carefully and critically examined as research tools.

The metamorphosis of oral history into video testimony also raises challenges for research. The early recordings (oral histories) were driven by a desire to expand the historical record, but as the years passed, preserving eyewitness accounts (testimonies) while there was still an opportunity to do so took precedence. The notion that "time was running out" has motivated many video testimony projects. The goal to capture so many stories has served important needs for survivors and families, and yielded thousands of video testimonies that reflect a range of academic value to which researchers must be especially sensitive.

Holocaust historian Christopher Browning uses the term "collected memories" to refer not to a collective retrospective memory of the Holocaust but to survivors' individual accounts of the Holocaust taken together. "How may a historian of the Holocaust use a variety of different, often conflicting and contradictory, in some cases clearly mistaken, memories and testimonies of individual survivors as evidence to construct a history that otherwise, for lack of evidence, would not exist (39)? Browning argues that historians must use a subjective source such as testimony with care and be conscious of the inherent pitfalls as well as advantages.

Browning's concerns about the proper use of "collected memories" must be applied to the study of the postwar experience. Similarly, one must approach case files and oral histories with a discerning and critical eye. Indeed, this has always been the task of the historian: to gain critical perspective using any and all records available. To be sure, there are always potential stumbling blocks. In the case of this study, one must recognize that records and testimonies, such as those outlined above, are the elements of history; still, they cannot be accepted without careful scrutiny and analysis as history themselves. By critically weaving a multiplicity of sources together, one may endeavor to create a tapestry of depth and richness. Perhaps we should not be surprised that the picture that results is more complex and darker than some might have wished or expected it to be. Still, this more nuanced view does honor to those who endured the Holocaust and illuminates their first years in America.

Notes

1. This figure is based on statistics in Dinnerstein, *America and the Survivors of the Holocaust*, and records from the National Refugee Service and the United Service for New Americans, the postwar Jewish communal agencies involved in the resettlement effort.
2. For a discussion of the Anglo-American Committee of Inquiry and US negotiations with Britain to lift restrictions on DPs to Palestine, see N. Cohen 73–78; Dinnerstein ch. 3; Kochavi 103–13; Grose 202–05; and M. Cohen.
3. For more information about the White Paper, see Berman 66–70; Kochavi 60–64; and Marrus 152–53, 274–76.
4. Based on my work at the Rhode Island Holocaust Memorial Museum from 1988 until 1998, as an interviewer for Survivors of the Shoah Visual History Foundation (now the USC Shoah Foundation Institute for Visual History and Education) from 1996 until1998, and from analyzing testimony collections at the United States Holocaust Memorial Museum.
5. According to the United Service for New Americans records from 1946 through 1954.
6. The one earlier exception to this was permitting affidavit-granting status to organizations sponsoring "unaccompanied minors" during the war years.
7. For a contemporary study of the National Refugees Service and USNA, see White.
8. There were a proportionately large number of slots for Germans even though the number of German Jews who survived was proportionately (and numerically) far lower than surviving Polish Jews, for whom there was a relatively smaller quota.
9. At this time the federal minimum wage was seventy-five cents per hour. At a weekly salary of twenty dollars, Mr. G's pay was considerably less than minimum wage.
10. Denver was a center for the treatment of respiratory diseases, including tuberculosis.
11. The JFCS in Boston offers another example of a more sensitive approach and one that took the newcomers' experiences into consideration. See B. Cohen ch. 5.
12. See Mintz; Novick; and Shandler, which describe the Holocaust and its reception in American popular culture.
13. Based on my own experience as director of education at the Rhode Island Holocaust Memorial Museum (Providence, RI) and conversations with other museum leaders at that time through the Association of Holocaust Organizations (AHO). The AHO Annual Meeting in 1992 had a session devoted to oral history programs to meet the growing interest of centers and museums.
14. Eliach is the author of *Hasidic Tales of the Holocaust* and *There Once Was a World: A 900 Year Chronicle of a Shtetl*.
15. For more about the first oral history projects see Eliach and Gurewitsch 67.
16. Joanne Rudof, archivist of the Fortunoff Video Archive, National Endowment for the Humanities Seminar.

17. From 1988 until 1998, the author was director of education at the Rhode Island Holocaust Memorial Museum, where an oral history project was initiated in 1987.
18. The Fortunoff Video Archive for Holocaust Testimony at Yale offered training. The Association of Holocaust Organizations, established in 1985, served as an important resource for Holocaust centers wishing to establish local oral history projects.
19. This collection is housed at the United States Holocaust Memorial Museum (USHMM).
20. In November 2005, the Survivors of the Shoah Foundation Visual History Foundation merged with University of Southern California to create the USC Shoah Foundation Institute for Visual History and Education.
21. From the USC Shoah Foundation Institute for Visual History and Education website at www.usc.edu/schools/college/vhi/.
22. I was a trained interviewer for the Shoah Foundation from 1996 to1998 and conducted twenty interviews in the greater Boston area.
23. B. G——, interview 43565, 3:18:05 with Survivors of the Shoah Visual History Foundation. She also discussed this with me during a telephone interview.
24. In this case he was referring to the American Jews in his community. He had no relatives.
25. The author wishes to thank the Center for Advanced Holocaust Studies, USHMM, for supporting my research with a "Life Reborn" Fellowship in 2004, and Dr. Joan Ringelheim, director of oral history at the USHMM, for directing me to this collection.

Works Cited

Berman, Aaron. *Nazism, the Jews, and American Zionism*. Detroit: Wayne State UP, 1990.

Browning, Christopher. *Collected Memories: Holocaust History and Postwar Testimony*. Madison, WI: U of Wisconsisn P, 2003.

Case file 306-49. New York: New York Association for New Americans Archives, 1949.

Case file 312-49. New York: New York Association for New Americans Archives, 1949.

Case file 320-49. New York: New York Association for New Americans Archives, 1949.

Case file 322-49. New York: New York Association for New Americans Archives, 1949.

Case file 323-49. New York: New York Association for New Americans Archives, 1949.

Case file 347-49. New York: New York Association for New Americans Archives, 1949.

Case file 361-50. New York: New York Association for New Americans Archives, 1950.

Case file report, record group I-065. Jewish Family and Children's Services, Denver. Newton Centre, MA and New York, NY: American Jewish Historical Society.

Case file report, box 3, file 1766B, record group I-065. Jewish Family and Children's Services, Denver. Newton Centre, MA and New York, NY: American Jewish Historical Society.

Case file report, box 9, file 1943, record group I-065. Jewish Family and Children's Services, Denver. Newton Centre, MA and New York, NY: American Jewish Historical Society.

Cohen, Beth. Case Closed: Holocaust Survivors in Postwar America. New Brunswick, NJ: Rutgers UP, 2006.

Cohen, Michael. *Palestine and the Great Powers*. Princeton: Princeton UP, 1982.

Cohen, Naomi. American Jews and the Zionist Idea. New York: KTAV, 1975.

Dinnerstein, Leonard. *America and the Survivors of the Holocaust*. New York: Columbia UP, 1982.

Eliach, Yaffa. *Hasidic Tales of the Holocaust*. New York: Vintage, 1988.

———. There Once Was a World: A 900 Year Chronicle of a Shtetl. Boston: Little Brown, 1998.

Eliach, Yaffa, and Brana Gurewitsch. *Holocaust Oral History Manual*. New York: Museum of Jewish Heritage, 1991.

Faulk, Mildred. "Modern-day Pilgrims Happy." *New York Daily Sun* 25 Nov. 1947.

Fitzdale, Ruth, Director, Family Service Department, NYANA. Letter to Dr. Alfred Neuman, Executive Director, JFCS, Denver. 9 May 1951. JFCS case file report, 1944–48, record group I-065. Jewish Family and Children's Services, Denver. Newton Centre, MA and New York, NY: American Jewish Historical Society.

Interview 43565, 3:18:05. Interview with Survivors of the Shoah Visual History Foundation. Columbia, South Carolina. 18 June 1998.

Genizi, Haim. America's Fair Share: The Admission and Resettlement of Displaced Persons, 1945–1952. Detroit: Wayne State UP, 1933.

Grose, Peter. *Israel in the Mind of America*. New York: Knopf, 1983.

Gurewitsch, Brana. "Transforming Oral History: From Tape to Document." Johnson and Strom 284–87.

Hartman, Geoffrey H. "The Fortunoff Video Archive for Holocaust Testimonies, Yale University." Johnson and Strom xxv–xxix.

Johnson, Mary, and Margo Stern Strom. *Facing History and Ourselves: Elements of Time.* Boston: Facing History and Ourselves, 1989.

Kaplan, Morris. "7 Young Refugees Getting Diplomas: Freedom Here is Blotting Out Concentration Camp Horrors for High School Seniors." *New York Times* 18 June 1948.

Kochavi, Ariyeh. Post-Holocaust Politics: Britain, the US, and Jewish Refugees, 1945–1948. Chapel Hill: U of North Carolina P, 2001.

Langer, Lawrence. *Holocaust Testimonies: The Ruins of Memory.* New Haven: Yale UP, 1993.

Marrus, Michael. The Unwanted: European Refugees in the Twentieth Century. Oxford: Oxford UP, 1985.

Mintz, Alan. Popular Culture and the Shaping of Holocaust Memory in America. Seattle: U of Washington P, 2001.

Mr. G. Letter to Jewish Family and Children's Services. 20 May 1951. JFCS case file report, 1944–48, record group I-065. Jewish Family and Children's Services, Denver. Newton Centre, MA and New York, NY: American Jewish Historical Society.

Novick, Peter. *The Holocaust in American Life.* Boston: Mariner, 2000.

RG-50.091*0004. National Council of Jewish Women, Cleveland Section, Oral History Project. Washington, DC: United States Holocaust Memorial Museum Archives.

RG-50.091*0005. National Council of Jewish Women, Cleveland Section, Oral History Project. Washington, DC: United States Holocaust Memorial Museum Archives.

RG-50.091*0019. National Council of Jewish Women, Cleveland Section, Oral History Project. Washington, DC: United States Holocaust Memorial Museum Archives.

RG-50.091*0073. National Council of Jewish Women, Cleveland Section, Oral History Project. Washington, DC: United States Holocaust Memorial Museum Archives.

RG-50.091*19. National Council of Jewish Women, Cleveland Section, Oral History Project. Washington, DC: United States Holocaust Memorial Museum Archives.

RG-50.091*198. National Council of Jewish Women, Cleveland Section, Oral History Project. Washington, DC: United States Holocaust Memorial Museum Archives.

RG 50, 233*0073. Postwar Testimonies. Washington, DC: United States Holocaust Memorial Museum Archives.

RG 50_549, 02*00. Postwar Testimonies. Washington, DC: United States Holocaust Memorial Museum Archives.

RG 50_549, 02*0026, 33. Postwar Testimonies. Washington, DC: United States Holocaust Memorial Museum Archives.

RG 50_549, 02*0064. Postwar Testimonies. Washington, DC: United States Holocaust Memorial Museum Archives.

RG 50_549, 02*0070. Postwar Testimonies. Washington, DC: United States Holocaust Memorial Museum Archives.

RG 50_549, 02*0117. Postwar Testimonies. Washington, DC: United States Holocaust Memorial Museum Archives.

RG 50_549, 03*0004. Postwar Testimonies. Washington, DC: United States Holocaust Memorial Museum Archives.

Rosenberg, A. "A Summing Up." *New Neighbors* 3 (1950): 4.

Rudof, Joanne. Lecture. Yale University, August 1996.

Samuels, Gertrude. "DP Chief Arrives in Land of Choice." *New York Times* 17 Feb. 1949.

———. "DP's in America: 'We Have Become Alive.'" *New York Times Magazine* 28 March 1948.

Sandelowski, Molly. Taped personal interview. 3 March 2000.

Shandler, Jeffrey. *As America Watches*. New York: Oxford UP, 2000.

Shoah Foundation Institute for Visual History and Education. U of Southern California. 4 Oct. 2008 <www.usc.edu/schools/college/vhi/>.

"U.S. Citizenship Won by Most Jews Who Came Here on D.P. Ship in '46." *New York Times* 16 Sept. 1952.

White, L. C. *300,000 New Americans*. New York: Harper, 1957.

Wyman, Mark. DPs: Europe's Displaced Persons, 1945–1951. Ithaca: Cornell UP, 1998.

Survivors as Teachers

By Michael Berenbaum

*in collaboration with
Martin Goldman, Linda Hurwitz,
Rositta Kenignsberg, Dale Daniels,
Barbara Appelbaum, Noreen Brand
and Miriam Klein Kassenoff*

This article got its start over a breakfast in June, 2003.

I had a morning meal with a survivor-friend of mine, Sig Halbreich, who, having just returned from another of his numerous speaking engagements, wanted to tell me about his activities as an educator of the Holocaust. At ninety-three plus,[1] Sig is a survivor of several camps. First arrested as a Polish army officer in 1939, he spent more than five years in German incarceration including three winters at Auschwitz. He has what Primo Levi has described as a "low number" (28) at Auschwitz—indicative of the early date of his arrival there—and he thus had developed a well-earned respect due to the mere fact that he had nonetheless endured. As such a veteran prisoner, he was that rare *Capo* (concentration camp foreman) who protected his prisoners, most especially the children, whom he brought into his barracks and to whom he gave lighter assignments, treating them with as much decency as conditions permitted. Thus, by any measure, even though he was beginning to be a bit slowed by advancing age, he remained a formidable personality well worth giving one's time to.

Conversations with Sig tend to become intense. He talks, and, in part because his hearing is diminished, I have learned to listen. But more importantly, I listen to try to gain a better sense of what it was like to spend one's thirties—arguably the prime of one's life—in the living-death of the Nazi concentration camps.

Sig handed me a list of the more than 2,000 speaking engagements where he had spoken about the Holocaust; I was astounded by both the volume of his speaking engagements and by their diversity. He has spoken in schools of all kinds, from universities and colleges to high schools—public and private; Catholic, Jewish, evangelical and elite prep schools as well as junior high schools and even elementary and Hebrew schools. If invited, he came. No longer able to drive, he braved Los Angeles's far from user-friendly public transportation system when no one could drive him. As a concession to age, only, he began to take with him another Los Angeles survivor, a fellow Auschwitz inmate, the late Fred Diament, who was more than fifteen years Sig's junior. In Sig's mind, this served a second purpose: When the day finally came when he no longer would be able to get to the schools, he wanted to train a successor so that his educational agenda could continue. Alas, Fred predeceased him, and finally now at ninety-five, after a heart attack, open heart surgery and the slight depression that followed, Sig has been forced to give up his teaching and lecturing.

Sig has also written a book entitled *Before, During and After* and has been the subject of a children's book, *The Number on My Grandfather's Arm*, which tries to explain the Holocaust to young children, those young enough to sit on their parent's or grandparent's lap to be read to before bedtime. He has also been instrumental and deeply involved in creating the Los Angeles Museum of the Holocaust, which was previously know as the Martyrs Memorial Museum (not to be confused with the more prominent and well-known Beit Hashoah Museum of Tolerance—the Hebrew and the English names are deliberately different; only the Hebrew makes explicit reference to the Holocaust—established nearby more than a decade ago by the Simon Wiesenthal Center). For years, Sig addressed school groups and adult visitors, spending his retirement years in service to the community and dedicated to the preservation of memory. This, then, was the man with whom I was honored to share breakfast on that summer morning.

By chance, when I got to my office later that same day, I was asked to read a draft of Joe Brandt's memoir. Joe is from Rancho Mirage, nearby Palm Springs, California. A Rumanian by birth, he is a child-survivor of Auschwitz and came to the United States alone in 1946, where he began a career that led to wealth and prominence. This has in turn given him the opportunity to spearhead the creation of the Memorial to the Holocaust, a sculpture and garden in Palm Springs, which serves as one of the sites of his own educational activities speaking to students, teaching in classes, addressing teachers' workshops. His educational efforts thus dovetail with Sig Halbreich's efforts.

As I thought about it that morning, both Sig and Joe reflect a pattern: Survivors—many of whom are now in their seventies, eighties and, in Sig's case, even in their nineties and long retired—have been volunteering in increasingly significant numbers to tell their stories to audiences, large and small, in public and private school classrooms and in museums, in Holocaust educational institutions and elsewhere. Over the past decade, in particular, they have been dedicating themselves to this work with an intensity that does not seem to diminish with age. Once they were less prominent and more silent, as Beth Cohen has suggested in her new book *Case Closed*, perhaps because they thought we were unwilling to listen. But they are no longer silent; indeed, they are actively engaged in conversation with the third post-Holocaust generation and even the fourth—a conversation that is eagerly welcomed by both by classroom teachers and their students.

Survivors were the first to instruct me about the Holocaust, when I was a young student in a New York Hebrew-speaking Yeshivot and when they were known not as survivors but as refugees. So as a gesture of gratitude, I now often read, comment upon, and write forwards to their memoirs. So I looked over Joe's memoir much as I might read a new edition of Mel Mermelstein's more well-known memoir, *By Bread Alone*. Mermelstein achieved a measure of fame a quarter century ago by challenging Holocaust deniers—the self-styled "Liberty Lobby"—by taking them to court in order to gain the reward they had offered to anyone who could prove that Jews were actually gassed at Auschwitz. The Jewish establishment, Jewish Defense Organization and even public relations specialists had all advised against it. After all, no one knew what could be gained, but everyone understood what could be lost. Yet Mermelstein prevailed. The court took judicial notice of the Holocaust, and he received his reward. After his triumph, a made-for-television film was broadcast telling his story (*Never Forget*). Subsequently, Mermelstein established a mini-Holocaust museum at his lumberyard in Orange Country, California, where he receives school groups on a daily basis. Now in his late seventies, he worries what will happen to his collection of materials relating to the Holocaust and to his teaching after he is no longer able to carry on.

One can go from city to city in the United States and witness similar dedication, similar efforts by survivors to ensure that the meaning and message of the Holocaust will not die. But as each year passes, age is taking its inevitable toll on these vital, personal witnesses to a horrific past. So I thought I would take the occasion of this collection of articles on the impact of the Holocaust on America to take a closer look at and assess the role of the survivor-teacher today—while there is still time to do so. For this survey I have not only called upon my own personal experience with survivor-teachers but have also have queried a number of my colleagues across the country (whose collaborative efforts with me are acknowledged in the authors' credits), who are actively involved in education with regard to the Holocaust. The accounts that follow reflect our collective understanding of the role of the survivor-teacher of the Holocaust—what these remarkable people have done and are doing to bring a vital message to a broad range of students. It will further consider the special, even unique strengths of these witnesses in shaping the attitudes of our youth as well as a few of their weaknesses.

Let's begin with a few brief profiles that well illustrate the extraordinary roles that survivor-teachers have played in supporting education on the Holocaust. Mike Jacobs labored hard to build the Holocaust Museum in Dallas. He even brought a railroad car of the sort used to transport the Jews to the camps from Poland to stand at the entrance to the museum, which was originally built at the Jewish Community Center and subsequently moved downtown. The museum is now in the process of building an entirely revamped exhibition. He showed that it was possible to preserve and bring such a railroad car—and all the tangible presence that it carried with it—so long a way. So it was to him that we later turned to for advice, as we contemplated bringing such a boxcar to the United States Holocaust Memorial Museum. He was, as always, enthusiastic and helpful. He was at the Dallas Museum of the Holocaust (before it moved from the local JCC) so often that it is fair to say that his spirit always will remain a part of it.

In Phoenix, Arizona, one finds Gerda Klein, who wrote her marvelous memoir, *All But My Life,* soon after the war and spent the next five decades speaking to organizations and groups on behalf of Israel and on behalf of memory. She later achieved even greater prominence when the film *One Survivor Remembers: The Gerda Weissman Klein Story* appeared on HBO and went on to massive recognition, winning an Oscar, an Emmy and a Cable Ace Award. Having been co-producer of that film, I can testify first-hand that it took no special talent from the filmmakers to accomplish their task and, in turn, to win their much-coveted awards. All we had to do was stand aside and let Gerda speak to the camera. She was—and is—a natural. A small part of her story serves as the ending of *Testimony,* the film by which we conclude the permanent exhibit at the United States Holocaust Memorial Museum. Her late husband Kurt Klein, who was also her liberator, was her partner as his own story made its way into television in "America and the Holocaust." The child of German Jews murdered in the Holocaust, Kurt came to the United States in the 1930s and attempted without success to bring his parents over, confronting obstacle after obstacle to their immigration. He returned to Europe as an American GI and participated in the liberation of the woman who later became his wife.

The prominence that Gerda and Kurt gained allowed them to address audiences on several continents and work indefatigably to tell the story of the Holocaust. Gerda was instrumental in taking the story of the Holocaust to new arenas, such as Columbine High School, which she visited shortly after the 1999 massacre, when she was uniquely able to address the student survivors in a way that was particularly credible and healing.

In Los Angeles, Rene Firestone, a Hungarian survivor of Auschwitz, served for more than a decade as a teacher at the Simon Wiesenthal Center. She then volunteered to work at the Survivors of the Shoah Visual History Foundation (now the USC Shoah Foundation Institute for Visual History). Her own story and her journey was featured in the Academy Award-winning film *The Last Days*. Together with the stories of four other colleagues, she described the last stage of the "Final Solution"—the destruction of Hungarian Jews in the spring and summer of 1944. This was three years after the killing of Jews in German-occupied former Soviet territories began, two years after the destruction of Polish Jewry in the death camps of German-occupied Poland and well after everyone knew that the defeat of Germany was only a matter of time. Rene subsequently became a much sought-after speaker at high schools and colleges, conferences and symposia. She, too, had a significant impact on students by the sheer force of her story and her way of communicating with them.

Also in Los Angeles one encountered a Polish survivor, the late Henry Rosmarin, whose presence was manifest throughout the Survivors of the Shoah Visual History Foundation, most especially as the foundation was interviewing survivors on six continents. Soft and gentle, he had so much personal warmth that one always had the sense of being in the presence of a uniquely caring person. Describing his own mother he said, "She awakened me to the world not by yelling but by caressing, by hugging me, embracing me, even moistening my eyelids." As she had done to him, so he did to others. One could not imagine that a man of such warmth had had so difficult a life. He had endured the Shoah, suffering, pain, anguish and loss, and yet he found the love of his life within that darkness; he thought he lost her but then they were later miraculously reunited. Like a Hollywood movie, only for real: Love found, love lost, love reunited. He had two children, sons who brought him great pleasure, but they had special needs that would endure into his old age and extend beyond his lifetime. His world was not rich in material possession—he barely squeaked by—but abundant in all that mattered, rich with love and friendship, music and spirit, *Yiddishkeit* and *Menschlichkeit*. He would often pose the question "why?" Why all this suffering? And he would question the Holy One, not with the rage of Job, but with a depth of humanity, a warmth and a passion that was singularly his own. If God were listening, tears should have been shed in the heavenly court and not only below.

Still, there was no pretense. He knew who he was; he knew what had been given to him in life: what had been taken away from him in life, and what ordinary pleasures and *nachas* (blessings) would never be his in life. His language of communication always included music. When he played the harmonica at my daughter's wedding, the melody of "Shalom Aleichem," the Sabbath queen entered the room even though it was Sunday. When he played at the dinner celebrating the 50,000th interview of the Survivors of the Shoah Foundation, we were enveloped in majesty and mystery, holiness, and sacredness. He had created community with all of us, and we were also connected as one with those who entered the camps and did not leave. As a living representative of the non-survivors—one more link in the long chain of Jewish history—Henry served as our means of continuity.

Henry described his survival, even his time in the camps, as a series of miracles. When he was close to death, the harmonica saved his life or a potato sack saved his life or reciting the *Shema Yisrael* saved his life. He did not allow suffering to dominate his being even though he has every right to claim he had suffered greatly. Most importantly, he was able to teach in classrooms and in boardrooms with an authority that came from his very being—even as his strength waned toward the end of his life.

I knew that I was not alone in perceiving the survivors as teachers and that no one had written seriously of their role except in passing, so I e-mailed a request to colleagues who work in Holocaust institutions large and small asking them to add to my own perceptions of the survivor as teacher.

In Washington, DC, survivors have had an important impact on school audiences that visit the United States Holocaust Memorial Museum. They form the core of the Museum's volunteer corps, serving tens of thousands of hours in an institution that is open seven days a week, 363 days a year. (It is closed on Yom Kippur and Christmas.) During the non-winter months (when many survivors go south for a warmer climate) their first person accounts are a staple of the Museum's educational programs.

As my former colleague Martin Goldman, who retired as the Director of Survivor Affairs at the Holocaust Museum notes, Nesse Godin can serve as one significant example. Nesse was a child survivor (with her mother) from Lithuania who can relate to children by the simple power of her story. Her presence in the classroom is majestic despite the fact that her English is heavily accented and she is more forceful than eloquent. There is a simplicity to her humanity, but also a power that gives voice to her decency and determination. She tells the story of her marriage after the war. Nesse would get angry at the thought of her mother ever getting remarried, even though her mother had no such plans. Instead, her mother suggested several possible suitors for Nesse. As she told Martin, "I looked at Jack and thought he was cute. Who proposed? How did we decide to get married? I cannot remember. I don't remember us even being in love before we got married. We needed each other. But let me tell you," she assured her interviewer, "we are very much in love now."

Martin further notes:

> Nesse was invited a couple of years ago to speak at a women's penitentiary. At the end of her presentation an inmate came up to speak with her. She told Nesse that she was in prison because she had a terrible temper and regularly beat up people. Nesse told her that the next time she felt like hitting someone to think of her (Nesse) and the terrible experience that she had during the Holocaust and to let that thought overcome her desire to hit someone. About a year later Nesse got a letter from the woman in which the inmate reported on what she was doing. She wrote to Nesse that in the previous year she had not hit anyone, but that during that same year she had said the word "Nesse" quite a few times.

Martin recalled a second survivor, Manya Friedman, who was born in 1925 in Chmielnik, Poland, and was in the Sosnowiec ghetto. She was in the following camps in Germany: Gleiwitz, Rechler and Ravensbrück. In January 1945 she somehow survived a death march. She was given to the Swedish Red Cross in April 1945 and taken to Sweden. In the last couple of years Manya has bloomed into a wonderful speaker. She speaks all over the country as part of the museum's Speakers Bureau to children, adults, to the military and to policemen.

Manya was asked to speak to the Naval Academy cadets a couple of years ago during one of their annual visits to the Museum. As the survivors that speak to the military and to policemen often do, Manya spoke about the need for them to understand the power that they hold in their hands, the trust that the people that they are protecting place in them, and the important role they play in keeping our country free and safe. Manya was really pleased to get an e-mail recently from one of the cadets, now an ensign, to whom she had spoken. He told her that the short presentation she had made that day had made a big impact on him. When he wrote, he was aboard a ship off the coast of Iraq. He wrote to her about how he remembered what she said about how young people in uniform, who were considered to be protectors of the people, suddenly could become their persecutors. He said that he was conducting himself and making decisions that could affect the lives of so many people based upon her words.

In Pittsburgh, the former director of the local Holocaust Center, Linda Hurwitz, reports:
At the Holocaust Center of Pittsburgh, local Holocaust survivors have been effective presenters of their personal stories as well as teachers. If a teacher is one who transmits information, motivates interest, inspires the listener to want to learn more about a subject and motivates one to examine the value of life's relationships, then the Holocaust survivor, an eyewitness to history, is surely such an educator.

Though the survivors have been told to focus on their personal experiences and not feel compelled to tell the history of the war, the most effective presenters are intelligent and informed and can set the place and time in history for students. They are also often called upon to relate what they went through to events today.

Three of the most active survivor teachers are Shulamit Bastacky, Marga Randall and Jack Sittsamer.

Shulamit was an infant when she was placed in the basement of a house in Vilna where she survived three years of deprivation with little human contact. Because she does not really remember the experience but knows her story from her parents, who did find her at the end of the war, I suggested that she take courses on Holocaust history as well as read others' literature about the Holocaust to supplement her presentation. She annually sits in on the course I offer each summer for teachers and was an interviewer for the Shoah project, too. She is able to tell her account of being helped by non-Jews, as well as about life in Poland for Jews and the aftermath of remaining in Poland until the late 50s. She arouses a great deal of interest and empathy among younger kids and recently initiated a teddy-bear project. Because she emphasizes her lost childhood, students in appreciation sent her a teddy bear after one of her presentations. That gave her the idea to give teddy bears to nearby family shelters for children being deprived of a home today. The newspaper even picked up a story about this. She never married or had children of her own, but she really has inspired many young people with a sense of interest in the topic and has always shown a deep caring for child-victims of deprivation in particular.

One thirteen-year-old from West Virginia became so attached to her that the family includes her in their personal events and the young woman has now graduated from Boston University, majoring in Holocaust studies.

Marga Randall, another active presenter to students, was only eleven in 1941 when she arrived in the United States from Germany. She recalls the way her beautiful life changed when Hitler came to power—how her father died, how her mother was forced work in another town, how she was sent to grandparents and then to Berlin and how she finally arrived in America. Although she has a grateful and keeps a positive attitude about life, the effects of her disrupted childhood on her life are indelible, obvious and permanent. She continues to love the German language and foods and has gone back to visit in recent years many times. Recently she took a group of college students there and even spoke in her German home town as one whose life was deeply transformed by the injustices of the 1930s and 40s. I sent her to Yad Vashem to take their course a few summers ago, and she prides herself on her learning about the history that complements her personal story.

She has completed a book, *How Beautiful We Once Were*, which captures relationships maintained, developed as well as those that were irrevocably lost. Students connect to her and learn a great deal about the impact of those formative years of life. Marga is a fine example of a survivor who has been very willing to learn and to improve so she could become a better and better storyteller. Her teaching ability can be measured by the overwhelmingly positive feedback of students and teachers over the years.

Finally, Jack Sittsamer, a survivor of several concentration camps and the only survivor of his family, has been giving presentations since he retired. He has a much more subdued, quiet personality than the two women previously mentioned; and, at first, I was not sure he would be a strong speaker who could do justice to his compelling life-experiences. However, in the beginning I went with him to schools, and we discussed how to respond to often-asked questions such as "Why didn't you fight back?" and personal inquiries about members of his family which were emotionally difficult for him to answer.

Survivors should be willing to get a bit of training, if they really have a commitment to being speakers. Jack has a soft-accented voice but strongly moves through the years from before the war, to his teen years in the war "when

I was your age," to the concentration camps, work experiences, the search for his brother and his ties to his buddies. He has become the president of the survivors group and has gone on the radio, written letters-to-the-editor, spoken to adult groups, had his sister remembered by a *bat mitzvah* girl, etc. As a teacher, he always exemplifies someone to admire for his values and the simple manner in which he has persevered. He has effectively now reached thousands of people in the greater Pittsburgh area. He teaches that one must respond to whatever life presents you with strength of character, flexibility, a willingness to learn new things, and with a kindness that evil cannot destroy. Who could ask for a better teacher?

Barbara Appelbaum from Rochester reports in a similar manner regarding the survivors she uses as teachers in her upstate New York community:
Many believe that the study the Holocaust entails looking at the horror, the piles of dead bodies, the end process of unthinkable evil as shown in liberation photographs and film footage. What the survivor does when he or she enters the classroom is put flesh back on the bodies of those victims, allowing students to see them not for what was done to them but for who they were in the fullness of the lives they led.

It is only by seeing a person's humanness—and realizing how much was taken away—that one can fully appreciate what must be done to preserve life and prevent such evil from happening again. That is why it is so important for students to be in the presence of these survivors, to hear them tell their stories, to experience them in the fullness of their being. The survivors remind students of their own grandparents but with a difference.

This is especially true of Czech child survivor Henry Silberstern who in his early seventies has no accent and has a very casual demeanor. This survivor of Terezin, Auschwitz and Bergen-Belsen does not stand in front of a classroom and give testimony, but engages students in a dialogue. Although not a trained teacher, he answers student questions skillfully in ways that allow them to understand what Henry's experience was like. Henry was one of eighty-nine boys, mostly from Terezin, that Dr. Josef Mengele singled out to work at Auschwitz. Henry gives a vivid picture of Auschwitz as a thirteen-year-old boy experienced it—doing odd jobs for the Nazis, playing games in the midst of dead bodies, getting used to seeing bodies hanging from nooses as they went about their daily lives. He describes the daily routine of camp life, tells how he dealt with extreme hunger, what he talked about to the other boys and what he dreamed about. Henry is extremely honest and open about his feelings. In a matter-of-fact way he explains how he got so used to the scenes of mass carnage around him, that after the war he was amazed to find that people will hold a funeral when one someone died.

Henry will sometimes tease students, challenging them to think how they can know he really is a survivor. Yet when Henry tells, without much emotion, what it was like to discover that his mother had also survived Bergen-Belsen and to be united with her there, only to lose her again—this time to typhus, students know he is for real. Before he comes into the classroom students have the benefit of seeing a documentary made locally that records his reunion with over thirty of the Birkenau boys, returning to Auschwitz. After seeing the movie, the students are awed to be in Henry's presence and delighted to discover that he is so approachable.

Why do survivors make such effective teachers? Appelbaum cites several reasons:

Survivors tell amazing stories; they give students perspective on their own lives; they teach students about what is means to be discriminated against and the lasting impact of discrimination; and survivors show students how to cope with trauma, how not to hate those at whose hands one has suffered.

Of the amazing stories, Appelbaum further writes:

Helen Epstein once remarked that the literature that she read in school always paled in comparison to her parents' stories. Likewise, students are fascinated with the stories that survivors tell of their lives during the Holocaust—the close calls, the situations that called for quick decisions that were a matter of life and death. These stories are so fantastic that they could not have been dreamed up.

This is especially true of Ellen Arndt who survived with her mother, as well as with Erich, who eventually became her husband, and his family. Ellen and Erich convinced Erich's father, a physician, to seek help from his former patients in going underground in Hitler's Berlin. Dr. Arndt had practiced in a working class section of Berlin and some of his patients were very indebted to him for the care he gave their family members, sometimes without payment.

Ellen is an excellent storyteller. Even though she speaks without benefit of notes, without photographs or other visual aids, students quickly tune into her quiet voice and her quick wit and listen intently as she relives the events of her life in hiding.

Unlike Anne Frank, Ellen hid out in the open by walking incognito through the streets of Berlin. Blonde and blue eyed, she told how the stereotypes of Jews that portray them as having dark complexions and bulbous noses worked to her advantage, because no one suspected that she could possibly be Jewish. Students admire Ellen's daring, her sense of humor, and her ability to outwit the Nazis and live a lawless life. She tells them about how, cold and hungry and not able to ride the subway another time without arousing suspicion, she and her mother emerged from the subway and noticed that the Nazis were holding a Christmas party in a dark, cabaret-like setting. Her mother readily agreed to attend with her, asking, who would look for Jews in such a setting?

That is not the only stereotype that Ellen talks to students about. She and her family, the largest to survive intact in hiding, are proof that not all Germans were willing executioners. She owes her life to the efforts of fifty to sixty people who risked their own safety to feed, shelter and protect her family. Some of these people were strangers; many were poor, but all defied Hitler. Ellen through her testimony breaks down many of the stereotypes that the students may have about Germans and the Holocaust.

She also tells about Dr. Arndt's fears that their lawless life would become a habit after the war, but she quickly assures students she hasn't stole anything since. She spoke about how they would go into a small grocery store and give a large bill to the clerk who was then forced to go into the back room, usually the owner's living quarters, to get change. In the meantime they would steal food, ration coupons, whatever they could.

Ellen has recently completed a memoir of her life in hiding in Berlin, one of at least three such narratives that are currently to be published, that detail not only dramatic accounts of survival but the nexus of support from Germans opposed to Hitler and willing to facilitate the survival of a Jew, often at great risk to themselves and their families.

Appelbaum continues by making telling points regarding how survivor-teachers can make their stories relevant to today's students:

Survivors give students perspective on their own lives. Students today are dealing with problems that can overwhelm them. Yet when they listen to how a survivor coped with slave labor, starvation, separation from family, death of parents, students realize that they cannot take their families and their comfortable lives for granted. Angie Suss Paull tells students how the Nazis in the Lodz Ghetto selected her mother to be deported. Angie desperately tried to accompany her, but was shoved aside. Later she tried to fill her mother's role by trying to provide meals for the family from whatever food they had. She always tried to give a little bigger portion to her father whom she could hear crying at night. She tried to comfort him. Ultimately, Angie lost both her father and brother at Auschwitz, but survived with her sister.

Survivors teach students about what it means to be discriminated against and how lasting is its impact. Survivors' stories highlight where hatred and discrimination can lead if it goes unchecked. Evie Jacobson, a *mischlinge* (of mixed Jewish and non-Jewish ancestry), remembers how easily she was indoctrinated into believing the lies about Jews, until she found out that her father was Jewish and she then became herself the object of discrimination. She tells of the courage of one of her classmates, who remained her friend in spite of the taunts of others who claimed that in befriending a Jew her friend was just as bad. Evie shares with students that after the war she learned that her teacher tacitly praised Evie's friend for sticking by her and confided that as a teacher she could not say anything publicly but that Evie needed friends more than ever.

Evie also emphasizes how her experiences during the Holocaust impact on her today. She is still seeing a therapist and has problems of identity. This was exacerbated when she was sent on the *Kindertransport* (a group of 10,000 mostly Jewish youngsters who were sent from Nazi Germany to England prior to the war to be adopted by English families and await the war in relative safety.) An only child who was pampered by her German family now had to adjust to a rather stern adoptive father and a family that was very reserved. Evie lived in fear of being sent back to Germany if she misbehaved. When the English bombed Germany, she didn't know whether to be happy or sad. Her father was still living in Germany.

Evie shows children how she still suffers from the trauma of having been separated from her father and forced into a strange culture over sixty years ago. And she wasn't even in a concentration camp.

Survivors show students how to cope with trauma, how not to hate those at whose hands one has suffered. Survivors are invited into the classroom because they can make the events of the Holocaust come alive for the students. Once there, however, survivors do more than teach about the Holocaust. Students see these people, who are like their grandparents except they have lived through unbelievable horrors. Yet they have come through the experience and remain compassionate human beings. Students learn that survivors who suffered unimaginable cruelty at the hands of the Nazis and their sympathizers can pick up the pieces of their lives and start over. Even those who lost entire families in the war have chosen to go on, get married, raise children and lead productive and seemingly happy lives.

Students can see that the worst can happen to survivors, and yet they need not be filled with hatred or a desire for revenge. They can be gentle and whole human beings, who take delight in their children and grandchildren. They may have dreams that continue to haunt them, but they are not filled with hate. As Angie tells them, hate is a waste of time. If you hate someone else, that hatred will end up ruining *your* life rather than the life of the person you hate. Students from the inner city especially are moved by these comments. Many feel that, because their ancestors were slaves here in the United States, they have a right to continue to feel bitter and resentful. The students were visibly moved by Angie's comment to them: "If I go out and shoot a German because of what his ancestors did to me, I will go to jail."

Survivors make a particularly powerful impression on new immigrant students who are refugees from such places as Bosnia and Rwanda. Frequently these students cry, as painful memories emerge which they share with the survivors. Sometimes they tell the survivors, "If you can make it, I can make it."

Angie frequently shares with students her reluctance to tell her story to her own children, fearful that it would turn them toward hatred. Her youngest son came home one day and asked, "Mom, can you buy me a German dictionary?" When she inquired why, he said, "because I like the language." Angie knew she had succeeded. She had not taught her child how to hate.

Rositta Kenigsberg of the Holocaust Documentation Center in Southern Florida reports on her experience with survivors in the classroom and at teacher training seminars:

Sitting at a table with ten high school students representing a variety of ethnic and religious backgrounds, Esther, a survivor of Bergen-Belsen, introduced herself as a survivor of the Holocaust and began to talk to them about her life as a teenager.

> I was your age when the Holocaust broke out. Maybe we didn't have fast cars and computers and video games, but I had the same hopes, dreams, and desires that you do today. As a young girl, I, too, wanted to meet someone special, fall in love, have a family. Suddenly my life was interrupted. Everything was taken away from me—my family my home, my friends—just because I was Jewish. This is what prejudice, hatred, and bigotry have done to me. How many of you have ever experienced prejudice and hatred?

At that point in the conversation, there wasn't a student who didn't relate and become totally engaged in what Esther had just said.

A survivor becomes a unique kind of teacher—one who bears his/her soul and recounts the darkest and most tragic time in his/her life, and whose honesty, sincerity, resilience, compassion, heroic defiance, and optimism all become a profoundly effective message. The students quickly realize and are tremendously touched that the survivors are there for them and the students immediately "get it" as they begin to tell Esther, "I promise I will remember everything you told us and I will tell it to my friends and family, so that it never happens again to anyone."

The student comments we have received for almost two decades always make mention of the fact that what they learned from a survivor, they never got in books or in films. They also mention how amazed they are that the survivors didn't just give up but rebuilt their lives. They admire the survivors for having the courage to tell their story. Many students have also commented that they will never say they are hungry after listening to survivors describe the reality of the hunger they experienced.

Halina, a survivor of Auschwitz, always says to her students, "I am not here to teach you to hate. I am here to teach you what hate can do." Halina also stresses, "You don't know how lucky you are to live in a democratic county like the United States, where you are free to practice your religion and very privileged to vote for your country's leaders. Don't ever take it for granted."

Dale Daniels of the Holocaust Center in Brookdale, New Jersey, reports:

Holocaust survivors can be the most effective teachers of the lessons of the Holocaust. Bringing the survivor into the classroom gives each student a chance to touch history. The survivor shares her/his personal experience, so that Holocaust history becomes more than simply comprehending numbers of victims or catastrophic events. The personal story provides an opportunity for a child to come to know the face, heart and spirit of an individual eyewitness. Students identify with the child-survivor and thus make a personal connection to history. More than that, students recognize the effect of prejudice and discrimination in these personal experiences and can then link this to their own life experience.

For the survivor the experience of sharing his/her history is understandably a most difficult one. Survivors repeatedly say they do not tell their story, but rather with each recounting they live it again. They are flooded with the emotions and fears of the past, a response that is palpable to the students witnessing the story. Nevertheless for those survivors able to share their history, the opportunity to speak to students is their gift to the present and the future. They know the impact they have on children and this helps them overcome their fears.

There are pragmatic concerns when connecting survivors and students for a meeting. The survivor needs to be able to articulate his/her story and tailor it to the needs of the audience. Not all the facts can be shared, whether it is due to time constraints or suitability. Awareness of the age, emotional and developmental level of the audience is needed in planning for a survivor's presentation. Especially important is appropriate preparation prior to the survivor's visit, so that the student has a framework for listening to the survivor's experience. Of equal concern is sensitivity to the needs of the survivor to insure the quality of the experience for all participants. The time frame needs to be structured so that the story can be shared with appropriate period for questions and discussion.

Child-survivor Erica speaks to groups of all ages but is especially effective with middle school students. Erica left her family and her home in Germany on the *Kindertransport* in 1939. She was twelve years old. When Erica speaks, she paints a portrait of her life as a young child. As she relates her experiences in the 1930s, the evolving persecution is communicated on a very personal level. Her description of her return from kindergarten on April 1, 1933 to find her parents' business boycotted conveys the confusion and fear of a child in a tangible fashion that her audience can readily grasp. Soon after, she tells them how, as a witness to a car accident, she saw a policeman collecting blood on a blotter. She explains how she needed to see if the victim's blood differed from her Jewish blood. Later, she speaks out to her teacher, a severe offense, to question why she is a "dirty Jew" when her dress is clean, pressed and white. The spiraling persecution leads to a growing isolation as she must leave all she knows and loves. Erica reaches out and touches students, her experience presented on an emotional and developmental level nuanced so that the students easily identify with her. There is no longer a woman in her seventies before them, but rather a twelve-year-old sharing with them a past that seems immediate and real. The students learn that name-calling, stereotyping, discrimination and isolation all have painful, far-reaching results.

Lisbeth, a native Austrian, was living in Hungary when the war broke out. She survived by hiding in a coal cellar. Her world for months was one of almost total isolation and severe limitations. Her story is punctuated with episodes of paralyzing fear and strength. Lisbeth conveys her determination, extreme self-reliance, and spirit, as she recounts her story. Lisbeth speaks often to middle and high school students, but her greatest success is with special education classes. Students recognize in her experience the strength of the human spirit in overcoming endless frustration and limitation. Discrimination is accepted as a challenge overcome by her personal strength to survive despite victimization.

Fred was just six years old when he, his mother and sister left Germany to live in Holland following *Kristallnacht*—a large-scale mob attack by stormtroopers and civilians on Jewish homes, businesses and synagogues in many German cities and parts of Austria, November 9–10, 1938. His mother escaped to England to work as an *au pair* on September 1, 1939. He and his sister remained behind with relatives only to be caught by the invading Germans. After a period of internment at Westerbork, Fred was placed on a train for Sobibor. His hysterical cries disrupted the orderly boarding process, so he was removed from the train to the death camp. He was left in Westerbork for a year and was then deported to Bergen-Belsen where he remained until the end of the war.

Fred speaks to students from grade five through adult. He weaves the story of his childhood, given from a child's perspective, so listeners can sense his growing need but inability to escape the web of persecution surrounding him. This child, saved merely by a cry, evidences the idiosyncrasy of survival. Fred's description of his life in the camps is detailed and visual, giving a unique perspective on day-to-day survival by a child all alone. His story speaks of themes of isolation, discrimination and persecution. Listeners can feel the confusion and overwhelming losses of one small boy caught in the Holocaust. Fred often punctuates his story with, "Do you understand what I am saying?" When he is finished, his listeners always do.

Noreen Brand, formerly the educational director of the Florida Holocaust Museum, and now serving in the same capacity at the Illinois Holocaust Museum and Educational Center in Skokie reports:

To allow history to come alive is a daily pattern at the Florida Holocaust Museum in St. Petersburg, Florida, where survivors stand in front of 160-plus young people who are at the museum for a tour and to learn about the past. What better way than to learn from an eye- witness? These unique individuals, our survivor-teachers, give of themselves and harness energy from their memory that runs deeply throughout their being. Yad Vashem's large maps mounted on foam-core board, along with precious few photographs from before the war years, are displayed next to the podium, reflecting a time that was stolen from their past. With these props and memoirs, our survivors present the stories that only they can tell.

Entering the museum (or alternatively, when some of our survivors visit a school or classroom), the attendees encounter a well-attired person carrying an attaché case or tote bag. After warm greetings from the museum staff, off they go to their classroom, on the third floor, our education gallery. Approaching the podium, carefully setting out maps, personal photos and identification cards (that were designed and written by our second generation group) our incredible survivors prepare their plan for the next forty-plus minutes—to teach their story, to integrate a geography lesson, to touch on connections to current day. Each is an historian in his or her own unique way. Students arrive (from grade five through adult) and find an opportunity to learn, to be enriched and to be left with a charge to move forward and teach the lessons learned. These students will learn details not written in a report or published in a memoir or diary; they will learn geography through a personal dialogue as the audience travels through time with our teacher.

Felix, one of our teacher-survivors, not only works with students, but with the Juvenile Justice Boot Camps, and the prison system in the state of Florida. He teaches about hatred and man's inhumanity to man; he shows the number on his arm, scars on his back and chest, and tells why one should not hate, but care for mankind. He explains why it is important to treat others as you would like to be treated.

Frank stands before youngsters telling them of his teacher, calling him to the front of the classroom to model "what a Jew looks like." In a soft demeanor he tells about the changing tide of the early 1930s, how his life and dreams were shattered, but also of his success as a humane person, encouraging all to make the most of their education and life—something he lost. Frank uses maps, shares enlarged photographs and reads vignettes from his published memoirs. Young people are mesmerized, questions abound and many stay behind waiting to speak to him, to offer a hug, to thank him for what he has taught them.

How does one learn about ghetto life? Who could possibly embrace what it means to smuggle food, weapons, supplies? How does one learn to take a stand, and actively participate in society? Enter a ghetto survivor—this individual had been involved in the Warsaw Ghetto Resistance and Uprising, a member of the *Oneg Shabbat*, an organization in the Warsaw Ghetto dedicated to chronicling and documenting life there, one who knew the value of education as a young college youngster, who had her life turned upside down. Her desire to take care of the younger people in the ghetto led to the formation of a secret school, where she told the story of *Gone With the Wind*, taught Latin, wanted to have these young people find a venue to find strength to go on in light of the worst conditions, wanted them to survive. The lessons are lessons for living life, for caring for others, to never give in or give up. Her attempt to provide a semblance of normalcy during the most abnormal times, lessons for all future generations to hold tight too.

These are examples of lessons that seldom get taught effectively in the classrooms. Often the focus is on lifelong lessons, which get lost in the "mandated" testing. The teacher needs to understand the integration of these lessons within the testing venue, to consider the narrative, to think about the persuasive, to allow one to think critically and to understand the relationship of history and English and geography through testimony.

Still, Brand correctly cautions:

Survivors and witnesses offering testimonies do not always have correct dates or chronology of events, and as the years since the Holocaust pass, there may be a "drifting of memory," in which some of the less painful memories are recounted while the more painful ones are omitted or only partially recovered. Thus, Holocaust testimonies must be verified by examining other sources. Archival materials, diaries, artifacts, and art used in conjunction with testimonies offer a fuller picture of the era. These other sources help to validate information in testimonies and at times correct misremembered dates or chronologies. These other mediums are offered in the museum visit as docents carefully and sensitively integrate the testimonies into their teaching through the museum.

Museums, with their diverse professional staffs, are far better equipped than individual classroom teachers to modify, correct, clarify and, when necessary, even verify what survivors have said. Miriam Klein Kassenoff, the director of education for the Miami Beach Holocaust Memorial, in a city that is the home of numerous survivors, writes more cautiously about the role of survivors as teachers. She is, herself, a child-survivor of the Holocaust, and consequently her critical view is also self-critical.

Miriam Klein Kassenoff, the director of education for the Miami Beach Holocaust Memorial:
The role of the Holocaust-survivor as educator is complex. It is true that probably the most valuable experience the student can have and the one that will leave its biggest and most profound impact is the day he hears the testimony of the Holocaust survivor. Even today, after twenty years of being a Holocaust Educator, I hear from students, now in their early adulthood, say that they have never forgotten the first time they heard a Holocaust survivor speak. Debra Messing, the famous actress of the popular TV show *Will and Grace*

was so touched by her experience in high school that she has narrated a film for students and teachers called *Marion's Triumph* about Marion Blumenthal, a Holocaust survivor Ms. Messing met in her public school year. Steven Spielberg frequently speaks about the first time he met a survivor and saw the Auschwitz number on his arm. That vision has remained with him all his life, and thus the production of the now famous *Schindler's List*. There are many stories such as these testifying to the impact of the Holocaust-survivor and his testimony on the students in the classroom. Whether testimony is the same as education of the Holocaust is the question I wish to pursue here.

First, we must recognize that Holocaust-survivors are all too human. Their experiences are diverse, so too, their backgrounds and expertise, their ability to reach students, their recollection of events and their familiarity with the history. Their experiences during the Holocaust also differ. Some survived by escaping and "being on the run" throughout eastern Europe as early as 1940, fleeing from country-to-country to the safe haven of Lisbon. Some were able to catch a ship to America, having had no idea of what was going on in the rest of Europe until many years after the war and then learning of the Holocaust only through newspaper reports and relatives' reminiscences. Some survived by going to England as young children on *Kindertransports* and only know about the history through other means. Some survivors spent years in ghettoes. Some were actually in the death camps. Some were in Russia. So basically most survivors qua survivors—excluding the professional historians—do not have the overview of the Holocaust knowledge as would the historian/scholar.

Although many survivors have studied the history and are sufficiently knowledgeable to present it to the student, in many instances the limits of their knowledge can pose a problem. For example, there are instances where survivors will tell students about the "soap" that was made from the Jewish victims when there is no documentation to support this—of course the students are fascinated, none the less—or some survivors, wanting to be "professorial" and a bit tired of their own stories, will tell the history of how the Holocaust happened. This approach can present a few problems, since there is never enough class time for the history and the testimony—and what the teacher wants the student to hear is the testimony. Survivors frequently don't present their accounts in a chronological manner and history, if it is to be best understood needs a clear chronology. Otherwise, a student can be left confused, and the survivor often may not have the exact historical knowledge to clarify such confusion; as a result, misinformation is presented.

Still, the survivor is the teacher, the one who teaches all of us the lessons to live life: to understand the value of never giving up, to move forward, to forgive, to appreciate each new day, and to pass these lessons onto the next generation.

The focus of the survivor-visit should be within the allotted time given to discuss how life before the Holocaust affected him or her, how life during the Holocaust changed that experience. Most importantly, I feel the survivor needs to focus on the return to life—how he or she was able to rebuild after tragedy. This is the most important lesson a holocaust-survivor can contribute in his testimony to the student of today. How does one go on with indomitable spirit after such a tragedy? How does one find a way to live in a positive manner, still believing in the possibility of human decency, in God (if the survivor is questioned about this), not seeking revenge but justice, not seeking retribution but instead doing good charitable work to keep this kind of tragedy from happening to other cultures? In almost all instances, holocaust-survivors become role models for the students and, yes, " heroes" (and we surely need many of those today for our students to use as models their own life. This then is the role of the holocaust-survivor as an educator—a mentor of "character education," and social responsibility.

Kassenoff is correct. Still, several cautions are in order.

Survivors are not historians even though they have lived history intensely through an intense period of history. Few of them had access to what was happening elsewhere. As one survivor told me, "Do you think we had newspapers in Auschwitz?" Few also could or can even today perceive the Germans, except through the lens of their own victimization. Thus, the best survivor-teachers are those who were willing to undergo rigorous training and to work with scholars and educators to understand their own limits and then to go beyond them. And the best questions to pose to survivors are those that relate to their own experience. For example, to ask a child-survivor of the Holocaust about the causes of Nazism is unhelpful. The student should learn that elsewhere, as the survivor *per se* has no particular expertise regarding the answer. But to ask what it was like to attend school and interact with classmates as the Nazi regime was developing is something that some survivors can speak on with great authority.

Sometimes survivors generalize from their own experience and establish it as a principle. When Gerda Klein says in *One Survivor Remembers* that "only those with imagination could survive," she is singularly convincing even though what she really is describing is the way that she employed her imagination to insulate herself from the harsh reality of the camps and thus to protect a part of her own humanity. When she speaks of suicide as "the final solution to a temporary problem," she is equally convincing but she is also generalizing—rightly or wrongly taking upon herself the "Role of Survivor" who has the right to speak on behalf of all survivors.

Furthermore, we must heed the uncompromising warning of the distinguished Holocaust scholar and literary critic Lawrence Langer that the presentations by survivors can easily obscure the more prevalent story of the other victims—and I insist that survivors are also victims—the many more people who did not emerge from the camps and did not live to see the liberation. After all, the survivor did *survive*, and this fact inevitably colors the way a survivor's story is told and how it is perceived by his or her audience.

Nor does the survivor in the classroom often present with the intensity it deserves the story of the ongoing wounds, what Langer in his important book *Holocaust Testimonies* calls in the listing of his chapters "Humiliated Memory: The Besieged Self," "Tainted Memory: The Impromptu Self," "Unheroic Memory: The Diminished Self." Even if they speak of defeat, the students perceive victory and triumph. The very presence of the survivor in the classroom intensifies the sense of heroism and, even if muted in the presentation of the survivor, it is almost uniformly present in the responses of the students and their teachers.

I have deliberately not emphasized the experience of some of the most prominent of survivors, such as Elie Wiesel, the preeminent voice of his generation, and Miles Lerman, who spearheaded the campaign to built the United States Holocaust Memorial Museum and later chaired the Holocaust Memorial Council, its governing body. I also omitted Benjamin Meed, who has headed the American Gathering of Jewish Holocaust Survivors for the past quarter century, devoting his entire life to remembrance, to organizing gatherings of survivors, to building Holocaust museums in Washington, DC, and New York and to chairing Holocaust commemorations in the Capitol Rotunda and in Temple Emanuel in New York City, two of the largest commemorations in the United States. Nor do I feature Vladka Meed, his wife who was active in the Warsaw Ghetto Resistance as a courier purchasing weapons and smuggling them into the ghetto and who later wrote an early important account of the resistance entitled *On Both Sides of the Wall*, which has recently been translated into German and Japanese among other languages. For more than fifteen years, until the Second Intifada (the Palestinian-Israeli conflict that began in September, 2000) made travel to the Israel seem too hazardous to attract a constituency, Vladka took groups of teachers to Poland and Israel for an annual seminar on the Holocaust and Resistance. Survivor-led, the groups traversed the camps and heard from distinguished professors in Israel and survivors' testimonies from life inside the camps and, of course, the Resistance. She became the teacher to teachers.

Nor have I dealt with the survivors who have achieved major economic success in the United States and used their position of influence and affluence to build the great institutions of remembrance, from the Holocaust museums in Jerusalem, Washington, DC, New York, Los Angeles, Houston, Detroit and elsewhere as well as university chairs in Holocaust studies and other impressive attempts at remembrance.

My reasons are specific. In each community where Holocaust education activities have been conducted, survivors have come forth—ordinary men and women, who lived through extraordinary times and who give voice to a unique experience that resonates in the lives of students. This is an experience not confined to the United States or Canada but from first-hand observation is true as well of Australia and South Africa (also the homes of Holocaust museums and of important educational outreach programs), England and France as well as in Israel.

If you asked most survivors why they survived, the most frequent answer was through luck; in truth, they survived because of a number of factors, including age and physical condition, their ability to perceive and respond to danger and the resources that they had—inner resources as well as material resources. Many also required assistance from family and friends, acquaintances and even strangers. So luck is a partial answer which indicates that every survivor knows someone wiser and stronger, more deserving, resourceful and capable who was at the wrong place at the wrong time and met with death. So the accidental nature of their survival conferred no meaning and offered no lessons. Some—perhaps even a considerable number—felt guilty for the very fact of their survival. I have often heard it asked by survivors: "Why did I survive, when so many others did not?" That question could neither be answered immediately after the war nor easily in the years thereafter. But for some survivors the most compelling answer is found not in answering why they survived, but in what they have done with the accident of their survival. In the cases of the survivor-teachers, they have borne witness and thus *ex post facto* endowed their survival with meaning. They have used their "luck" to speak to conscience, to enhance human dignity and to plead for human decency. It is an important part of their moral legacy, an attempt, however inadequate it may be, to rescue something from the ashes and overcome some of the evil that shaped their youth and thus their life.

This generation will be the last privileged to be the direct beneficiary of that decision to embrace the world and to compensate for loss by testimony. The unanswered question for all is, what will happen once living memory has been transformed into history?

Appendix

STUDENT COMMENTS FROM THE HOLOCAUST DOCUMENTATION CENTER[2]

"After today, I realize how lucky I am, how much I took for granted, and how fortunate I am to have all the opportunities that I do."

"I expanded my knowledge through this program, but more importantly, I learned to appreciate life more and to live with more happiness for what I have."

"I can see that what I learned today will help me to be kinder to others and not allow myself to hate."

"Now I understand that ignorance is the only thing anyone should fear. I realize that just because everyone is from different backgrounds, we can still unite. We just might start a beautiful thing. I am taking home a profound, heart-changing experience."

"If we pass on the knowledge that prejudice will lead to hostility and war, maybe, just maybe, our children can grow up to see a peaceful world."

"I think what I learned will make me think twice before I judge a person. Yes, today's experience will help me."

"Now I understand how one person, me, can make a difference."

"I learned that I have the opportunity to make things better in this world."

"This day taught me how to change my thinking toward people and treat them better."

"It made me realize that when I am going through tough times, it is nothing in comparison to what the survivors had to endure."

"I now know that prejudice and hatred have no place in our world."

"The survivors' courage really touched me deeply."

"From now on, I will try to be more courageous to stand up for what is right."

"It is amazing for me to hear the survivors talk about all they lived through in their lives and still be able to see the good in the world."

"I have learned not to discriminate against others because we are all equal."

"I was given a vivid description of what life was like in a concentration camp."

"I will no longer tolerate prejudicial remarks others make."

"I will try to educate those who don't know or who just don't care to know about what happened in the Holocaust."

"The survivor and liberator's speeches were emotional, and despite the fact that I was not in Europe, I got some kind of idea of what took place."

"What moved me the most about today was when the survivor at my table showed me the numbers, which had been tattooed on his arm. It was a sign of the pain he had been through."

"I learned that racism and hatred is the true root of evil."

"I now understand that it is important for our generation to make a difference and pass down the history that we learned today."

"This is the most important day of our students' school year".—A teacher

"The survivor told us what happened to her. It wasn't a movie or a book. It was reality."

"The most interesting and helpful part of the program was knowing that I am right when I tell people that being prejudiced is wrong."

"I will hand this information down to my children."

"Thank you for this gift of education."

"I learned that being a survivor is such a superhuman effort—something admirable and encouraging."

"It is vital that victims of all sorts speak out against evil."

"I found a deeper meaning in love for one another."

"The images of children's faces are a reminder of how important tolerance is."

"I became totally aware of the entire truth today."

"It's unbelievable to me to think that people would really do this to another individual. I also think the survivors are brave to go through whatever pain they endure to retell their stories."

"I think this qualifies as a top-rated educational experience."

"What a great way to educate us about prejudice and violence and their dangers."

"The survivors bared their souls and reopened painful wounds to teach us. I am most grateful to them for that."

"I hope that every student in our country will have the opportunity to participate in a program of this nature. It is very important."

"It was an honor to speak to and listen to a survivor. There is nothing like a firsthand experience like this one was."

"This is the first step to making this world a better place."

"Thank you for the life lesson."

"I hope that this program can continue so that one day my children can be lucky enough to be a guest here and experience what I did."

"We need to remember the Holocaust and tell the stories so people won't forget and let something like the Holocaust happen again."

"This program made me more aware of what's going on around me."

"Keep this program going for as long as you can because we students take this to heart and will remember this for the rest of our lives."

"Just keep doing the work of God and know that if you take care of his work, he will take care of yours."

"Listening to a survivor is a wonderful experience that everyone can learn from."—A teacher.

"This experience has shown me to open my eyes to horror and will allow me to open my mouth to change evil and hatred."

"What I learned today will remain in my mind and my heart until the end."

"I became aware of the importance of living today as if it is the last day—enjoying every possible moment."

"I learned that in life there are many struggles but that one cannot give up the fight."

Survivors as Teachers 57

"I learned that in order to come together as one, the people of this nation must neither love nor like one another but must learn to respect and communicate with each other."

"I learned more in a day than I have in my whole life."

"I learned that the Holocaust wasn't something that simply happened sixty years ago. It's something that lives on with us. It is something that teaches us that we have to make a difference in the world."

STUDENT RESPONSES
TO STUDENT AWARENESS DAYS—2001[3]

"Because of the information I learned today, I will not judge people just because of their race or religion." (Grade 10)

"Today I learned that one person can help other people change their thoughts. I will pass on my knowledge to others." (Grade 9)

"It is s one thing to read from a text book, but it is another to see and hear actual events from those who lived through this terrible time in our history." (Grade 11)

"Student Awareness Days taught me not to judge people or discriminate against them as a group or as an individual simply because they are different." (Grade 11)

"It is unbelievable to think that people would commit such horrors on one another. Having lived through it, I think that the survivors are extremely brave to come and tell us their stories." (Grade 11)

"This was the most intellectual experience in my life. It qualifies as a top-rated program which provided me with some incredibly meaningful information." (Grade 12)

"I feel as though I have grown as a person through taking part in this program." (Grade 10)

STUDENT AWARENESS DAYS—2000

"I am thankful for my freedom now more than ever. I will always think of the experience of the survivors." (Grade 9)

"I can now help others understand what happened during the Holocaust because of what I've learned." (Grade 9)

"This is one of the most memorable field trips that I've been on. It was more exciting than I ever thought it would be. I have a lot of respect and admiration for the survivors that had the courage to share their experiences with us." (Grade 10)

"I will never forget this experience. I will pass it on to my children." (Grade 9)

"I learned that horrible events towards people are caused by people. It all starts with us. We have the power to stop or end violence." (Grade 12)

"Student Awareness Days are specifically important because many of the survivors will not be with us much longer. More people should have the opportunity to hear them speak. The program was great." (Grade 11)

"I learned that hatred can lead to horrible things and what's worse is that we are still surrounded by this hatred today." (Grade 11)

"The part I found most interesting and helpful was the table discussions (with the survivor). I think this is a wonderful experience and I'm glad that you have this program for high school students to attend." (Grade 10)

"I learned that there were resistance groups that helped to fight against the Nazis. These people were very brave." (Grade 11)

"Prejudice has to stop and I can definitely see myself looking beyond a race or religion to truly see and have a friendship and respect for others who are not like me." (Grade 12)

"More groups like yours must be created to increase world understanding and to show those younger students that extreme prejudice as the Nazis showed to the Jews will forever be present in our world unless *we* stop it." (Grade 9)

"I will try as hard as I can, and even harder than I think I can to take a stand against bias/prejudice or any other harmful acts I see taking place." (Grade 10)

"What I learned today changed me because it showed me never to stay silent in the face of injustice." (Grade 10)

"I want to stand up for all races when I hear people make racial jokes and slurs, or when people call each other names, I want to be able to say that is wrong." (Grade 12)

ADULT RESPONSES TO STUDENT AWARENESS DAYS
March 29 and May 9, 2000

"At the beginning we discussed the survivor's story. Later, we discussed hatred and racism and its prevention."

Mimi Klimberg, Facilitator

"They (the students) became more open, more willing to talk personally. They grew in respect for one another. It was a wonderful and productive experience."

Susan Weiner, Facilitator

"(The survivor at my table was) always attentive and patient. She listened carefully to student comments and concerns and encouraged continued interest and positive action."

Al Rosenthal, Facilitator

"The survivor was inspirational. The students learned a great deal about the Holocaust, prejudice and hatred."

Elizabeth Feldman, Facilitator

"I hope you are able to expose children in elementary school to this program. The earlier we can teach our children not to be prejudicial, the better their lives will be."

Sonia Ramirez, Parent/Chaperon

"At first they (the students were) kind of uninterested but after I spoke, they couldn't believe they were hearing and seeing a survivor in person. I think it was a very good thing for all."

Helen Hecht, Survivor

"The students acquired a deeper knowledge of the Holocaust and their involvement in tolerance. The magnitude of the Holocaust challenged them the most."

Maurice Krakowsky, Survivor

"The students at my table were deeply touched. It made a deep impression on them. They thanked me for telling them all I experienced and told me they had learned a lot."

Leo Rosner, Survivor

"The students thanked me a lot for sharing and enlightening them with my past."

Brenda Senders, Survivor

"I will give as much time as I am able to this program after experiencing the feeling of the group of students at my table."

Sonia Klein, Survivor

"They asked very good questions. The students became increasingly more attentive and interested. The facilitator at my table was excellent."

Lisl Bogart, Survivor

"Students talked about (their) own prejudices. Table discussion centered around doing good and doing the right thing. They all said meeting a survivor meant a lot."

Magda Bader, Survivor

At our most recent institute on Holocaust studies,[4] survivors also sat with teachers. As they shared their painful stories with them, the teachers reacted. Later, they wrote in their journals to and about the survivors. The following are a few excerpts of their reactions:

"To the survivors . . . Thank you so much for reliving all this for us so that we can learn valuable lessons and live to say that we met you and spoke to you—a living history lesson. I love you all for not giving up, for hanging in there, enduring the worst pain so that your brothers and sisters who did not make it could be assured that you honored your promise to them. You challenge all of us to be more humane."

"Where did they find their strength to get through each ugly, dark day? It is beyond my understanding except to know that only God can give someone the reason and strength to survive this horrendous experience and become a wiser, more compassionate, and more tolerant human being because of it. These survivors have a mission to teach all of us, so that we will keep the lessons alive even after they are gone."

"At lunch, Lisl told us her story, showed us the yellow star, and shared her brother's story. What courage. It is absolutely awe inspiring to look at this woman's face and realize a tiny portion of what she endured. What a marvelous testament to the courage of the human spirit. I must pass along all that I've learned to my students." [Lisl is a survivor of Terezinstadt.]

"It was very interesting to listen to Rita and her personal story of survival. She talked about being pulled out of summer camp and returned to a different life. It was a surprise to learn that her life was so normal one day and the change that occurred the next. I was surprised at how easily she told her story of survival and how much she remembered. She is a testament to humanity." (Rita is a survivor of the Warsaw Ghetto Uprising)

"Everyday I have been cold in class. So, I wear a jacket. I complain how cold it is, but I wonder what a survivor would think about my complaints. 'How dare she complain. She has no idea what cold is'. I also feel hungry since it has been many hours since my last meal. Again, if a survivor knew what I was thinking, would they believe me to be spoiled and complain about something that is nothing compared to the hunger they have felt or would they be understanding and realize that since I didn't live through their experience, this is all I know? Maybe they expect a person like myself, one that experiences these minor, insignificant problems to be bothered by them. I think of how strong these individuals are. Do they ever complain about cold or hunger now? Are they so extremely grateful that they lived that they would never complain about the unimportant again? I will ask and maybe learn for myself to be satisfied to have only lived through these small problems and be thankful for them. Can I teach my students empathy and compassion? It is something I take away from being with the survivors."

"As a teacher, it makes me feel that I need to repeatedly emphasize racism, intolerance, and bigotry. It is important for everyone to be educated about the Holocaust so that this never happens again."

"We often hear about the Warsaw Ghetto and the uprisings, which occurred there. But hearing it from Rita Hofrichter, who actually experienced it, was just such a privilege. I cannot fathom how much fortitude and will she must have had to endure the hunger and working conditions of her youth. To be exposed to such horror at such a tender age and to be able to talk to us now, in the autumn of her life, of all her experiences is such a beautiful thing. I know how many survivors and liberators remained silent about their experiences for many, many years. I am grateful to Rita for her sharing her memories with us. I will pass them along to my students."

"We were asked specifically why we are taking the course. Reaching deep into my soul, I search for reasons that are meaningful . . . to gain knowledge, information about the Holocaust so I can better inform my students—to gain deeper insight into prejudice in general. What affects one, affects all."

Notes

1. Sigfried Halbreich passed away in September 2008, but weeks before his 99th birthday.
2. The Holocaust Documentation and Education Center, located in Hollywood, Florida, is "is non-sectarian, non-profit, multifaceted organization ultimately devoted to teaching today's youth the evils and dangers of racial hatred, bigotry, and indifference through the lessons of the Holocaust" (www.hdec.org/).
3. See www.hdec.org/student_awarness_day.htm.
4. See www.hdec.org/teachers_institute.htm.

Works Cited

Adler, David A. *The Number on My Grandfather's Arm*. Illus. Rose Eichenbaum. New York: URJ, 1987.

"America and the Holocaust." *American Experience*. Dir. Martin Ostrow. PBS. 6 April 1994.

Cohen, Beth B. *Case Closed: Holocaust Survivors in Postwar America*. New Brunswick, NJ: Rutgers UP, 2007.

Halbreich, Siegfried. *Before, During and After*. New York: Vantage, 1991.

Klein, Gerda. *All But My Life: A Memoir*. New York: Hill and Wang-Farrar, 1995.

Langer, Lawrence. *Holocaust Testimonies: The Ruins of Memory*. New Haven: Yale UP, 1991.

The Last Days. Dir. James Moll. Perf. Renee Firestone, Alice Lok Cahana, Bill Basch, and Irene Zisblatt. Alameda Films, 1998.

Levi, Primo. *Survival in Auschwitz*. New York: Summit, 1986.

Meed, Vladka. *On Both Sides of the Wall*. Intro. Elie Wiesel. Trans. Steven Meed. New York: Schocken, 1993.

Mermelstein, Mel. *By Bread Alone: The Story of A-4685*. Huntington Beach, CA: Auschwitz Study Foundation, 1981.

Never Forget. Dir. Joseph Sargent. Perf. Leonard Nimoy, Dabney Coleman, and Blythe Danner. Theatre Communications Group, 1991.

One Survivor Remembers: The Gerda Weissman Klein Story. Dir. Kary Antholis. Narr. Peter Thomas. HBO, 1995.

Randall, Marga. *How Beautiful We Once Were: A Remembrance of the Holocaust and Beyond*. Pittsburgh: Cathedral, 1998.

A Jewish Perspective on the Global Economic Revolution in a Post-Holocaust World

By Steven Windmueller

Jews are experiencing a fundamental change in their social and financial position both within American society and, more broadly, in the context of the global community (Windmueller, "Second American Jewish Revolution"). What one may characterize as a "key-nexus" appropriately describes the particular and unique role that Jews have played over the course of their history as well as a role they continue to perform in the global marketplace. That is, Jews, especially American Jews, frequently serve as key generators of new ideas, playing prominent roles in shaping and promoting the arts and culture, supporting and participating in scientific advancements, and marshalling resources for new business and civic initiatives. This notion of a nexus-community involves the special interplay of three factors: the presence of significant networks of influential contacts; access to financial and intellectual resources; and the creation and deployment of critical information. These elements represent some of the ingredients especially central to the American Jewish experience and relevant to the development of the current global environment.

In these special connector-roles Jews can perform two core functions in the advancement of ideas and in the development and management of capital. They can be described as among the first people to serve as knowledge-workers, and they may be further seen as interpreters of ideas in their role as writers and teachers and as knowledge-creators who advance new ideas as researchers and scientists.

As entrepreneurs over the course of history Jews not only have had occasion to move and manage economic resources but have also played significant roles in the assessment of financial and business trends and in the development of theoretical principles and economic policies about how markets work. Jews in America today can often be seen to be highly entrepreneurial, directing their resources and creative energies toward such cutting-edge notions as global markets, hedge funds, venture investments in new technologies, and an assortment of real estate and business interests. Indeed, a new social and economic revolution has redefined the place and prominence of Jews both within the marketplace and the civic arena, in many ways returning Jews to their unique place in history as social *networkers* and economic connectors within the global system.

GLOBALISM AS THE REFUTATION OF NAZISM

This phenomenon takes on added significance in a post-Holocaust environment. The Nazis defined ethnic identity in terms of the nation-state, which was therefore central to their concept of power and order. For them, the "fatherland" *alone* embodied the essence of their identity and civilization. Globalism serves as the precise counter-point to this Nazi model of nationalism and racially focused politics. The global enterprise is best understood in terms of a broad-based collective engagement of the world in the economic marketplace. It thereby extends beyond and thus refutes the centrality of the state, while at the same time affirming the essential intellectual value and inherent economic importance of the individual rather than the nation in advancing ideas and marketing goods and services. Such economic involvement in the world has served as a central theme during different time frames of Jewish history. Indeed, for Jews, the rise of nationalism has all too often represented a significant, even deadly, threat to their status as a minority within assertive national cultures. Such an historically precarious status stands in significant contrast to the freer flow of ideas that naturally tend to grow out of global economic and social participation.

In the years immediately following the Second World War, Jews along with other middle class citizens, especially in America, became fully engaged in the national economy; such participation positioned them, in turn, to become key participants in the opportunities afforded American investors and the business sector to enter the global market several decades later. A number of factors contributed to the advancement of this Jewish participation in America's economy in the years following the Second World War. The GI

Bill provided educational incentives for returning service personnel, allowing them to enter college and subsequently build professional and business careers. Returning soldiers, settling in America's expanding urban suburbs during the 1950s, were often able to launch new and innovative businesses or alternatively, reinvigorate their family businesses. As a result, these enterprises grew into regional and at times national service and consumer industries. The three immediate post-war decades (1950–80) represented a period of heightened economic growth and social change, affording a significant number of Jews an array of professional opportunities in such fields as medicine, law, and accounting. As universities and graduate centers welcomed in an unprecedented manner the influx of young Jews, the Jewish "baby-boomer" generation was afforded an opportunity to have a profound impact on each of these and other disciplines. In the process, Jews significantly expanded their intellectual contributions and economic influence throughout American society. In his study on Jewish occupational patterns, Barry Chiswick has further demonstrated the increased earning power of Jews, as a result of their "white-collar" professional status and their choice of managerial and proprietorship positions within the economy (Chiswick, "Labor Market Status" 136–37).

This post-war generation in many ways provided the framework for the American Jewish engagement within the global arena, as Jews, along with other entrepreneurs and investors transferred their domestic focus to these new international marketing opportunities. The communications and technology revolutions enhanced and supported this economic transition, facilitating its development by accommodating to the demands for global access.

Upon reflection, United States foreign and economic policies for Germany and, more broadly, for Europe in the immediate post-war and Cold War eras, nurtured the uniting of the continent, leading to the creation of the Common Market and the European Union. This successful focus on super-regional governance and shared economic and social interests on the continent must be seen as a policy designed to counter any initiatives designed to reinstate nationalistic ambitions or intentions, and more specifically, a strategy constructively to redirect Germany's role away from its Nazi-induced past and to bring it within a transnational European orbit.

THE CONCEPT OF A "NEXUS COMMUNITY"

This idea of creating such points of intersection has been central to Jewish roles as the quintessential diaspora people. To be sure, transnational connectedness, boundary crossings and diversity are not unique characteristics to Jews; nonetheless, these characteristics have been clearly prevalent in their varied historic experiences and so recognized both within and outside of Jewish culture. In their work on *Jews and Port Cities*, David Cesarani and Gemma Romain suggest that Jews throughout history were "perpetually crossing geographical, political, linguistic and cultural boundaries" (3). Unlike many other ethnic groupings, Jews, as a result of their long experience as a diaspora culture, had acquired marketable skills and have continued to pursue the goal of financial sustainability—regardless of national context. Other cultures have centered their attention on protecting their physical place or ensuring their social and economic status within that space, whereas Jews have directed their energies toward educational achievements and building trade and social networks without the same focus on physical, national space.

For example, in medieval European centers such as Holland, France and Britain, Jews have played central roles in key industries and in forging trade connections. This was particularly the case in Amsterdam, where Jews played dominant roles in such industries and international markets as diamond-cutting and sugar refining (Arkin 87–102). Contrastingly, England's limitations on Jews and their economic and political rights was challenged by a number of eighteenth century writers and business persons, who saw the advantages of inviting Jews to settle in England, arguing that a liberal naturalization policy would contribute to national wealth (Arkin 116–17).

Viewed from the perspective of the twenty-first century, Nazism in many ways reflected the very worst tendencies in a traditional economic system. Anti-Semitism clearly played a role in shaping how Jews positioned or protected their resources (Chiswick 146–47). Chiswick suggests that in response to persecution, Jews avoided investments that could be seen as "geographically specific," namely investments that would have been beneficial to one specific location versus another. " 'Human capital' is embodied in the person and is therefore portable. . . . European Jews would have an incentive to invest in human capital rather than in other assets."

Jews have been uniquely successful in parlaying their education into income-capacity. The appreciation and application of learning has been a particularly significant factor in defining their economic standing (Ruppin 51). Chiswick also proposed that "persecuted groups will invest in transferable and liquid assets rather than assets that are merely portable" (147), suggesting that legal and business knowledge are highly transferable skill-sets.

Global participants focus on building and sustaining networks of relationships. Such networks over the course of Jewish history are related to trade, employment, and business and have been the essential ingredients that have allowed diaspora communities to succeed. In the past such connections have been critical to Jews and other groups in allowing them to trade products and services as well as to transfer key social ideas across political boundaries. "Indeed, Jews were for centuries the only representatives of international commercial activity" (Abrahams 214). "Globalization intensifies the need for cosmopolitanism, or for an awareness of being citizens of the world.... Globalization—namely, migration and technological sophistication—fuels an array of substate and trans-state attachments and identifications that challenge any state's capacity to draw upon cultural homogeneity as the basis of identity or belonging" (Croucher 189, 191). This statement by Croucher reaffirms this success of the new economic order, especially as compared to any prior nationalist system.

Access to and the use of information has been a significant factor in Jewish history and represents in this time of global environment a particular marker of Jewish engagement with ideas. Throughout the past Jews have played significant transmitter-roles within the societies in which they lived, bringing new ideas and resources into a culture, providing particular core services and in the process supporting and contributing social, economic and political change. In the course of Jewish history, these often assigned transmitter-roles resulted in an all too predictable reaction: the emergence of anti-Semitism.

In response to the extraordinary achievements and roles performed by Jews, Charles Murray in a recent *Commentary* article[1] addresses these issues by trying to understand and quantify *Jewish intelligence* or genius throughout history. For Murray and others the focus has been on seeking intelligence markers as a way of explaining or justifying these high levels of performance. Others have written about the "high achievement levels" found among Jews as a push-factor in accelerating their involvement in such arenas as business, professional and civic enterprises. The need to excel, it has been argued, grew out a response to the longstanding patterns of religious hatred and discrimination directed against Jews.

In his latest book, *Five Minds for the Future*, Howard Gardner introduces several mind-types that are necessary for the global market place of the twenty-first century. These particular characteristics, according to some sociologists, may reflect how Jews see themselves in the modern world. "The synthesizing mind" selects information from disparate sources and puts them together in ways that make sense to others, while "the creative mind" goes beyond existing knowledge to pose new questions, offer new solutions, and come up with new ways of thinking.[2]

There might well be an immediate tendency for one to fear reactions to concepts that express any such notions related to a Jewish presence and influence in the world of business, as the accusation of economic domination is one of the oldest anti-Semitic diatribes directed against Jews throughout history. However, the case being developed here is *not* really about control and power. Instead, it rather more reflects and reflects on the significant changes that have emerged in American society, especially in a post-Holocaust world, and how these changes have enabled opportunities for Jews (and many others) to compete for positions in the American marketplace and beyond that had previously seemed unattainable. This fundamentally represents the basis of a revolution in which this Nexus Community of Jews was particularly well suited to participate.

CHANGING SOCIAL REALITIES: THE AMERICAN EXPERIENCE

In contrast to other historical experiences, and more specifically the Nazi atrocities, Jews in contemporary American society have been able to carry out effectively those functions that have allowed them to play a much more significant role in the American and global communities. Three factors in post-Holocaust America have set the stage for a socio-economic transformation within a Jewish context. First, the diminution of any stigma associated with being Jewish. This is most prominently reflected in the general absence of (both official and unofficial) state-sponsored or government-sanctioned anti-Semitism. It also may be seen in the gradual minimization of executive-suite discrimination within America's corporate business systems and the related removal of restrictive barriers to social clubs and civic organizations. The dropping of these national and institutional barriers has made it possible for Jews to penetrate all levels of the American economic system and its corresponding social networks. A second factor involves the demise of the college quota system that had systematically limited the participation of Jews in the intellectual centers of American academic life. Finally, the shedding of the Jewish immigrant experience and the corresponding rapid assimilation of the next generation(s) into American society further facilitated Jewish entry into elite educational, social and business structures during the post-Second World War period.

As the American economy developed during this time, numerous centers of wealth were created, permitting Jews to play creative and supportive roles in the building and developing of capital enterprises. Correspondingly, Jews gained credibility through their demonstrated high levels of philanthropy and their contributions in support of culture, health research and services, as well as education initiatives. To achieve the success that has defined the American Jewish experience in a post-Holocaust world and to arrive at this point of engagement, this community had to move through a series of three economic developmental stages:

The Era of Labor was dominated by four core characteristics: Unionization among Jewish workers, the presence of small family businesses, the presence of a cadre of Jewish artisans, and the presence of a small but growing element of Jewish mid-level managers and administrators. As Nathan Glazer suggests:

> "During the period between 1920 and 1940 a great social change was under way made up of workers into one that is today . . . largely made up of middle-class people: white collar workers, businessmen, and professionals. Initially masked by the arrival of large, new, working class elements, the change was further delayed by the great depression of the thirties. But it was being prepared by intense education and by significant shifts in occupations" (80–81).

The Entry Point was a period when Jews were able to access the corporate sector, expand their business interests and holdings and enter key professions including medicine, academia, and mid-level government service. Simon Kuznets writes about the post-Second World War period, as trending "toward greater concentration in professional and technical pursuits; toward an increase in employee status among officials and managers and within the professional-technical group proper; toward a decline in the share in industrial blue collar jobs; and since 1950 toward a lesser concentration in trade, particularly of small proprietorships" (17–18). In the post-war era, Jews accounted for 9% of all university faculty members, and among Ivy Colleges and other elite institutions of higher learning, Jewish academicians represented 19–22% of these faculties (Lipset and Ladd 92–93).

Chiswick reports on the significantly high percentage of Jews who are self-employed. During the period immediately following the Second World War, more than half (56%) were so classified. While that number had dropped to about one-third of the Jewish labor force by 1990, Jews remain far more likely than other Americans to identify their work status in this manner (Chiswick, "Economic Status" 253ff.). "American Jewish men had higher levels of schooling, occupational attainment and earnings . . . than non-Jewish men"

(Chiswick, "Postwar Economy" 97). During the post-war years and beyond, these educational and career differentials between Jews and non-Jews have continued to widen. Chiswick goes on to conclude that the "entrepreneurial spirit remains strong among Jews" ("Postwar Economy" 98).

These prior socio-economic positions held by Jews revolved around four principles:

1. Each generation of Jews in this country tended to move one step ahead of their parent's generation in terms of socio-economic advancement and personal status.
2. Status was defined and measured in terms of middle class social values. "Wealth" was measured in comparative class terms.
3. In the past break-through career or professional achievements in the work force (high level career appointments, contributions to scientific advancements, and social recognition) in such areas as commerce, medicine, and the public policy arena were seen as the exception rather than the norm.
4. Both specific governmental policies such as the GI Bill and more recently, the opening of global marketplace provided special opportunities that few other constituencies so fully embraced as effectively as American Jews.

The Global Marketplace marks the present level of Jewish economic participation. There is evidence as well that the traditional business and professional fields selected in the past as careers of choice have given way to investment banking, international trade, technology research and production, etc. In this current phase in the development of professional options, Jews play an influential role in the global business environment. They frequently serve as key investors and managers of hedge and venture capital funds and have facilitated access to the creation and distribution of new technologies, as they continue to aspire to compete for senior level positions in government, academia, business, and the arts. Current employment and career patterns suggest the growth of Jewish economic and professional involvement is centered in ten core fields of industry and business: building and construction; real estate; television, theater and film; technology; manufacturing; investment and banking; biomedical research and health care services; international trade and commerce; arts and culture; and information services.

THE MEGA-WEALTH FACTOR

The impact of this new status and wealth can be measured in part by the number of Jews who are identified as part of *Forbes'* listing of the world's richest people. Of the 415 Americans who hold assets in access of one billion dollars, 24% on this list are Jewish (Popper). Worldwide, one finds an additional group of twenty billionaires representing Europe, Russia, Canada, Latin America, Australia, and Israel. Jews account for more than 10% of this particular category of international wealth (Popper).

Similarly, a significant number of prominent Jewish women made *Forbes* 2007 "100 Most Powerful Women," including such key players as ninth-ranked Irene Rosenfeld, who serves as the CEO of the $34 billion Kraft Foods; Safra Catz, President and CFO of Oracle; Orrit Gadish of Bain and Co.; and Rochelle Lazarus of Ogilvy and Mather, along with Supreme Court Justice Ruth Bader Ginsburg and Israeli Foreign Affairs Minister, Tzipora Livni ("100 Most Powerful Women").

If one were to examine, for example, five major corporations that were either founded by Jews or are currently led by Jewish CEOs, it may provide some insight into the scope of influence that this mega-wealth sector has on the international economy (McGregor 52–63):

1. Michael Dell of Dell Computers, whose company was ranked last year by *Business Week* as the 14th most innovative company in America
2. Howard Schultz of Starbucks, whose company was ranked last year by *Business Week* as the ninth most innovative company in America
3. Arthur Levenson, Chairman and CEO of Genentech Inc., "the world's foremost biotechnology company, . . ." whose company was ranked this year by *Business Week* as the twenty-third most innovative company in America
4. Steven Cohen, manager of SAC Capital Advisors, whose company *Business Week* named as one of the nation's top performing hedge funds
5. Sergey Brin and Larry Page, co-founders of Google, whose company was ranked this year by *Business Week* as the second most innovative company in America.

The case of thirty-three year old Sergey Brin and his partner thirty-four year old Larry Page, co-founders of Google, offers some insights into this new class of wealth. Today, it is estimated that Google is worth in excess of $150 billion and each partner holds assets in access of $15 billion. The two entrepreneurs have recently pledged one billion dollars of company profits to Google.org, their philanthropic arm. As someone who came to the United States from the FSU (Former Soviet Union), Sergey's family has taken a particular interest in HIAS (Hebrew Immigrant Aid Society), the agency responsible for the resettlement of Jews in the United States (Malseed 39–45, 66–69).

The economic interests of the Jewish mega-donors varies greatly, encompassing such core industries as banking and investments (Sandy and Joan Weill), real estate (Robert Meyerhoff), insurance (Peter Lewis), Home Depot (Bernard Marcus), computers and technology (Michael and Susan Dell), SunAmerica and KB Homes (Eli and Edythe Broad).

Based on the 2005 list of the fifty most generous philanthropists in America, 33% have been identified as Jewish (Woolley 61). Similarly, a significant percentage of the largest family foundations in this country are held by Jewish families, among them are the Annenberg Foundation with assets in access of $2.5 billion, the Harry Jeanette Weinberg Foundation, with $2.1 billion, and the Michael and Susan Dell Foundation with resources in excess of $1.2 billion.[3] Among new entrepreneurs one finds as well a disproportionate number of Jewish individuals who are engaged in such start-up businesses. One half of the top ten "most generous philanthropists" in the United States are Jewish with a total pledges between 2001 and 2005 in access of $6 billion and whose collective lifetime giving has acceded $13 billion. For this group of donors, the range of their philanthropic interests, while varying significantly, involves, for example:

1. Biomedical education and research (Mann)
2. Open and democratic societies (Soros)
3. Public Education, arts, culture and science (Broad) (Bloomberg)
4. Children's health care (Dell)

The impact of this new wealthy class has also revitalized the Jewish communal system both through individual donations and foundation-giving as reflected in these five family foundations (Foundation Center):

1. Sheldon and Miriam Adelson Foundation, $200 million
2. Harry and Jeanette Weinberg Foundation, $60 million
3. Avi Chai Foundation, $46.8 million
4. Charles and Lynne Shusterman Foundation, $34.8 million
5. Jim Joseph Foundation, $25 million

Examples of individual gifts to Jewish institutions, worldwide:

- Ronald Stanton (Yeshiva University), $100 million (2006)
- Sheldon Adelson (Yad Vashem), $25 million (2006)
- Sheldon Adelson (Birthright), $30 million (2007)
- Jacobs Family (Technion), $30 million (2006)

Charles Lemert and Anthony Elliott have suggested that a new individualism is emerging as a result of globalization: "The culture of advanced individualism has ushered into existence a world of individual risk-taking, experimentation, and self-expression. . . . It is also in the expansive emotional literacy and cultural cosmopolitanism of its people who, in their diversity, have developed ways of living that are more open, experimental, and privatized than was the case in the past" (Lemert and Elliott 11, 13). This seems evident in both how the mega-donor class has directed given resources, often by-passing traditional institutions by either creating new funding structures such as Birthright Israel[4] or by directing their giving to special interest areas, revitalizing older, established institutions or embracing specific programs within these entities.

The mega-donors are not the only class of Jewish wealth that is asserting its presence and profile. Today, there are Jews who can be described as "wealthy" or "near-wealthy" who hold assets in the multi-million dollar range, and similar to the top donor base, have created an array of philanthropic instruments to carry out their social and communal interests. Even middle-class Jewish households reflect some of the same patterns of economic achievement and charitable participation.

The distribution of household income among Jews, especially at the high end of the income scale, reflects their relatively high educational levels and the high status of their jobs. More than one-third of Jewish households (34%) report income over $75,000, compared to 17% of all United States households. Proportionally fewer Jewish households (22%) than total United States households (28%) report household income under $25,000. The current median income of Jewish households is $54,000, 29% higher than the median United States household income of $42,000. In 1990, the median income of Jewish households was $39,000, 34% higher than the median income of $29,000 for all U.S. households.[5]

Economist Barry Chiswick writes: "American Jews are more likely to be employed in higher-status occupations, such as professional and managerial jobs. In 1957 one-fifth of employed male Jews were professionals, as compared with about one-tenth of the other white males; over three-tenths of Jews were managers and proprietors, almost double the proportion of other whites" ("Labor Market Status" 135). Similar patterns are reflected in later studies including the 1970 Census where the higher earnings of Jews could be in part attributed to higher levels of education and urban residence ("Labor Market Status" 138–39). This American Jewish economic success can be tied to their immigrant past. "Each cohort of Jewish immigrants, within 10-15 years of assuming residence in the United States, matched the earnings of native-born American workers of the same age and occupation" ("Labor Market Status" 142–43).

In referencing these categories of Jewish wealth, there is significant evidence that these individuals and families have embraced the economic opportunities afforded investors and entrepreneurs over the course of the past twenty years. Three factors would appear to be particularly significant:

1. Taking advantage of new business options and tax incentives designed to encourage and promote entrepreneurial investments, Jews among other investors have been especially adept at exploiting these opportunities and have thereby moved to enter the global marketplace.
2. Marshalling of resources from an array of funders, Jews have used their business and communal networks to build these funding streams which are a significant vehicle for raising critical revenue in the changing marketplace.
3. Building on existing investment portfolios and growing these funding bases in order to compete in world markets has permitted the accumulation of mega-wealth.

As a result of these new economic conditions, Jews are and will continue to play a profoundly significant role in participating in and shaping elements of the American economy. This specific access to and interest in both business and financial markets and the corresponding policies related to global trade and investment are particularly significant. Anecdotal evidence suggests that younger Jews today are selecting business degree programs over law and medicine as further evidence of this engagement with and interest in the global economy or are employing their professional training in areas aligned with these new career trends.

The more significant story here may well be the core roles Jews play within the modern, post-Holocaust American society as connectors, functioning as key interpreters of economic and social developments and trends, in addition to being seen as prominent writers, consultants, managers, and advisors to those handling corporate policy. This revolution is less about the increased acquisition of wealth and more about the manner in which Jews are both deploying their resources and in turn how their particular professional roles have changed within this society and more specifically within the economy. Jews who hold significant roles in senior management are shaping business investment practices, while others have influence over the formation of government economic and social policies. Similarly, Jews in key intellectual centers are contributing to the creation of new industries, disciplines and arenas of research.

Such economic transformation for Jews could only happen in a society that has afforded its citizens full access in all areas of the economy. In the post-Second World War era, America has opened up its social, intellectual and economic infrastructure to Jews. Whether this "open door policy" was created in part as a reaction by American elites to Hitler's assault on European Jewry or whether other social factors were at work in the consciousness of Americans, this era has elevated the state of Jewish economic participation.

THE GLOBAL JEWISH COMMUNITY
As the economy expands, involving new professional and business opportunities in trade and technology, Jews will continue to take advantage of the economic options that have opened up for them during the post-Holocaust era in America. As a result, one of the key outcomes involving these social and economic realties will be the creation of a new "global Jewish community," as emerging centers of Jewish life are being formed or recreated both within this country and around the world. Portions of the American South, Southwest, and West have become the new business and high-tech regions for the nation and then, by extension, for the world. Quietly but significantly whole new sets of "mini-communities" are being created worldwide by this new Jewish global class. At least ten new communities have been formed or strengthened as a result of this new international market focus. China with over one thousand new Jewish residents in such cities as Shanghai and Hong Kong has been joined by such other emerging global participants as India, now with five thousand individuals, followed by South Korea, Japan, Thailand, Singapore, Kenya, and Nigeria, each with smaller but nonetheless significant new Jewish residents. Jewish entrepreneurs are playing key roles as well in such emerging economies as Russia, Brazil, and South Africa. In addition, the rebirth of Jewish life in Germany has been driven in part by the new economic opportunities afforded

to Jews and others through their participation in the European Union's largest economy. Similarly, Sydney Australia continues to show growth as a destination point for Jews leaving Southern Africa.[6]

Five factors seem to play a role in the choices that Jews are now making in their selection of countries of choice:

1. The absence of significant and overt anti-Semitism;
2. The presence of a stable and democratic political system;
3. A commitment on the part of the government to open market policies;
4. Open immigration policies and/or a commitment to welcome foreign residents and to receive professionals with skill-sets that are in high demand;
5. The presence of both growth markets and access to global communications.

Within the past twenty-five years, Jews with significant wealth from Central and South America, France, South Africa, Iran and Israel have relocated to the United States and other centers of global economic development.[7] The new global economy is contributing to a renewal of the redistribution on a worldwide scale of the Jewish people and in turn having profound impact on the reshaping of the American Jewish communal system.

CONCLUSION

Throughout history Jews have played significant roles in the world's key economies. This pattern continues today as a result of globalization and the corresponding access to new business opportunities and markets, along with the demise of traditional economic forms of anti-Semitism, and the high levels of educational achievement afforded Jews living in western societies. Jews have readily embraced these opportunities. These changes have refocused how Jews see themselves as social connectors, contributing to the evolution of a new global economy.

To a great extent, Jewish participation in the global experiment we have come to call the global economy has served as a powerful refutation to the Nazi enterprise directed against world Jewry. This profound engagement with the world in many ways serves as a tangible triumph over Hitler's intent to destroy the Jewish people. "Globalism" can be seen as the countervailing theme to German ideology; the former represents an affirmation of the individual in the marketplace of the world, free of class or group distinction and discrimination, where one is evaluated in terms of business acumen and social entrepreneurialism rather than on ethnic grounds. This can be seen in contrast to the Nazi construction of racial beliefs and nationalistic themes that were principally designed to deny to their enemies a place within German society. Perhaps that is just the point: the Nazis wanted to turn the world into an environment subservient to German identity and need. The global economy was to be a *German* national economy on a world scale, in which Hitler and his Nazi allies stood at the pinnacle. What has emerged instead is an economy that transcends nationalism and thus an economy in which Jews could successfully compete. Drawing upon the successful post-war experience of Jews, one can observe over the past fifteen years not only the significant movement of Jewish investors into international markets but also many of this community's leading professionals and business consultants as central figures in helping to define and shape the global arena.

In the process of acquiring new wealth, this new class of the mega-rich is reshaping the Jewish communal system and in turn contributing to the reinvention of the larger philanthropic enterprise. The impact of this growth of personal wealth cannot be underestimated and the emergence of new global opportunities to accrue financial capital has afforded Jews among others a window in time to build fortunes and in turn to use those resources for social good.

Notes

1. Murray, see 32 and 33 in particular as they address the question of Jewish intelligence.
2. Gardner 45 with reference to the "Synthesizing Mind" and 77 with reference to the "Creative Mind."
3. Key Jewish Foundations were extracted from the list of major national and local foundations, Foundation Center, "Top 100 U.S. Foundations by Asset Size."
4. Taglit Birthright Israel was created by several major donors as a means of providing a quality, free ten-day Israel educational program for individuals 18–26 years of age. The program was founded in 2000 and since then some 160,000 individuals from fifty-two countries have participated, with 70% from the United States.
5. The data represents a compilation of information reported in the "2000–2001 National Jewish Population Survey"; also see Sheskin 66–69.
6. Data extracted from the "World Jewish Population" materials provided in the *American Jewish Year Book*.
7. Jewish population patterns as reported over time in the American Jewish Year Book reflect these movements.

Works Cited

"The 100 Most Powerful Women." *Forbes.com* 30 Aug 2007 <http://www.forbes.com/lists/2007/11/biz-07women_The-100-Most-Powerful-Women_Rank.html>.

"2000–2001 National Jewish Population Survey." New York: Unitied Jewish Communities in Cooperation with The Mandell L. Berman Institute-North American Jewish Data Bank, 2003.

Abrahams, Israel. *Jewish Life in the Middle Ages*. New York: Antheneum, 1978.

Arkin, Marcus. "Amsterdam Jewry: During the Age of Mercantilism." *Aspects of Jewish Economic History*. Philadelphia: Jewish Publication Society, 1975. Ch. 10: 87–102.

Cesarini, David, and Gemma Romain, eds. *Jews and Port Cities, 1590–1990*. London: Vallentine Mitchell, 2006.

Chiswick, Barry R. "The Economic Status of American Jews." *American Jewry: Portrait and Prognosis*. Ed. David Gordis and Dorit Gary. West Orange, NJ: Behrman, 1997. 247–60.

———. "The Labor Market Status of American Jews: Patterns and Determinants." *American Jewish Year Book* 86 (1985): 131–53.

———. "The Postwar Economy of American Jews." *A New Jewry? America Since the Second World War*. Studies in Contemporary Jewry 8. Ed. Peter Y. Medding. New York: Oxford UP, 1992. 85–101.

Croucher, Sheila L. *Globalization and Belonging*. Lanham, MD: Rowman and Littlefield, 2004.

Foundation Center. "Top 100 U.S. Foundations by Asset Size." 28 June 2007 <foundationcenter.org/findfunders/topfunders/top100assets.html>.

Gardner, Howard. *Five Minds for the Future*. Cambridge: Harvard UP, 2007.

Glazer, Nathan. *American Judaism*. Chicago: U of Chicago P, 1957.

Kuznets, Simon. *Economic Structure of U.S. Jewry: Recent Trends*. Hebrew U, 1972.

Lemert, Charles, and Anthony Elliott. *Deadly Worlds: The Emotional Costs of Globalization*. New York: Rowman and Littlefield, 2006.

Lipset, Seymour Martin, and Everett Carl Ladd, Jr. "Jewish Academics in the United States: Their Achievements, Culture and Politics." *American Jewish Year Book* 72 (1971): 89–128.

McGregor, John. "Most Innovative Companies." *Business Week* 14 May 2007: 52–63.

Malseed, Mark. "The Story of Sergey Brin." *Moment* Feb. 2007: 39–45, 66–69.

Murray, Charles. "Jewish Genius." *Commentary* 123.4 April 2007: 29–35.

Popper, Nathaniel. "Rapid Rise of Mega-Donors Reshapes Communal World." *Forward* 2 March 2007 <www.forward.com/articles/10246/>.

Ruppin, Arthur. *The Jews of To-Day*. London, 1913.

Sheskin, Ira M. "How Jewish Commuities Differ: Variations in the Findings of Local Jewish Population Studies." New York: City U of New York Grad. School and U Center and Mandell L. Berman Inst., North American Jewish Data Bank, 2001. 66–69.

Windmueller, Steven. "The Second American Jewish Revolution." *Sh'ma Magazine* June, 2006 <www.shma.com/june_06/second_american.htm>.

———. "The Second American Jewish Revolution." *Journal of Jewish Communal Service* 82.3 (Fall, 2007): 252–60.

Woolley, Suzanne. "The Top Givers." *Business Week* 28 Nov. 2005: 59–61.

"World Jewish Population." *American Jewish Year Book* 102–07 (2002–07). New York: American Jewish Committee.

Bringing the Holocaust to America[1]

By Richard Libowitz

The United States maintained its neutrality through the first years of the great conflict which had been raging across Europe since 1914. Supporters of President Woodrow Wilson used the slogan, "He kept us out of war," as a refrain in his successful campaign for re-election. The tune changed in 1917, however, as America entered the fray on the side of England and France. American doughboys joined the struggle with a now supportive American public singing that "the Yanks are comin' over there," renaming sauerkraut "Liberty Salad" and calling frankfurters hot dogs. Once the armistice stopped the fighting, the troops came home and the Treaty of Versailles ended the war, the country turned its back on Europe and the world in general. Despite Wilson's most strenuous efforts, the United States rejected membership in the League of Nations, passed rigorous immigration restriction laws and generally maintained an isolationist policy for the next two decades that even so astute a politician as Franklin Roosevelt could not easily change.

A similar pattern seemed to develop at the end of World War II. With peace attained, many Americans preferred to put the war, its memories and lessons behind them. Elie Wiesel has often said the most important action to be taken about the Shoah is "to tell the story." Stripped of mind-numbing statistics, multiple names on an overfull map and the names of politicians, generals, perpetrators, rescuers and bystanders, the Holocaust is a story of human tragedy and moral failure rarely approached in human history. When the war ended, it was a story few were willing to tell or even approach. The United

States had new goals, a new president and a new enemy—the Soviet Union. The beginning of the Cold War and subsequent anti-Communist inquisitions had major impact on domestic thinking as well as on American foreign policy. There seemed neither time nor place to reflect on an uncomfortably brutal past.

No matter how moved some Americans may have been by the visual and written testimonies beginning to emerge from the concentration camps, there seemed to be no great impetus to deviate from the policies that had limited immigration quotas from Eastern Europe since the early 1920s and had placed additional stumbling blocks in the path of would-be refugees in the 1930s. Post-war America, including the Jewish community, failed to welcome survivors of the Holocaust with open arms. Thousands of Jews lingered in Displaced Persons' Camps, applying for visas and waiting for something to happen. Those who were permitted entry received assistance from various Jewish agencies concerning their physical needs, but their psychological concerns were ignored; no one wanted to hear the survivors' stories, no one seemed willing to listen. Again and again, the survivors were told they were in America now, that they had to make a new life in the new world, and that the past should be forgotten. And, for the most part, the survivors took the hint; many would not discuss their experiences for decades.

Still, the past had not been completely forgotten nor had it been totally ignored. Photojournalists and reporters had been posting stories since the first concentration camps were liberated, most notably, Margaret Bourke-White's photographs of Buchenwald survivors published in the May 7, 1945 issue of *Life*. Gruesome pictures were included in newsreels playing in movie theaters even before the war had ended. The International War Crimes Trials at Nuremburg were covered by a legion of reporters representing various wire services, newspapers, magazines and radio networks. Even the new medium, television, included aspects of the Holocaust in both its dramatic and public affairs broadcasts. However, the fact that some materials were available to the American public did not mean that the public took great note of them. Just as in the 1930s, while it was possible, if one looked hard enough, to read about the entire history of the Third Reich as it developed (Ross; Baron), the general public, nonetheless, was not inclined to include the Shoah among its major concerns. It would take more than two decades and the rise of a new generation to bring the Shoah to the prominence that we tend to take for granted today.

THE 1950s

By 1950 most people felt that the United States had left behind the struggles of 1930s Depression and 1940s world conflict. The GI Bill had provided the resources to quit the crowded streets of the northern cities for the new housing developments and open spaces of the suburbs. From one Levittown to another,[2] America was engaged in a building explosion; new streets lined by tract housing, occupied by veterans whose growing families attended new schools and worshipped within the churches and synagogues that had followed their flocks to larger, airier quarters. Television had become a central facet of family life, with network programming filling the evenings and uniting diverse sections of the country to watch *I Love Lucy, The Ed Sullivan Show, Gunsmoke* and *The Mickey Mouse Club*.

Conventional wisdom, writes Jeffrey Shandler in his study of the presentation of the Holocaust on American television, is that the Shoah was a subject to be avoided by the networks for several decades after the war. Shandler counters that the Holocaust "as a concept . . . developed since the middle of the twentieth century in a dynamic and complex process, which has produced an extensive public debate over what may be considered a legitimate work of Holocaust memory culture, whether on television or in any other form" (xvii). The Holocaust was not an unknown topic for the new medium, but many of the discussions were reserved for Sunday morning religious programming, not likely to attract large or heterogeneous audiences.

A network of interstate highways was being built, to tie together north, south, east and west, supplying pathways for the automobiles being produced by Detroit in ever increasing numbers. The cars themselves reflected the growing optimism of the country—ever-lengthening, fins, bigger, more powerful engines that allowed drivers to take on ever greater distances. Airline travel was still a luxury for most people but newer planes, able to carry larger payloads of passengers farther in shorter time, were bringing down the costs, and Americans were on the move. Further atomic and hydrogen bomb tests proclaimed America's dominant military power to the world. Still, tens of thousands of GIs were fighting in Korea and the Soviet Union also had atomic weapons. The infamous McCarthy investigations and House Un-American Activities Committee hearings generated a paranoia focused on Communist sympathizers and their plots, resulting in damaged reputations, ruined careers—all in the name of patriotism.

The American Jewish community, as well, was undergoing a rapid metamorphosis in this decade. The postwar period was one in which American Jewry achieved a greater blending into general American society, as Will Herberg affirmed in his groundbreaking study of religion in America, *Protestant-Catholic-Jew*. There was a new acceptance of Judaism as a legitimate American religious faith, so long as it was practiced unobtrusively, in a manner that did not challenge Protestant norms. Many young Jewish veterans used the GI Bill to attend college, married and joined the movement to the suburbs, leaving the urban Jewish neighborhoods of their youth. Native born and confident of their identity as Americans, this generation was leaving the blue-collar jobs of the sort that had employed many of their parents; they moved on to white-collar professions, ownership of independent businesses and entry into the upper echelons of the medical, legal and teaching professions. They joined Reform or Conservative synagogues with parking lots, playgrounds, gymnasia and swimming pools, became members of lodges, bowling leagues and the PTA. They tended to vote Democratic, the party of Roosevelt, and they also supported many social causes. Their children joined the Cub Scouts and Brownies, played Little League and complained about going to Hebrew School on weekday afternoons. Israel was largely viewed as a faraway land, populated by Jewish farmer-soldiers who danced the *hora* and sang "*Hava Nagila*"; while they bought Israel Bonds and proclaimed the wonders of a people who brought water to the desert, few actually made *aliyah* to the new state. The various American Jewish defense organizations were more concerned with domestic situations involving anti-Semitism than lobbying the federal government for support of Israel.

Research pertaining to the Shoah advanced throughout the decade. The number of scholarly monographs on the Third Reich and the Holocaust increased annually, some becoming early standards within the field (Baron 68–71), but few penetrated into the consciousness of the general public. The popular American literature of the 1950s included many books of special Jewish interest, several even making best seller lists (Asch; Baruch; Golden), but two books with Holocaust themes or sub-themes attracted particularly significant audiences, Anne Frank's *Diary of a Young Girl* and Leon Uris' novel, *Exodus*. While neither book can be said to have created a ground swell of interest in the Shoah among American readers, each would increase a general awareness of the event itself, particularly among younger, more impressionable readers.

Anne Frank's diary attracted a large readership in the United States, as it would in many other translations around the world. The poignant words of the child in hiding, her saga of the relationships and clashes among the people who lived with her in the secret annex, her optimism about the eventual triumph of good in the world and her tragic end all touched sensitive chords in the audience, as would the stage play and film that followed within a decade. Although a foreign story, Anne's hopes and dreams were typical of teenaged girls everywhere; and, while she may have been Jewish, that term seemed more adjective than noun. Hence she could be broadly accepted as a kind of Jewish persona of every young girl. The diary mentioned the Franks observing a holiday or two, but there was not a lot of concern with the details of Jewish life and theological distinctions between Christianity and Judaism were not a topic of her discourse. "Jew" was little more than a synonym for "victim." Anne and her family were victims an audience could accept, pity and embrace—a fact not lost on those who later wrote the stage and cinematic adaptations of the story. The transmutation of Anne Frank from Jewish victim to universal symbol of tragically lost youth fostered the continuing acceptance of her story. Anne Frank became a universal martyr, but the reading and acceptance of her story by the public cannot be said to have advanced American knowledge of the Holocaust beyond the most subliminal level.

Exodus appeared on bookstore shelves in 1958, spent nineteen weeks atop the best-seller lists and was the best selling book in America for 1959.[3] The topic of many a rabbi's sermon and sisterhood luncheon, Uris' novel contained all the ingredients a general readership might want; a strong and handsome hero, a beautiful heroine with a tragic past, ill-fated lovers, feuding brothers, evil villains, action scenes galore—all set against an exotic foreign backdrop. Although the central story was a fictionalized account of the postwar years leading up to the creation of the State of Israel, the opening subplot centered on *Aliyah Bet*, the illegal immigration efforts to resettle Holocaust survivors in Mandate Palestine in defiance of British immigration restrictions. Again, most of the characters were Jewish, but few were portrayed as religiously observant; the Jewish hero, Ari Ben-Canaan, was a determinedly secular Palestinian, while the heroine, Kitty Fremont, was a Christian from the American Midwest. A film version was released in the early 1960s; perhaps with an eye on the larger audience, several of the primary roles were portrayed by performers who did not appear stereotypically Jewish.[4]

Exodus, though a story about Israel, included several characters who had experienced the Holocaust—in particular, Karen Clement, hidden and protected by a Danish Christian family, and Dov Landau, a young survivor of Auschwitz who sought revenge for his suffering and joined the terrorist Irgun as soon as he reached Palestine. Karen seeks to soften Dov's hatred and mistrust of non-Jews by recalling the goodness of the Hansen family, while Dov comforts Karen when her search for her scientist father concludes in a psychiatric hospital, German torture having left only a shell of the man she had long sought. *Exodus* was, most of all, an action story about tough Jews, playing against and cutting across stereotypical images of Jews as passive rather than active, cerebral rather than physical, victims rather than heroes. The American Jewish audience loved it and the general audience accepted it.[5]

As the 1950s drew to a close, William L. Shirer published his massive *The Rise and Fall of the Third Reich*, the first major history of Hitler's Germany to be written for an English-speaking audience. The author had been a correspondent stationed in Germany, beginning in the 1930s; his book became a best seller, despite its 1,245 page length.[6] It remained a standard source of information for decades and remains in print today.

A second book which appeared at the time was quite different in length, style, and tone from Uris' novels or Shirer's chronicle. *Night* was an English translation of the French version of a Yiddish book, *Un die Welt Hot Geshvign* ("And the World Was Silent"). Published in Argentina, the slender text was written by a young Hungarian-born Israeli newspaper correspondent named Elie Wiesel. Still selling after forty-five years (and recently on the best-seller's list, thanks to an endorsement from Oprah Winfrey), there is nothing optimistic in *Night*, nothing positive, nothing hopeful. The fight for survival waged by Eliezer and his father through their months in Auschwitz and on the death march thereafter exhaust one, leaving the reader filled with sadness and despair. The book was not a best-seller; it did not inspire anyone, but it became a somber presence in Jewish literature, to be turned to when one was ready to go beyond the optimism of Anne Frank to the now familiar chilling words:

> Never shall I forget that night, that first night in camp, which has turned my life into one long night, seven times cursed and seven times sealed. Never shall I forget that smoke. Never shall I forget the little faces of the children, whose bodies I saw turned into wreaths of smoke beneath a silent blue sky.
>
> Never shall I forget those flames which consumed my faith forever.
>
> Never shall I forget that nocturnal silence which deprived me, for all eternity, of the desire to live. Never shall I forget those moments which murdered my God and my soul and turned my dreams to dust. Never shall I forget these things, even if I am condemned to live as long as God Himself. Never (44).

But if Wiesel was unable to forget, the American public was not yet prepared to remember with this level of intensity.

THE 1960s

In the early 1960s, America's attention was focuses upon the space race and the Communist threat. The inauguration of John F. Kennedy marked a transition—the accession to power of a new generation, born in the twentieth century, tested by Depression and tempered in world war. The optimism of what would come to be called "Camelot" would soon be offset, however, by the failure of the Bay of Pigs invasion of Cuba, the building of the Berlin Wall and the Cuban Missile Crisis of October 1962. On the domestic front, civil rights demonstrations—begun in the 1950s—filled southern streets, sidewalks, and jails as well as northern newspapers. Many rabbis spoke from their pulpits in sympathy with the cause of civil rights, and young Jews joined in, as marchers, Freedom Bus riders, voter registration activists and—as in the case of Andrew Goodman and Michael Schwerner—the victims of racist backlash.[7]

The activism of the Kennedy administration and the moral passion of Martin Luther King, Jr. further stimulated these young, largely second-generation native-born American Jews to participate in causes that Jewish tradition or teachings might have endorsed. The image of Abraham Joshua Heschel standing next to Martin Luther King, Jr., during the march in Selma, Alabama, a rabbi and a Baptist minister together as Americans, underscored the findings of Will Herberg from 1955 and 1960, that a non-specific empathy with Judaism was being accepted by American culture as a legitimate—if not quite equal—American identity (231–53). This involvement of the first members of the Baby Boom Generation—with their elder brothers and sisters—was only a foretaste of the turbulence that would envelope the country by decade's end. Before the morass that was the Vietnam War, three events occurred that helped to invigorate Jewish identity, raise public concern for the well-being of the State of Israel and arouse unprecedented American interest and investigation about the Holocaust.

In Buenos Aires, Argentina, on the evening of May 11, 1960, agents of the Mossad, Israel's secret service, kidnapped a middle-aged man shortly after he alit from a bus on his way home from work. Initially insisting his name was Ricardo Klement, the man soon admitted he was SS officer Adolf Eichmann, former head of the Central Office for Jewish Emigration in Berlin and the Reich Central Security Office (dealing with Jewish affairs and evacuation) and among the most wanted of Nazi leaders.[8] Secreted out of Argentina, Eichmann was brought to Israel where, despite protests from the Argentine government, he was held for many months leading up to a public trial that presented the facts of the Holocaust before a world that had either never been very familiar with them or had long before put them out of mind.[9]

In Israel, interest in the trial was so great that the Israel Broadcasting Authority used the event to establish the country's first television station, and television receivers were placed in storefronts so that the citizenry—most of whom did not own a TV—could view the continuing broadcast of the trial.

In the United States, the ABC television network regularly devoted several minutes of its late-night news broadcast to the day's events at the trial and made available to the public a copy of the charges levied against Eichmann. For a younger generation, too young to remember or born after World War II and the horrors of the Shoah, the trial served as an introduction to an event largely unmentioned at home or in their school history books (see Epstein). It may have been difficult for many to believe that the ordinary-looking man with the dark-rimmed eyeglasses who sat, day after day, in a bullet-proof glass cubicle in the court room, had worn the Death's Head insignia and bore responsibility for millions of deaths in the camps. For survivors and some other members of the generation who had lived through that period, the trial reawakened memories and raised consideration of the events for the first time in years, if ever.[10]

While the story of Eichmann's capture, his trial and subsequent execution began to stir memories, a later series of events in Israel created the impetus that led to an upsurge in Jewish identity and inquiry in America of the Shoah, including a much more systematic investigation of the darkest times in modern Jewish history. The growing tensions and fears of May, 1967, followed by the seemingly miraculous events of the Six-Day War awakened among young American Jews. Largely third-generation Americans—the baby boomers—were not yet old enough to have experienced the remaining social and professional prejudices with which their parents were so well acquainted. Many had grown up in the new neighborhoods, sharing with their Gentile friends Cub Scouts and Brownies, Davy Crockett hats and hula hoops before the folk music revival and then "Beatlemania" put guitars in their hands and love beads around their necks. Now, they had begun attending college, in numbers incomparable to those of previous generations. For them, the Six-Day War fostered an upsurge in Jewish identity and a personal identification with the State of Israel—even among otherwise secular young Jews—that had not manifested itself before, nor had it been apparent in many of their elders. Oddly enough, a remark by Martin Luther King, Jr., uttered just prior and in a context unrelated to Israel or the Six-Day War, played a contributory role in this new Jewish positivism. Following the lead of previous speakers, King had used the phrase "Black is beautiful" in a speech, meaning that a Negro seeking equal rights and opportunities in America need not abandon his or her distinctive African traditions and cultural identity. King's apparent approval of African cultural particularism—an apparent rebuff of the melting pot theory that had excluded Blacks anyway—gave an imprimatur to distinctiveness that many minority groups—and donors to liberal causes—quickly embraced. By midsummer of 1967, a number of groups were asserting their cultures with buttons—bearing declarations of "Black Power," "Irish Power," "Italian Power," "Indian Power," "Polish Power," and "Jewish Power"—which began to be worn on the shirts and jackets of largely youthful advocates of each cause. Over the next few years, growing numbers of young American Jews traveled to Israel, as tourists and volunteers to work on the kibbutzim, or as students in the suddenly burgeoning semester and one-year programs sponsored by American and Israeli universities as well as by the Israel government and the Jewish Agency.[11]

We have already noted how the box office success of the 1960 motion picture *Exodus* spread a positive and sympathetic portrait of Jews and Israel to a large viewing audience. A second film released during this period created a different mood. An adaptation of a telecast from *Playhouse 90* in 1959, *Judgment at Nuremburg* (1961) was unlike the many World War II battle films that continued to be produced during the 1960s; attention focused upon a segment of the Third Reich's leadership and, therefore, upon Holocaust perpetrators. An international cast brought star power to this fictionalized version of the War Crimes Trials held in the immediate post-war years. Spencer Tracy starred as Dan Haywood, an American jurist presiding as Chief Justice during the trials of former judges in the Third Reich.[12] The audience was presented with a variety of defendants, from the staunch Nazi Emil Hahn (Werner Klemperer) to the noble Ernst Janning (Burt Lancaster), who had known his actions were contradictory to the legal system to which he had devoted his life but who continued to act in accordance with Party policies and now was prepared to confess his acts and accept his punishment. Director Stanley Kramer included actual film footage of the concentration camps, which was utilized as evidence during the trial. For many in the audience, too young to have seen the newsreels fifteen years earlier, this was the first time these now-familiar images were giving broad public viewing. In the film's final scenes, after the Nazis have been found guilty and sentence has been pronounced upon them, Haywood is depicted visiting Janning. The convicted Nazi-judge thanks the American for the manner in which the trial had been conducted and gives him a stack of papers, files on as many of the Nazi-era cases as he can recall. Haywood accepts the papers but again rebukes the German for having acted as he had.[13]

The film was well received by audiences and critics alike, garnering many awards around the world.[14] Its acceptance by the American public may have been as much a response to the A-list cast as to the story itself, but the fact remains that a producer (Stanley Kramer) felt he could include actual scenes out of the Holocaust in a major commercial film.

Two highly controversial dramas reached Broadway during the 1960s. While Richard Burton was starring in *Hamlet* and Carol Channing dominated the stage in *Hello Dolly*, *Der Stellvertreter*, a lengthy work by West German playwright Rolf Hochhuth, debuted in Berlin, and had its initial English-language performances as *The Representative* in London. In a shorter version, it opened on Broadway February 26, 1964 as *The Deputy*, where it ran for 316 performances. Incurring audience catcalls, demonstrations and picketing in Europe, the play is the story of Father Riccardo Fontana, S. J., a naïve young priest whose father, Count Fontana, is counsel to the pope. Father Fontana has been sent to Berlin, where he meets Gerstein, a Christian SS officer with a conscience. Gerstein informs Fontana of the massacres of Jews and asks for papal intervention. Having been confronted, the pope agrees to make a general statement of concern for the oppressed, but refuses to make any direct reference to death camps. Disheartened by the refusal to help, Father Fontana eventually sacrifices his own life, substituting himself for a Jewish prisoner selected for the gas chamber. The young priest's passionate anguish stands in sharp distinction to the pope, making the play a clear condemnation of Pope Pius XII and his public silence throughout the Holocaust. Conservative Catholics were quick to condemn the play and rushed to the defense of the late pontiff.[15] Coming so soon after the invitations to ecumenical and inter-religious dialogue of Vatican II, *The Deputy*, written by a Lutheran, was seen by some as a step backwards. Other critics were more positive in tone. James H. Nichols, a Protestant who served as an observer at Vatican II, was critical of the theatrical merits of the play, calling the portrayal of the Pope "dramatically unconvincing," but he added, "The function of such a play as this is precisely to make men acknowledge and test their deepest religious differences in a dialogue, not to deny they have any" (112).

Jewish reactions to the play have varied. In 1999, in an essay devoted to the Vatican statement, "We Remember: A Reflection on the Shoah," David Novak wrote:

> Rolf Hochhuth's 1963 play *The Deputy* ... [which] builds on the plausible assumption that the Pope did know about the mass extermination of the Jews from 1942 on, raised the question of why the Pope didn't publicly condemn what the Nazis were doing to the Jews. On that question, the jury is still out. If we assume that the Pope knew what was happening, then the question is whether his public silence was an act of moral cowardice or an act of moral prudence.
>
> Those who make the case for moral cowardice argue that the Pope feared to upset the Nazis under whose control he was living during the German occupation of Italy. Furthermore, he had always seemed more concerned with the danger of communism, with its explicit anti-Christian and anti-Catholic bias, than he had been concerned with Nazism. ... Those who make the case for moral prudence note that the Pope reasonably feared that many other Catholics, especially the clergy (who would be taken as his agents), would be killed if he spoke out. There is also, of course, the question of whether public criticism by the Pope of Nazi policies would have had any positive effect. It might well even have been counterproductive.
>
> Because moral judgment in this case requires much more historical inquiry, one can hardly be conclusive about either judgment. The case is further complicated by the fact that we are dealing with a moral judgment that if unfavorable would be for a sin of omission rather than a sin of commission. No one could say that the Pope actually spoke or acted positively on behalf of the Nazi regime (as did some bishops), and certainly not on behalf of the crimes of the Nazis. (24–25)

The second play to induce consternation among some viewers, *The Man in the Glass Booth*, opened on Broadway September 26, 1968, and enjoyed a run of 269 performances, closing May 17, 1969.[16] British actor Donald Pleasance starred as Arthur Goldman, a Jewish businessman with a proclivity for making anti-Semitic remarks. Convinced he is actually SS Colonel Adolf Dorff, Israeli agents capture Goldman and, when he does not refute the charge, bring him to Israel for trial. Goldman/Dorff seems to revert to his Nazi past; he wears an SS uniform as he sits in his bulletproof box during the trial, boasting about Hitler and atrocities, until a spectator announces that the defendant really is a Jew. Goldman, it seems, wishes to be a martyr, to provide some sort of atonement and retribution for the crimes done to his people.

The play, so clearly based upon events of the Eichmann capture and trial, was not well received by the critics. Donald Pleasance received rave reviews for his performance (and won a Tony as Best Actor), but the reviewer for *Time* wrote that the play "recapitulates the past without transforming it. It raises the stale questions of German guilt, Jewish passivity and the paranoiac personality of the archkiller, along with a recital of atrocities. But it offers no fresh illumination."[17]

Television presentations concerning the Holocaust were not numerous in the early portion of the decade; although former Nazis and concentration camp survivors would appear as characters in various episodic television series, usually detective mysteries or court dramas, and references to the camps became more common, as some terminology became familiar to American audiences. One different and notable exception to this norm was an episode of the series *The Twilight Zone*. Airing on CBS on November 10, 1961, "Death's Head Revisited" told the story of the unrepentant SS Captain Lutze, who makes a nostalgic visit to Dachau many years after the war. Intending to reminisce, he is instead confronted by the ghosts of the men he tortured and killed. Tried and convicted by the shades of his victims, he is sentenced to feel the pain they had known, a punishment which costs him his sanity.[18]

A far different view of the Third Reich debuted on the ABC network on September 17, 1965. *Hogan's Heroes* was a situation comedy about a group of Allied prisoners of war who were, in fact, the masters of Stalag 13 (their POW camp), from which, its bumbling Commandant, Colonel Wilhelm Klink, boasted, no one had ever escaped and within which the overweight and unaware Sergeant Schultz saw and heard "nothing." Led by the dashing Colonel Hogan (Bob Crane), the prisoners eat gourmet meals, maintain radio contact with London and constantly slip out of camp to romance local *fräuleins*, perform acts of sabotage, and rescue Allied fliers and spies, despite the efforts of evil Nazi generals and diabolical Gestapo agents.[19] A farcical production with little connection to history, the series generated some early complaints for making light of such dark times but enjoyed good ratings and a long television life (168 episodes) before beginning syndicated reruns.[20]

THE 1970s

Stirred by the Six-Day War and emboldened by the wave of activism sweeping college campuses throughout the late 1960s and early 70s, Jewish students joined in the call for curricular reforms, breaking away from the "canon" of traditional liberal arts subjects. Departments of history, philosophy, sociology, English, religion, and political science were requested, implored, and, in some cases, commanded to add course offerings recognizing the existence and significance of heretofore generally ignored groups. The three fields which most benefited from this expansion of the curriculum and about which, in some cases, student interest fostered a rapid growth from an additional course or two to programs, majors and departments were Women's Studies, Black Studies, and Jewish Studies. The 1970s witnessed a rapid increase in courses and even programs in Jewish Studies at colleges and universities throughout the United States. Many of these new courses began as expansions of units previously included within earlier offerings in history and religion departments. They tended to be broad rather than deep, usually involving surveys of a period or religious tradition. The historical surveys, if inclusive of the twentieth century, engaged in discussion of the Holocaust, on some campuses, for the first time. Department chairs and college registrars, pleased by the full enrollments the new courses were achieving and in a period when many departments were expanding their total course rosters, were inclined to accept proposals for further additions, more specialized in nature. In 1959, independent of one another, Franklin H. Littell and Yaffa Eliach had offered the first courses on the Holocaust at any American college or university.[21] In the ensuing decade, few followed their lead, but, as the 1960s yielded to the 70s and, especially, the 80s, Holocaust courses, the publication of books, and preparation of films became a growth industry, supported by endowed chairs in Jewish Studies, which also enjoyed a sharp increase in number.[22]

By the mid-1970s, courses and units devoted to Holocaust study were spreading across the country; *Night* was becoming standard reading in many of those courses, and Elie Wiesel was being seen more and more frequently on American television, serving, for all intents and purposes, as the voice of the survivors. The 1973 Yom Kippur War had put an end to much of the optimism that had been the prevailing Jewish attitude about the Middle East since 1967. The intervening years had also witnessed other events which darkened the mood of the country. Years of increasingly strident protest against the Vietnam War had divided the country and brought down the Johnson Administration. Many liberal Jews found themselves advocating for changes in federal policy in two different directions: urging Washington's support for Israel while demonstrating against American military actions in Viet Nam. The bipolar nature of these positions was not lost on some, as when Vice President Spiro Agnew publicly accused Jewish American student war protesters of dual loyalties and questioned their patriotism. This was a charge the students' immigrant grandparents might have feared above all others—America was for them *the* refuge, after all—but it was one quickly dismissed by the protesters.[23]

American television had tended to give minimal attention to the Holocaust during the opening years of the 70s although, by decade's end, the mini-series *Holocaust* (discussed below) would burst across the small screen. *QB VII*, a six-hour drama based on the Leon Uris novel, aired in two parts, April 29-30, 1974, on the ABC network. Ben Gazzara starred as Abe Cady, a journalist sued for libel by Adam Kelno (Anthony Hopkins), a physician whom Cady accused of committing medical atrocities in a concentration camp during the war. The program featured a well-known international cast, including Jack Hawkins, John Gielgud, Edith Evans and Anthony Quayle. Re-broadcast on several occasions, *QB VII* received thirteen Emmy nominations, winning five.[24]

The 1976 rescue by Israeli forces of Jewish passengers from a plane hijacked to Uganda was the subject of competing programs, each with internationally known lead performers, rushed through production for American television. *Victory at Entebbe* premiered on ABC, December 13, 1976, with a cast of extremely familiar faces, including Kirk Douglas, Burt Lancaster, Elizabeth Taylor, Helen Hayes, Helmut Berger and Richard Dreyfuss.[25] Less than one month later (January 9, 1977) *Raid on Entebbe* was broadcast by NBC. This version, the stars of which included Charles Bronson, Peter Finch, Yaphet Kotto and Sylvia Sidney, was better received by critics, garnering eight Emmy nominations.[26] Although not the primary subject, each film made references to the Shoah and made repeated mention that Holocaust survivors were among the passengers.[27]

American network television achieved its broadcasting high-water mark on April 16, 1978, with the premier airing of *Holocaust*. The eight hour miniseries traced the lives (and deaths) of two German families—one Jewish, the other Gentile—against the backdrop of the Holocaust in all its horrors. Following the now familiar pattern, fictitious characters were at the center of the story, surrounded by actual events and true historic figures. Once again, an international cast was assembled for the drama,[28] including a cohort of relatively unknown players who became extremely well known in subsequent years.[29] The characters represented a variety of types; the thoroughly assimilated Weiss family included a doctor and his wife, their artistic son (Karl) and his Christian wife (Inga), his sister (Anna) and athletic younger brother (Rudi). The primary German character, Erich Dorf, begins as a mild-mannered German Christian and ends as the cold organizer of mass murder.

The series was announced by NBC with great fanfare and publicized heavily in the weeks prior to its airing. The script, written by Gerald Green, was published as a novel and appeared in bookstores a fortnight before the initial episode; the music, composed by Morton Gould, was recorded and available for purchase. NBC also prepared a viewer's guide for educators, encouraging discussion following each episode. The broadcast itself began during the week before Passover and was scheduled to conclude on the anniversary of the Warsaw Ghetto uprising.

Jeffrey Shandler has noted, quite correctly, "Few critics championed *Holocaust* for making a significant artistic or intellectual statement about its subject—for some its greatest virtue was that it was produced at all" (159). As for the story itself, when all is said and done, it was a soap opera—lavishly produced on location, well acted, but a soap opera nonetheless. Every character meets a different fate; the Weiss parents witness *Kristallnacht* in Berlin, are deported to the Warsaw Ghetto, and die in Auschwitz. Daughter Anna is raped by German soldiers, loses her sanity and is sent to Hadamar, the "house of shudders," where patients are routinely killed. Karl, the artist son, survives Auschwitz and the death march to Buchenwald, reaching Theresienstadt, only to die at the moment of liberation, while younger brother Rudi leaves Germany and joins a partisan band, where he meets and marries Helena Slomova, a Zionist from Czechoslovakia, only to lose her in an attack. Captured and sent to the Sobibor concentration camp, Rudi is part of the uprising there and escapes. The sole surviving member of his family, Rudi is preparing to voyage to Palestine when he spies children playing soccer, his former sport. The series' final shot is a close-up of the handsome and healthy Rudi, smiling broadly.

Holocaust was accompanied by many controversies. Critics complained about the predictable (soap opera) format of the plot, while others decried the unrealistic appearance of the concentration camp inmates (the sole exception being the character of Karl, played by the gaunt James Woods). The fact that the series was filmed in color was objected to by some, who felt that black and white cinematography would have better projected the mood. Others worried that *Holocaust* would be the only major program on the Shoah many in the audience would ever see, leaving them believing the fictional presentation to be an accurate rendition of history. Elie Wiesel, perhaps the harshest critic, entitled his evaluation of the series "Trivializing the Holocaust."[30]

On a more positive note, discussions of the series and the event it portrayed took place in many venues, before a wide variety of audiences. *Holocaust* was the subject of articles in many Jewish and Christian journals, as well as in history, international affairs, and other publications, both scholarly and popular. Within a year, the program had been broadcast in Israel, South Africa, and a number of European countries, including West Germany, where it reached another large audience which had never discussed the Holocaust in so public a fashion.[31]

Perhaps the definitive affirmation of the Holocaust's entry into the American psyche also came in 1978, just several weeks after the airing of *Holocaust*, with the formation of the President's Commission on the Holocaust. Created by President Jimmy Carter and chaired by Elie Wiesel, the interfaith group was charged with making recommendations for an appropriate memorial to the Holocaust's victims. The commission met for the first time on February 15, 1979; on September 27 of that year it issued a Report to the President containing four recommendations; the creation of a "living memorial" with spiritual and educational components, national recognition of Days of Remembrance honoring victims of the Shoah, Senate Ratification of the Genocide Treaty, and American pressure on foreign countries to prosecute Nazi war criminals and care for Jewish cemeteries.[32]

On October 7, 1980, Carter signed Public Law 96-388, which established the President's Council on the Holocaust, the successor to the commission. The recommendation for a combined museum, memorial, and learning center having been approved, a site was chosen, the process of fundraising begun, and, on April 30, 1984, a symbolic groundbreaking was held, in which ashes from two concentration camps were mixed into the earth. Construction of the building was slow; the actual groundbreaking did not occur until October 16, 1986, while the cornerstone of the new edifice was laid October 5, 1988. Finally, on April 26, 1993, the United States Holocaust Memorial Museum was opened to the public, soon becoming second only to the Smithsonian Institution as a tourist attraction in Washington, DC.[33]

The creation of a national museum, the opening of similar institutions in Los Angeles and New York as well as many smaller museums and Holocaust memorials throughout the country, the observance of national Days of Remembrance by the Congress and military, and the many *Yom HaShoah* commemorations by Jewish and interfaith groups testify to the acceptance of the Holocaust not only as an unprecedented human tragedy, but one about which Americans should be concerned and remember. With a second and third generation taking courses, reading books, attending symposia, watching films and television programs, the victims' stories were finally heard and accepted. The Holocaust had become part of the American memory and was "silent no more."

Notes

1. For additional reading, see Novick, *The Holocaust in American Life*; Flanzbaum, *The Americanization of the Holocaust*; Baron, "The Holocaust and American Public Memory 1945–1960"; and Young, *The Texture of Memory: Holocaust Memorials and Meaning*.
2. The shared name of several large suburban developments across the northeastern United States created by developed William Levitt.
3. Its sales continued when a paperback version was published; by 1965 over five million copies had been purchased.
4. The cast included Paul Newman (Ari Ben-Canaan) and Eva Marie Saint (Kitty Fremont) with Sal Mineo, Valerie-Jill Haworth, David Opatoshu and Lee J. Cobb in the primary "Jewish" roles. Mike Cummings, in the "All Movie Guide," praises Sal Mineo for his portrayal of Auschwitz survivor Dov Landau but is more critical of Paul Newman, noting that he "performs well enough as Jewish leader Ari Ben-Canaan [but] his physical attributes—notably the blue eyes and light hair—rob him of a small measure of credibility."
5. In 1961 Uris published a more straightforward Holocaust novel, *Mila 18*. Set in the Warsaw Ghetto—the title was the address of the bunker in which resistance leader Mordechai Anielewicz and one hundred Jews were killed, May 8, 1943—the novel applied the same formula, blending fictional characters with historical events. Sales were good, although the commercial success of *Exodus* could not be duplicated.
6. The book was ranked seventh in sales in 1960 and second in 1961, its sales assisted, perhaps, by an increase in public interest due to the capture and trial of Adolph Eichmann.
7. Andrew Goodman and Mickey Schwerner were civil rights activists who, along with James Chaney, an African-American civil rights activist, were murdered by Ku Klux Klan members in 1964. Their story was the subject of the 1988 film *Mississippi Burning*.
8. For the story of Eichmann's capture and transport to Israel, see Harel.
9. See Hausner. Hausner, as Israel's Attorney General, was the lead prosecutor in the case.
10. Cf. Arendt 252 and her description of the "banality of evil."
11. The author speaks here from personal experience, having attended programs sponsored by Hebrew University and the Jewish Agency in the early 1970s.
12. In addition to Spencer Tracy, the cast included Burt Lancaster, Richard Widmark, Maximilian Schell, Marlene Dietrich, Judy Garland, Montgomery Clift, Werner Klemperer, and even the future "Captain Kirk," a young William Shatner.
13. Janning says, "Judge Haywood . . . the reason I asked you to come: Those people, those millions of people . . . I never knew it would come to that. You must believe it. You must believe it." Haywood replies, "Herr Janning it came to that the first

time you sentenced a man to death you knew to be innocent." See IMDB.com/title/tt0055031/quotes.
14. The film was nominated for the Best Picture Academy Award. Tracy, Schell, Clift, and Garland received nominations for acting. The film received a total of eleven nominations, and two Oscars. It also received awards in Denmark, Great Britain, Italy, and Spain.
15. More than forty years after the play's debut, a casual search of the Internet will uncover dozens of sites devoted to impassioned paeans to Pius and vituperations of Hochhuth's work as anti-Catholic, for example, "The Deputy was more than merely a play. It was a sustained exercise in character assassination that was resoundingly echoed in the popular press. The production of that play coincided closely with the publication of Anne Frank's Diary and the trial and execution of Adolf Eichmann. The world needed to give vent to its horror, and with no more real Nazis left to punish, the image of a pusillanimous pope offered just the right scapegoat" (Graham).
16. The play was written by British actor and author Robert Shaw and directed by Harold Pinter. A film version starring Maximillian Schell was released in 1975.
17. *Time* 4 Oct. 1968. Reviewing the play for the *New York Times*, Clive Barnes wrote: "Engrossing the play certainly is. But it has nothing to say about any of the subjects it hints it is going to illuminate. For its pretensions are based on totally false premises . . . We are in a lurid world of melodrama."
18. The set—which had been built as a frontier fort for an earlier production—did not look anything like Dachau, an inaccuracy unnoticed by the general audience which was satisfied by its decrepit appearance. *Twilight Zone* creator Rod Serling would include the character of Hitler in other episodes of the series, in stories that warned the audience of the dangers of hate.
19. Col. Klink was played by the same Werner Klemperer who had appeared in *Judgment at Nuremburg*. A German Jew and the son of conductor Otto Klemperer, the actor had come to America as a refugee in the 1930s and served in the American military. Robert Clary, who played the French POW, Cpl. Louis LeBeau, had an even stronger connection to the Holocaust. A child performer in his native France, Clary was captured in the second roundup of Jewish children in Paris and sent to Auschwitz, a fact he kept from public knowledge until the 1980s.
20. For some viewers, the program generated greater significance because of the character of Sgt. Kinchlow. Played by Ivan Dixon, "Kinch" was the first Negro character treated as an equal among an otherwise white ensemble cast. If *Hogan's Heroes* reduced Nazis to buffoons, Mel Brooks would transmute the horrors of the Third Reich to farce in his 1968 film *The Producers*.
21. Littell offered his course at Emory University; Eliach at Brooklyn College. Forty-five years later, each scholar was still offering courses on the topic.
22. In previous writings, I have discussed these survey-type courses as "phase one" Holocaust studies, the more specialized courses as "phase two," and, inevita-

bly, courses that use the Holocaust primarily as a hook for more general topics, as "phase three." By the 1990s, the total of phase one and two courses offered on American (and Canadian) campuses numbered in the many hundreds. See my article, "Teaching the Holocaust: End of the Beginning."

23. The author recalls spirited arguments with Israeli friends in this period about Richard Nixon: while I was excoriating the president for his Vietnam policies, my Israeli friends praised him for his support of their country.
24. John Gielgud and Juliet Mills won the awards for Best Actor and Actress; the program also received awards for music, graphic design and editing.
25. Outside the United States, it was exhibited as a feature film.
26. *Victory at Entebbe* received four nominations, for writing and technical achievements. See Marill 1: 176, 178, 235.
27. Even before either version of the Entebbe rescue story was broadcast, *21 Hours at Munich*, a dramatization of the murders of Israeli Olympic team members and coaches was aired on ABC (November 7, 1976). The film featured several well-known stars, including William Holden, Shirley Knight, Richard Basehart and Anthony Quayle, and received the Emmy for "Outstanding Special—Drama or Comedy." References were made to the earlier plight of Jews in Germany and the specter of the Holocaust was raised before an audience from whom sympathy for the victims could be expected.
28. Fritz Weaver, Rosemary Harris, Ian Holm and Nigel Hawthorne were among the better known cast members.
29. Performers within this category include Meryl Streep, James Woods, Tovah Felshuh, Michael Moriarty and Joseph Bottoms.
30. Shandler 155–78. Other objections extended to the sponsors; some felt commercials for a popular dog food were inappropriate.
31. The series had one NBC network rebroadcast before reaching cable, where it is shown on an annual basis.
32. See www.xroads.virginia.edu/~CAP/HOLO/commissi.html. The Convention on the Prevention and Punishment of the Crime of Genocide was adopted by the United Nations General Assembly December 9, 1948, and in force since January 12, 1951. Although President Harry Truman signed the treaty December 12, 1948, the Senate did not ratify it until 1998, making the United States the ninety-ninth nation to ratify the treaty.
33. See www.USHMM.org.

Works Cited

21 Hours at Munich. Perf. William Holden, Shirley Knight, Franco Nero, Richard Basehart, and Anthony Quayle. ABC. 7 November 1976.

Arendt, Hannah. *Eichmann in Jerusalem: A Report on the Banality of Evil.* New York: Penguin, 2008.

Asch, Sholem. *Moses.* London: Macdonald, 1952.

Barnes, Clive. Rev. of *The Man in the Glass Booth. New York Times* 27 Sept. 1968.

Baron, Lawrence. "The Holocaust and American Public Memory 1945–1960." *Journal of Holocaust and Genocide Studies* 17.1 (2003): 62–88.

Baruch, Bernard M. *Baruch: My Own Story.* New York: Holt, 1957.

Bourke-White, Margaret. Photographs of Buchenwald survivors. *Life* 7 May 1945.

Cummings, Mike. Rev. of *Exodus*, dir. Otto Preminger. *All Movie Guide* <www.allmovie.com/cg/avg.dll?p=avg&sql=1:16326~T1>.

"Death's Head Revisited." *The Twilight Zone.* CBS. 10 November 1961.

The Deputy. By Rolf Hochhuth. Perf. Emlyn Williams, and Jeremy Brett. Brooks Atkinson Theatre, New York. 26 February 1964. (Abridged version of *Der Stellvertreter;* also known as *The Representative.*)

Epstein, Joel. "The Holocaust as Non-History." *Methodology in the Academic Teaching of the Holocaust.* Ed. Zev Garber, Alan L. Berger, and Richard Libowitz. Lantham, MD: UP of America, 1988. 263–74.

Exodus. Dir. Otto Preminger. Perf. Paul Newman, Eva Marie Saint, Ralph Richardson, and Peter Lawford, and Lee J. Cobb. United Artists, 1960.

Flanzbaum, Helene. *The Americanization of the Holocaust.* Baltimore: Johns Hopkins UP, 1999.

Frank, Anne. *The Diary of a Young Girl.* Garden City: Doubleday, 1952. Golden, Harry. *Only in America.* Cleveland: World, 1958.

Graham, Robert A., S. J. "Pius XII's Defense of Jews and Others: 1944–45." <www.catholicleague.org/piusxii_and_the_holocaust/piusxii.htm>.

Harel, Isser. *The House on Garibaldi Street.* New York: Viking, 1975.

Hausner, Gideon. *Justice in Jerusalem.* New York: Schocken, 1978.

Herberg, Will. *Protestant-Catholic-Jew.* Garden City: Doubleday, 1955.

Hogan's Heroes. Perf. Bob Crane, Werner Klemperer, John Banner, Robert Clary, Larry Hovis, Richard Dawson, and Ivan Dixon. ABC. Released 17 September 1965.

Holocaust. Dir. Marvin J. Chomsky. Perf. Fritz Weaver, Rosemary Harris, Ian Holm and Nigel Hawthorne. NBC. Released 16 April 1978.

Judgment at Nuremburg. Dir. Stanley Kramer. Perf. Spencer Tracy, Burt Lancaster, Richard Widmark and Marlene Dietrich. United Artists, 1961.

Libowitz, Richard. "Teaching the Holocaust: End of the Beginning." *What Have We Learned? Telling the Story and Teaching the Lessons of the Holocaust.* Ed. Franklin H. Littell, Alan L. Berger, and Hubert G. Locke. Lewiston, NY: Mellen, 1995. 315–28.

The Man in the Glass Booth. By Robert Shaw. Dir. Harold Pinter. Perf. Donald Pleasence. Royale Theater, New York. 26 September 1968.

The Man in the Glass Booth. Dir. Arthur Hiller. Perf. Maximilian Schell, Lois Nettleton, Lawrence Pressman, Luther Adler. American Film Theatre, 1975.

Marill, Alvin H. *Movies Made for Television: the Telefeature and the Mini-series, 1964–1979*. Westport, CT: Arlington House, 1980.

Mississippi Burning. Dir. Alan Parker. Perf. Gene Hackman, Willem Dafoe, and Frances McDormand. Orion, 1988.

Nichols, James H. "*The Deputy* and Christian Conscience." *Theology Today* 21.1 (April 1964): 111–13.

Novak, David. "Jews and Catholics: Beyond Apologies." *First Things: A Monthly Journal of Religion and Public Life* (January 1999): 20–25.

Novick, Peter. *The Holocaust in American Life*. Boston: Houghton Mifflin, 1999.

"The President's Commission on the Holocaust." *American Studies at the University of Virginia*. 1998 <www.xroads.virginia.edu/~CAP/HOLO/commissi.html>. Path: The Capitol Project; Subject Index; Holocaust Memorial Museum: Analysis.

The Producers. Dir. Mel Brooks. Perf. Zero Mostel, Gene Wilder, and Dick Shawn. AVCO Embassy Pictures, 1968.

QB VII. By Edward Anhalt and Leon Uris. Perf. Ben Gazzara, Anthony Hopkins, Leslie Caron, and Lee Remick. ABC. Released 29–30 April 1974.

Raid on Entebbe. Dir. Irvin Kershner. NBC. 9 January 1977.

Rev. of *The Man in the Glass Booth*. *Time* 4 Oct. 1968.

Ross, Robert. *So It Was True*. Minneapolis: U of Minnesota P, 1980.

Shandler, Jeffrey. *While America Watches*. New York: Oxford UP, 1999.

Shirer, William L. *The Rise and Fall of the Third Reich*. New York: Simon and Shuster, 1960.

United States Holocaust Memorial Museum Web site. 30 Sept. 2008 <www.ushmm.org>.

Uris, Leon. *Exodus*. New York: Doubleday, 1958.

———. *Mila 18*. New York: Doubleday, 1961.

Victory at Entebbe. Dir. Marvin J. Chomsky. ABC. 13 December 1976.

Wiesel, Elie. *Night*. New York: Avon, 1969.

Young, James E. *The Texture of Memory: Holocaust Memorials and Meaning*. New Haven: Yale UP, 1994.

Imagining the Shoah in American Third Generation Cinema

By Lawrence Baron

As the Holocaust recedes further into the past, the number of survivors inevitably will dwindle until no one will be alive who endured its horrors. The stories they either recounted or withheld from their offspring as well as the lingering impact of trauma on their parenting provide oblique links to the calamity experienced by European Jewry during World War II (Berger; Hass).

How that legacy will be learned and transmitted by the grandchildren of survivors has become the subject of scholarly study only over the last decade.[1] Growing up at least forty years after the Holocaust and hearing as much as their grandparents and parents deemed appropriate to confide to them, members of this *Third Generation* must rely on "post-memory" to convey any semblance of the suffering inflicted on their ancestors. According to Marianne Hirsch, such remembrance results from a combination of a "generational distance" and "deep personal connection" to a traumatic event that scarred the life of a close relative. Recollecting an occurrence that one knows about second-hand requires an "imaginative investment and creation" (Hirsch 22–23). Though Hirsch applies this concept to explain the process employed by children of survivors to bear witness to their parents' ordeal, it seems equally valid for their grandchildren who are now assuming this role.

Several recent American movies such as *I Love You, I Love You Not* (1996), *The Devil's Arithmetic* (1999), and *Everything Is Illuminated* (2005) have dealt with Third Generation issues. They derive their plotlines from the post-memories of writers whose grandparents, other relatives, or family friends were survivors. The protagonists of these films eventually relive the Shoah by appropriating the identities of persecuted ancestors in flashbacks and time-travel scenes of incidents they had previously heard about in conversations, or by returning to the sites where relatives perished or evaded death at the hands of the Germans. Such narrative strategies replicate clinical findings about how some members of the Third Generation internalize the trauma of victimized loved ones. The three pictures illustrate a range of Third Generation responses to the Holocaust, including disassociation from a disturbing past, exaggeration of its influence on the present, and a realization that it is a relevant but not the determining factor in one's life (Chaitin, "Facing the Holocaust"; Chaitin, "Issues and Interpersonal Values"; Rosenthal).

For people with no personal connection to the Holocaust, movies provide the most common means to gain a sense of how it felt, looked, and sounded to be swept into its lethal vortex (Rosenstone 134–53). Since the vast majority of Americans fall into this category, films possess the capacity to function as "prosthetic memories," to borrow Alison Landsberg's term for widely disseminated media representations that enable contemporary audiences to grasp empathically, emotionally and sensually the travail of the "other" in a distant place and era (18–22). Indeed, Gary Weissman observes that some "non-witnesses," particularly American Jews, who belong to families unscathed by Nazi genocide, consider themselves part of the Third Generation and cultivate this vicarious kinship by interviewing survivors, reading their memoirs, touring sites where it was perpetrated, visiting museums, and watching motion pictures about it (2–27). In this regard, the perception of the Shoah represented in Third Generation films more closely resembles the perspective of non-witnesses than survivors.

Adapted from the play by Wendy Kesselman, *I Love You, I Love You Not* traces the emotional vulnerability of a teenage girl named Daisy to her internalization of her beloved Nana's anguish over losing her family and being interned at Auschwitz during the war. Their codependency has developed because Nana shares her haunted memories with Daisy but never speaks about them with her own daughter. While driving Daisy to visit Nana for an extended period, Daisy's mother warns her daughter against listening to Nana's stories, a sentiment echoed by her husband, who fears Nana will fill Daisy's "head with all these nightmares." Nana subsequently confesses to Daisy that she no longer resides with Daisy's parents because there were things she could not tell them.

Parenthetically, this pattern of preferential communication between survivors and their grandchildren and silence about the Holocaust when talking with their own children is not unusual. Many survivors preoccupied themselves with rebuilding their lives and starting new families after the war. They shielded their postwar children from the disconcerting details about the deaths of prewar family members and the tribulations of survival in ghettoes, hiding places, and concentration camps. Consequently, the passage of time and the popularization of the Holocaust made it easier for survivors to share their Shoah stories with their grandchildren rather than with their own offspring (Fossion et al.; Hass 161-62).

From the very beginning of the film, Daisy's entanglement with Nana heightens her identification with Nana's harrowing past. She feels estranged from her classmates at prep school because they seem so normal in comparison. In the opening scene, Daisy leans against a bathtub and draws Nana's identification number from Auschwitz on her own arm with a magic marker. When a Holocaust survivor speaks to her classes, Daisy weeps while the rest of the students gaze blankly at the slides the survivor is showing. After fielding several insensitive questions, the survivor asks if anyone has ever seen someone with numbers like those inscribed on her arm. Daisy is too ashamed to divulge her grandmother's secret, and Jesse, the sole African American at the school, chides Daisy for her timidity by reminding her that she is not the only one who is different there.

The intimate relationship Daisy has with Nana compensates for her social isolation among her peers. Although Nana emerges as a nurturing and strong character, she cannot conceal how psychologically wounded she remains from being abandoned by her Gentile girlfriend after she and her family were confined to the ghetto and being separated forever from her younger twin sisters by Dr. Mengele at Auschwitz. In the flashbacks to these incidents, Claire Danes, who stars as Daisy, also plays Nana as a teenager, symbolizing the mental bond that exists between the two characters. This is also apparent when Nana recalls voraciously reading books with her friend at her grandfather's while Daisy and she browse for books at a local shop.

Nana insulates Daisy and herself from the wrenching memory of losing her sisters by transforming the story into a fairytale about three sisters who had fled their home only to be captured by a white-gloved Angel of Death, who lured the twins away from their sibling. Kesselman often utilizes fairytale analogies in her plays because the "child or central figure in a fairy tale goes through terrible terrors, but fights against the terrors and survives in the end" (Interview, 266). Though Nana begins telling the story of the three sisters in the third person, she shifts to the first person by the end of it. Daisy asks what happened to the oldest sister, and Nana assures her she is "still here."

When confronted with crises, Daisy interjects herself into the accounts of the Holocaust presented by Nana and the survivor who spoke in her class: Daisy's popular boyfriend is taunted by his friends for dating such a shy and studious girl whom they dub Anne Frank. To stigmatize Daisy, they tape a photograph of an emaciated concentration camp inmate on the inside of her gym locker. They have written red numbers on the prisoner's arm and drawn an arrow pointing to them beneath the question "What's yours?" While waiting for the elevated train to take her home shortly thereafter, Daisy hears the voice of the survivor recalling how her mother tried to reassure her when they were deported. She envisions Nazi soldiers herding frightened Jews onto the transport. The infamous photograph appears in the hallucination, too.

After Nana retells the story of the three sisters later that night, Daisy worries that the Angel of Death will enter her nightmares. Of course, her fear quickly materializes. The synchronicity between grandmother and granddaughter is visualized in alternating close-ups of each tossing their heads as their sleep is disturbed by Dr. Mengele's sinister presence. Imagining herself behind a barbed wire fence, Daisy awakes and runs to Nana's bed, which is empty. Outside the house, Daisy sees Nana walking aimlessly in the dark. When the two hug, they look like twins dressed in their nightgowns.

The movie climaxes when Daisy's boyfriend callously jilts her for being too absorbed in the depressing past of her grandmother. Daisy lashes out at Nana as the source of her tainted Jewish identity and yells, "I don't want to be chosen like Marushya and Varushya [Nana's twin sisters]. I don't want to be taken away!" Hearing Nana recalling how her eyes burned from watching the atrocities in the camps, Daisy stands in the path of an oncoming train. For a moment, past and present coincide when Daisy serenely embraces the teenage apparition of her grandmother. The older Nana then yanks Daisy out of harm's way. Back in the safety of the living room, Daisy picks the petals from a real daisy, which confirm he "loves her not," and voices her disgust with how ugly the base of the flower looks when it is shorn of petals. Nana wisely points out, "It's a survivor, a yellow sun, a yellow star." Daisy regrets having to return home to her parents, but Nana reminds Daisy she will be around whenever Daisy needs her.

Critics of *I Love You, I Love You Not* accuse it of trivializing the Holocaust by comparing a "teenager's angst with genocide" (Haughton; Maslin). They charge that it is primarily a coming-of-age story. As Alvin Goldfarb puts it,

"Nana's experiences are meant to help Daisy grow up, not help her—or the audience—grapple with the experiences of a Holocaust survivor" (Goldfarb 121).

Though Kesselman concurs that her play is "more about adolescence than Jewishness," she drew upon stories told by friends who were survivors, particularly a cousin of her grandmother, for the film's plotline. Kesselman's grandmother, an immigrant from Riga before World War II, served as the model for Nana. If not literally a member of the Third Generation, Kesselman views herself as deeply connected to survivors as evidenced by her rewriting *The Diary of Anne Frank* for its recent Broadway revival (Vaughan 01C; Kesselman, Interview 272–73, 279–85).

Before dismissing *I Love You, I Love You Not*, critics and scholars should recognize that its target audience is teenagers. The film's PG-13 rating and casting with rising stars like Claire Danes and Jude Law indicate this, as does the synopsis on the DVD and videotape produced by Disney subsidiary Buena Vista Home Entertainment, which calls the movie "a passionate story about fitting in and falling in love." By identifying with Daisy's typical growing pains, adolescents unwittingly learn how psychic injuries inflicted on Holocaust survivors may still fester in the minds of their contemporary descendents. Goldfarb realizes that the "accessibility" of such works allows them to raise public awareness about the Shoah among groups who have little familiarity with it (120–21). As one reviewer remarked, *I Love You, I Love You Not* represents a "modern-day attempt to portray the events of more than a half a century ago in a format to give a minute understanding to a generation not even born when the atrocities were committed" (Salter). This is one niche that Third Generation films and literary works can fulfill.

Whereas Daisy filters her adolescent crises through Nana's traumatic memories, Hannah in *The Devil's Arithmetic* initially dissociates herself from the Jewish rituals and scarred past of her relatives. In Jane Yolen's novel upon which the film is based, Hannah's first utterance is "I'm tired of remembering" as she resists attending the family Seder at her Aunt Eva's home. The Shoah casts its pall on the gathering, where one of Hannah's grandfathers, who survived it, becomes agitated as he watches a television documentary about the Nazi crusade against the Jews (Yolen 3–10). In the film version, however, Hannah's uncles try to tell their distracted niece about prewar Jewish life in Poland and the public hanging of Yeshiva students caught trying to escape from their concentration camp. The wide age gap between Hannah and her uncles and aunt implies the latter are really her great uncles and great aunt.

The movie opens with popular actress Kirsten Dunst as Hannah hanging out at a tattoo parlor and deciding which design she prefers to be inked onto her ankle. Hannah suddenly realizes it is the first night of Passover and rushes home to join her parents for the family Seder. Nearing her Aunt Eva's apartment, Hannah contemptuously stares at the archaic garments and *peyes* of an ultra-Orthodox boy walking in the opposite direction. Eva warmly greets her niece and cannot believe how much she resembles Eva's deceased cousin after whom she was named. Curious about her namesake, Hannah wants to know more about her, but Eva demurs, "You wouldn't understand ... what it was like in the camps, what we lived through, if we lived, what it was like to be a Jew. This experience is so far from your world, I am afraid, though I so want to tell you what happened, it will mean nothing to you, and that would hurt me very much."

Hannah is noticeably bored with the rituals of the Seder, which are performed on screen in considerable detail. Her aunt kindles the candles; her uncle recites the blessing over the first cup of wine; the youngest children chant the Four Questions, and various members of the family narrate the biblical saga of how God freed the Jews from bondage and parted the Sea of Reeds (Red Sea) to let them escape Pharaoh's army. During the service, glimpses of the numbers tattooed on the arms of the survivors serve as a visual link between the bondage of the Jews in ancient Egypt and their status as nameless slaves in wartime Europe.

Towards the end of the meal, after Hannah has become tipsy from drinking too much wine, Aunt Eva urges her to open the door for the prophet Elijah, whose arrival will herald the coming of the Messiah. Hannah complies and finds herself in a hallway where a flash of bright light and the roar of howling wind whisk her back to the Polish *shtetl* where Eva's family dwelled until the Nazis deported them. Unaware of when and where she is, her cousin Rivka explains to Hannah that she (Hannah) had been stricken with typhus, which made her delirious for several weeks and killed her parents. Despite the strange surroundings, Hannah insists she is from New Rochelle, which prompts her relatives to ask where old Rochelle was. Rivka chooses a dress for Hannah to wear to a wedding, but Hannah finds her taste too "virginal." Rivka dismisses such remarks as side effects of Hannah's bout with typhus.

As the villagers congregate together for the wedding, Hannah is struck by the resemblance of the Yeshiva students to the boy she saw near her aunt's apartment. Director Donna Deitch pays as much attention to the marriage ceremony as she did to the Seder, and Rivka explains each custom to her confused cousin. German troops disrupt the wedding in a scene that parallels the pogrom at the end of the wedding in *Fiddler on the Roof*. It finally dawns on Hannah that this is the beginning of the Holocaust. She predicts that six million Jews will be systematically murdered by Germany, but none of her Polish relatives believe that something so barbarous will happen. As the town's Jews climb onto the trucks that will transport them to a death camp, the synagogue is set ablaze.

Hannah compares her memories of suburban life to the deprivations she faces daily in the camp where she and the Jews from the *shtetl* are interned. She realizes how shallow she had been, particularly when the Germans engrave her identification number on her arm, reminding her how she once had considered getting a tattoo to make a fashion statement. She regrets that she had ignored the unit on the Holocaust in her high school history class. In the nameless desolate camp where Hannah is incarcerated, the men and women converse with each other through the fence that separates their barracks. She befriends a young man who looks like the Orthodox boy she had snubbed earlier.

Since Hannah knows the outcome of the war, she assures the women in her barracks that some Jews will survive and immigrate to the United States. (Incidentally, in Yolen's novel, Hannah foresees the establishment of Israel: 156.) Hannah gives her bunkmates hope by regaling them with stories about the prosperity Jews will enjoy in America and recapitulating the plots of films she has seen, like *The Wizard of Oz*. The vulnerability of the Cowardly Lion and the melting of the Wicked Witch of the West serve as metaphors for the eventual defeat of Hitler.

Deitch does not spare her audience the horrors of daily existence in the camp. Hannah and all the other Jews are malnourished, overworked, and overcrowded. They live in constant dread of being selected for gassing. When several yeshiva boys conspire to escape, they are hung. A woman who had wrapped a belt around her stomach to hide her advanced state of pregnancy gives birth to a daughter. The commandant learns about the baby and sends the mother and newborn child to the gas chamber.

Yet interspersed among these moments of despair are instances when Judaism comforts the otherwise despondent inmates. Mourning the murder of his wife and daughters, a rabbi recites the Kaddish, whose Aramaic words resonate throughout the camp. At the fence Hannah asks her Orthodox boyfriend to teach her how to pray. During Passover, Hannah's compatriots secretly bake matzo and conduct a Seder that compensates for its lack of a meal with spiritual sustenance. Hannah reverentially performs the rituals that she previously had found meaningless.

As they break clumps of mud in a barren field, Rivka confides in Hannah that if she survives she will change her name to Eva. Hannah recognizes that Rivka is her future aunt and that she herself is destined to die and be reborn as Eva's niece. Thus, she exchanges places with Rivka when the commandant selects her cousin to be gassed. In the novel Yolen handles the gassing scene discreetly by writing that Hannah and the other women "walked in through the door into endless night" (160). Deitch, on the other hand, brings the viewer inside the gas chamber as cyanide pellets rain down onto the panicked women. After their screams subside, their nude torsos are positioned symmetrically next to each other like a collection of pretty dolls whose serene appearance undercuts the visceral terror that their gassing, gasps, and tumult had evoked up until that point.

Hannah awakes on her bed with her parents and relatives standing around it. The black and white shot of her regaining consciousness while still wearing a modest 1930s-style dress gradually becomes colorized. The scene intentionally reminds audiences of Dorothy's miraculous return from Oz in the film, as she comes out of the coma induced by being hit on the head during the tornado. Upon seeing her aunt, Hannah calls her Rivka instead of Eva. Astounded that Hannah knows her childhood name, Eva shows her niece a photograph that was taken of the two girls shortly before the German troops occupied their *shtetl*. Hanna vows to her aunt that she will never forget the Holocaust.

As the closing scene returns to the dinner table for the conclusion of the Seder, Hannah joins the family in a rousing rendition of the Passover song *Chad Gadya*. Whereas Dorothy had discovered that there's no place like home, Hannah has extended her concept of home and family to include all of the Jewish people, their traditions, and the six million whose martyrdom she had witnessed.

The cultivation of Jewish identity distinguishes *The Devil's Arithmetic* from *I Love You, I Love You Not*, which reduces being Jewish to a source of discrimination rather than a rich cultural or religious heritage. Many of the individuals involved in the production of the former, however, considered it a tribute to the lost world of European Jewry. Jane Yolen recalls that she used to be like Hannah, oblivious to the significance of Passover and the traumatic impact the Holocaust had on her uncle (167). Screenwriter Robert Avrech, a former rabbinical student, also scripted *A Stranger Among Us* (1992), a murder mystery set in a Chasidic community ("Robert J. Avrech"; "Biographies" 12). Donna Deitch established her reputation as a director of films about minority groups, like the lesbian couple in *Desert Hearts* (1985) and African American women in *The Women of Brewster Street* (1989); her interviews with survivors and research into the Holocaust for *The Devil's Arithmetic* enhanced her awareness of her own Jewish roots (Pepe; Shister; Wallace: "Cable TCA Press Tour" 7). Most of co-producer Mimi Rogers' relatives fled Germany, but others perished in the Holocaust. She hoped the movie would strengthen Jewish identity and memorialize the Jewish casualties of Nazi anti-Semitism (Atkin; "Cable TCA Press Tour" 9).

Dustin Hoffman, who collaborated with Rogers on this project, introduces the movie in a prologue. He recalls that when he brought the screenplay home to evaluate, his daughter pointed out that she was reading the book by Jane Yolen for school. He marvels at how the story has "touched the young readers making history come alive by combining harsh reality with the magic element of fable" (*The Devil's Arithmetic* DVD).

Honored with awards for children's literature and television, *The Devil's Arithmetic* has become a standard introductory work for teens learning about the Holocaust ("Awards," Jane Yolen Web Site; "Awards," *The Devil's Arithmetic*). Both the book and the movie have benefited from new communications technologies and the increased emphasis on the Holocaust and cultural diversity in private and public education. The film has been made available to schools through Showtime's Cable in the Classroom system, and students can download study guides based on the movie from Showtime's website ("Cable in the Classroom"). One recommended activity is to encourage "students to create their own storylines with a third generation non-Jew as the main character" ("*The Devil's Arithmetic*: A Guide for Educators" 3).

Unlike the previously discussed lead characters, who literally or psychologically relive the Holocaust, Jonathan in *Everything Is Illuminated* embarks on an odyssey to the Ukraine to locate the village of Trachimbroad, where his deceased grandfather had hailed from before emigrating to the United States. The movie opens with a close-up of a grasshopper trapped in amber, which symbolizes how memory freezes a moment in time, in general, and Jonathan's obsession with preserving memory, in particular. He has plastered the wall in his study with family photos and mementos stored in labeled baggies. When his dying grandmother leaves him a *Magen David* (Star of David) on a gold chain and a snapshot from 1940 of his grandfather with a pregnant woman named Augustine, Jonathan recalls seeing these items on his grandfather's deathbed. Since Jonathan had stolen the amber pendant off the nightstand in the same bedroom when his grandfather had died, he concludes that these three things are clues to his grandfather's survival in the Ukraine during World War II and decides to search for Augustine in the hope that she can decipher what these keepsakes mean.

When Jonathan travels to the Ukraine, Alex, his translator and alter ego, is portrayed as someone who has jettisoned his nation's history for American pop culture. He bluntly admits, "I was of the opinion that the past is the past, and like all that is not now, it should remain buried along the side of our memories." He sports American hip-hop fashions, break-dances in the discotheque, and "digs Negroes, most of all Michael Jackson." He inhabits a post-Soviet society where McDonald's, skateboard parks, and billboards are rapidly displacing indigenous Ukrainian landmarks. Alex's fractured English testifies to his hybrid identity, as does his esteem for Michael Jackson, who hardly epitomizes African-American manhood.

By contrast Alex's gruff grandfather (also named Alex) appears to be a genuine Ukrainian traditionalist who founded Heritage Tours to aid "rich Jewish people to search for their dead families." According to his grandson Alex, this was a strange career for him "because there's nothing he hates more than rich Jewish people or their dead families."

From the outset, the audience knows that the elder Alex is not what he appears to be. He claims to be blind but sees well enough to drive a car. His closest companion is his seeing-eye dog Sammy Davis, Jr., who is really just a vicious mutt "retrieved from the home for forgetful dogs." The only music that soothes this savage beast is Michael Jackson's "Billy Jean," a song about a man who denies he has fathered a child born to a woman whom he fantasized to be Marilyn Monroe. The grandfather is dismayed to learn subsequently from Jonathan that the namesake of his dog and favorite singer was Jewish.

Jonathan hires the two Alexes to help him find Trachimbrod. He yearns to see the place where his grandfather grew up and where he himself would still live if his grandfather had not immigrated to the United States. The first part of the film plays like a humorous road movie about the misconceptions these unlikely travel companions have about each other. Jonathan shocks the younger Alex, when he informs him that most Ukrainians were anti-Semitic even before Germany invaded their territory. His grandfather vehemently contests this generalization. The photo Jonathan carries mesmerizes the grandfather. When the terrain becomes familiar to him, the grandfather gets out of the car and stumbles upon discarded weapons from World War II that precipitate a dissolve to a moment when a German soldier aims his rifle at a man wearing a Star of David badge.

The next day the grandfather stops his car by a field of surreally beautiful sunflowers which tower above a dirt path leading to a small dilapidated home. He orders his grandson to inquire there about the location of Trachimbrod. Alex complies, but the taciturn silver-haired woman on its porch does not respond until she looks at the photograph Alex hands her. She then replies, "You are here. I am it."

In a room stacked to the ceiling with filing boxes, the old woman preserves what remained of the Jews who once dwelled in Trachimbrod. The labels on the containers chronicle the mundane and religious objects and events that comprised the life of the village, such as, weddings and celebrations, menorahs, silver cutlery, pinwheels, deaths of the first born, spectacles, underwear, wooden toys, and dust. She discloses that she is Augustine's older sister and discerns the resemblance between Jonathan and his grandfather Safran, who had married Augustine. The couple expected a baby before the Germans liquidated the Jews of Trachimbrod. The sister kept a picture of Safran's older brother Baruch. When the elder Alex sees the photo, he requests to be alone with her. Outside the younger Alex worries that his grandfather might have collaborated with the Germans in liquidating the Jews but insists that he is a "good person." His grandfather emerges from the house ready to go the site of Trachimbrod.

The woman then leads them to the banks of the river Brod, where a circle of stones surrounds a Soviet bronze plaque marking the spot where a thousand Trachimbroders died at the hands of "German fascism." She poignantly recounts the rounding up of the villagers, the burning of their synagogue, and the killing of all of them after the Jewish men were forced to spit on the unrolled Torah that the Germans had removed from the synagogue. Her father refused to desecrate the Torah despite the threat that Augustine and the baby she was carrying would be shot if he disobeyed.

She speaks as a witness, but her verbal account and the place serve as a catalyst for the elder Alex to envision the mass execution. Thus we learn that Alex is actually a Ukrainian Jew and was an intended victim of the Trachimbrod massacre—which he somehow survived. He stands erect before a firing squad. He catches a glimpse of a younger woman standing in the distance observing the impending bloodbath. He pictures the littered corpses as photographic stills rather than as the moving frames of a film. The young woman scavenges among the bodies to collect their belongings for posterity. Alex, now revealed actually to be Baruch, realizes he is not dead. His eyes meet the woman's, but both say nothing. He discards his coat with the Jewish star and leaves his bloodstained past behind.

Before departing from the woman's home, the woman tells the trio of searchers that Safran had gone to America a week before the Germans arrived in Trachimbrod. Jonathan gives her the amber pendant which originally belonged to Augustine. She reciprocates by entrusting him with the wedding ring Augustine had buried in a jar with the admonition "in case." They ponder what Augustine had meant by this phrase. Though Jonathan thinks Augustine hid it as proof she once had lived, her sister disagrees and surmises that Augustine left it "in case someone should come searching one day." In her opinion, the ring does not exist for those who seek it, but rather they exist for it. Her final question to her visitors is whether the war is over.

The movie reveals that both the younger Alex and Jonathan are members of the Third Generation. Baruch/older Alex had effaced his Jewish past and blended into the Ukrainian population by acting as though he were anti-Semitic. Now that he had returned to the scene of his near death and resurrection, he commits suicide at the inn near Trachimbrod. Perhaps he needed to be reunited in the ground with his community. Alex notices that, for the first time in his life, his grandfather appears to be content with where he was. Since Baruch was Jonathan's great uncle, Alex is Jonathan's cousin. Thus, Jonathan presents his *Magen David* to Alex to go along with the gold "bling" he wears around his neck. The final scenes parallel each other as Jonathan, back in the US, tosses soil from the Brod upon Safran's tombstone, and Alex does the same at Baruch's burial plot next to the Trachimbrod memorial. Not only does the grandfather's tombstone bear the name Baruch, a Jewish star, and a Hebrew inscription, but Alex, his father, and younger brother are all wearing yarmulkes. Alex's voiceover summarizes what was learned in the "rigid search" for Trachimbrod: "It has shown me that everything is illuminated in the light of the past. It is always along the side of us, on the inside looking out."

Alex's closing commentary reflects the obligation author Jonathan Safran Foer and director Liev Schreiber felt in trying to commemorate the lives of their grandparents. Foer attributes Jonathan's mania for collecting to his grandmother's habit of physically or visually "weighing" things and people, since she had been reduced to skin and bone as a fugitive from the Germans in war-ravaged Europe. Possessing a photograph of a woman who had rescued his grandfather, Foer went to Trachimbrod but abandoned his search when he found, in his words, "nothing—a landscape of completely realized absence." In lieu of any knowledge about his grandfather's story, he invented one which measured the discrepancy between "how things were [and] how they could have been" in an effort to articulate how he imagined the past impinged on his present ("Jonathan Safran Foer," Interview; Foer). Foer briefly appears in the film, clearing leaves away from graves with a blower.

Liev Schreiber's grandfather had immigrated from the Ukraine, as well. When he passed away in 1993, Schreiber panicked that he would soon forget what his grandfather had been like. His death prompted Schreiber to write a screenplay about a grandson seeking the origins of his grandfather in the Ukraine. When Schreiber came across a short story Foer had written as a precursor to the novel, he recognized the acuity of Foer's Third Generation insight into the quandary of remembering events he had never experienced (Fischer).

Everything Is Illuminated captures Hirsch's concept of "postmemory" in a more nuanced way than either *I Love You, I Love Not* or *The Devil's Arithmetic*. In those other films, the grandchild chronologically or psychologically recapitulates the ordeal of their respective grandparent or great aunt. To be sure, some grandchildren experience intergenerational trauma from knowing what their grandparents endured, and most would understand the didactic and dramatic purpose of a narrative strategy that presents the Holocaust as an imagined personal foray into the past. Members of the Third Generation, however, cannot claim to be the actual victims or survivors of the Shoah, as Daisy and Hannah vicariously do.

In *Everything Is Illuminated* the elder Alexander relives his loss of his community and his narrow escape from the same fate. Augustine's sister acts as a witness to the slaughter of Trachimbrod and curator of the artifacts that were woven into the tapestry of life there. Jonathan and Alex recognize they are tied to this history by lineage, memory, photographs, and their mutual journey to the burial ground of their descendents. Their encounter with the Shoah is mediated through the relationships they establish with each other, their memories of their grandfathers, the thoughts evoked by places where the latter almost perished, and the meanings they ascribe to the objects they have inherited. They are like the second carbon copy of an original document. Though the message has become fainter, they still can discern its essence if they are willing to expend the effort.

Perhaps it is particularly fitting that the creative artists of the Third Generation after the Holocaust exemplified here have resorted to film as the preferred means through which to grapple with their shadowy, attenuated memories. For these American-Jewish cinematic artists the Shoah is not so much real as it is surreal—something beyond reality to which they can no longer have direct contact due to the fading witness of actual survivors. Their third-hand encounter with an enormous, tragic reality has therefore necessarily become not only the stuff of a history, too often ignored by the Third Generation in contemporary America, but also a stimulus to an imagination that one might even characterize as an empathic fantasy. The medium of film—itself no more in physical essence than the projection of light and shadows on an otherwise blank screen—therefore seems an appropriate means through which the Third Generation can find its own way back to the Holocaust. The three films discussed here all show how imagination and images have become, perhaps *must* become, the best means through which to enter a world that no longer exists and about which there is nearly no one left to speak who was *really there*. The point these Third Generation cinematic artists might all make is this: the artifacts of the Holocaust—the historical records, mementos, commemorative plaques and museum exhibitions—alone are insufficient to make this crucial period of human history come to life again for an audience increasingly remote from the events. Rather, the most effective means to make a connection is through an exercise of imagination, and no better medium exists—especially for this American generation—to do this than the flickering light of film.

Notes

1. Dan Bar-On, "Transgenerational Aftereffects of the Holocaust in Israel: Three Generations." Bar-On and his students began research on this topic in 1988.

Works Cited

"Awards." *The Devil's Arithmetic*, Internet Movie Database. 18 Oct. 2002 <www.imdb.com/title/tt0179148/awards>.

"Awards." *Jane Yolen Web Site*. 18 Oct. 2002 <www.janeyolen.com/janeawards2.html>.

Bar-On, Dan. "Transgenerational Aftereffects of the Holocaust in Israel: Three Generations." Ed. Efraim Sicher. *Breaking Crystal: Writing and Memory after Auschwitz*. Urbana: U of Illinois, 1998. 91–118.

Berger, Alan L. *Children of Job: American Second-Generation Witnesses to the Holocaust*. Albany: State U of New York P, 1997.

"Biographies." *The Devil's Arithmetic* Press Kit. New York: Showtime, 1999.

"Cable in the Classroom." *Showtime Web Site*. 26 Oct. 2002 <http://www.sho.com/cic/html>.

"Cable TCA Press Tour." *The Devil's Arithmetic* Press Kit. New York: Showtime, 1999.

Chaitin, Julia. "Facing the Holocaust in Generations of Families of Survivors: The Case of Partial Relevance and Interpersonal Values." *Contemporary Family Therapy* 22.3 (2000): 289–313.

———. "Issues and Interpersonal Values among Three Generations in Families of Holocaust Survivors." *Journal of Social and Personal Relationships* 19.3 (2002): 370–402.

The Devil's Arithmetic. Dir. Donna Deitch. Showtime Networks, Millbrook Farms Productions, Punch Productions, 1999.

"*The Devil's Arithmetic*: A Guide for Educators." *Kidsnet Web Site*. 5 Dec. 2006 <http://www.kidsnet.org/pdf/da.pdf>.

Fischer, Paul. "Liev Schreiber—*Everything Is Illuminated* Interview." *Femail Magazine*. 23 Nov. 2006 <www.femail.com.au/liev-schreiber-everything-illuminated.htm>.

Foer, Jonathan Safran. *Everything Is Illuminated*. New York: Houghton Mifflin, 2002.

Fossion, Pierre, et al. "Family Approach with Grandchildren of Holocaust Survivors." *American Journal of Psychotherapy* 57.4 (2003): 519–27.

Goldfarb, Alvin. "Inadequate Memories: The Survivors in Plays by Mann, Kesselman, Lebow, and Baitz." Ed. Claude Schumacher. *Staging the Holocaust: The Shoah in Drama and Performance*. New York: Cambridge UP, 1998.

Greene, Alexis, ed. *Women Who Write Plays: Interviews with American Dramatists*. Hanover, NH: Smith and Kraus, 2001.

Hass, Aaron. *In the Shadow of the Holocaust: The Second Generation*. Ithaca: Cornell UP, 1990.

Haughton, Elspeth. Rev. of *I Love You, I Love You Not*. ApolloGuide. 2 Dec. 2006 <www.apolloguide.com/mov_fullrev.asp?CID=505>.

Hirsch, Marianne. *Family Frames: Photography, Narrative, and Postmemory*. Cambridge, MA: Harvard University Press, 1997.

I Love You, I Love You Not. Dir. Billy Hopkins. DVD. Buena Vista Home Entertainment, 2000.

"Joanthan Safran Foer on *Everything Is Illuminated*." Interview. 6 Dec. 2006 <www.jonathansafranfoerbooks.com/interview.html>.

Kesselman, Wendy Ann. *I Love You, I Love You Not*. Hollywood: Samuel French, 1988.

———. Interview in Greene 272–73, 279–85.

Landsberg, Alison. *Prosthetic Memory: The Transformation of American Remembrance in the Age of Mass Culture*. New York: Columbia UP, 2004.

Maslin, Janet. "Flower Girl Finds True Romance in Asphalt Jungle." *New York Times* 3 Oct. 1997.

Pepe, Barbara. "Ten Years Gone." *The Advocate* 20 Aug. 1996.

"Robert J. Avrech." *Internet Movie Database*. 4 Dec. 2006 <www.imdb.com/name/nm0043334/>.

Rosenstone, Robert. *History on Film/Film on History*. Harlow, UK: Pearson Longman, 2006.

Rosenthal, Gabriele, ed. *The Holocaust in Three Generations: Families of Victims and Perpetrators of the Nazi Regime*. London: Kassel, 1998.

Salter, James. Rev. of "*I Love You, I Love You Not*." 27 Nov. 2006 <http://www.cinemascreen.co.uk/filmdata/filmdata.asp?filmid=3600>.

Shister, Gail. "A Gay *Our Town*." *The Advocate* 1 Feb. 2000.

Vaughan, Peter. "Play Reflects Gentle Mood of Kesselman." *Minneapolis Star and Tribune* 7 Nov. 1986. 01C.

Wallace, Debra. "*The Devil's Arithmetic* Depicts a Surreal View of the Holocaust." *Jewish Bulletin of Northern California* 26 Mar. 1999.

Weissman, Gary. *Fantasies of Witnessing: Postwar Efforts to Experience the Holocaust*. Ithaca, NY: Cornell UP, 2004.

Yolen, Jane. *The Devil's Arithmetic*. New York: Puffin, 1990.

Thou Shalt Teach It to Thy Children: What American Jewish Children's Literature Teaches about the Holocaust

By Peter J. Haas and Lee W. Haas

Although a good deal has been written about Holocaust education at the college and university level, little attention has been paid to what is being taught in Jewish institutions for younger students, that is, in day schools, supplementary schools, synagogues, and the like. Even less is known about what Jewish children, who have no formal Jewish education after Bar/Bat Mitzvah age, know about the Holocaust. Our interest in this project was sparked by a desire to know what "Millennials"—children coming of age in the last decade or so—know or *think* they know about the Holocaust. It is our assumption that what they learn when they arrive on our college campuses is not so much a result of a Jewish education as it is a product of popular culture, be it films like *X-Men* or material read in high school, such as the diary of Anne Frank. There is, however, a third medium that may also be highly influential and yet has hardly been studied by scholars, namely, books about the Holocaust written especially for children below the seventh grade. What follows is our first step to survey this literature and to draw some preliminary conclusions about its history, development, and message.

We want to stress at the outset that in no way are we claiming that this study is comprehensive. The amount of material out there that could arguably be included in "Children's Holocaust Literature" is immense. What we have aimed to do here is to look at a varied enough sample so that we may be able to draw some reasonably accurate, if tentative, conclusions. The conclusions themselves lead to a further consideration of some interesting broader questions about how the Holocaust might well be seen and understood by children today, and thus about the nature of Holocaust-awareness in the next generation of American Jewish leadership.

Before turning to our discussion, we wish to focus on several important issues. There is, first and foremost, an inherent tension in the genre of children's Holocaust literature. On the one hand, the Holocaust is such a significant part of the contemporary Jewish narrative that it cannot, and should not, be ignored. The younger generation needs to be made aware in a responsible way of this formative event that has had such an impact on contemporary Jewish culture. On the other hand, the very nature of the Holocaust is such that it may not be suitable as a topic for all children, especially those below fourth grade. Jewish educators and librarians thus find themselves in an awkward situation. In essence, they have to decide whether or not to make aspects of the Holocaust available to children below fourth grade, and if so, how to present a proper sense of the Shoah to young children without exposing them to the horrific aspects of these atrocities.

This is an issue for parents as well, which in turn creates some market demand for writing Holocaust books for ever younger audiences. The Holocaust is usually not taught until fifth grade, whether in secular or synagogue schools. As a result, many educators and librarians do not discuss the subject before fifth grade, leaving parents with the task of determining whether to shelter their children from this information or to inform them about it in some manner, a job for which they may or may not feel prepared. For a variety of reasons, many parents do feel a need to expose young children to the Holocaust in some way at some time. They feel this need so as to socialize their children into the Jewish community and give them some background for the classes they will have during the middle school years and for the many books about the Holocaust that were written for preteens. So one major question is, what should be presented (and what should not be presented) in children's books on the Holocaust for this younger age group?

A second concern has to do with what one hopes to accomplish through a children's book on the Holocaust. At all grade levels, there is the issue of how accurate and detailed an author wants or needs to be when dealing with the Holocaust. It is important, of course, for children's textbooks and novels to be accurate, but how graphic should one be especially in relation to atrocities? And if one makes the story age-appropriate for young readers, then is one really being faithful to the event and to its victims? We have found books that fall virtually everywhere on the possible spectrum, indicating that this question is far from having a universally accepted solution. An example of this tension is found in the work of the author Carol Matas, who broke the normative boundaries in her well-known children's Holocaust book *Daniel's Story*. According to Adrienne Kertzer:

> Matas insisted on retaining the following passage even after readers of the manuscript suggested that it was too much for children: "After living for a while in the Lodz Ghetto, Daniel was sent to Auschwitz. There, he said that 'he almost committed suicide after seeing burning bodies in a pit.'" This passage goes against the traditional image of children's books as a place for "simple heroism, resistance, and spiritual uplift." But Matas felt that the need to inform children about atrocities (the "unbelievable") took precedence over the need to console and inspire children. (255)

Matas made a choice for accuracy over delicacy or what might generally be regarded as age-appropriateness. Our goal here is not so much to judge the decision Matas made as to point out that this is an issue many of the authors discussed below have had to weigh and consider.

The main question we propose to explore here, then, is how authors and illustrators of Jewish children's books have navigated through hazardous, dangerous literary shoals as they strive to find a safe passage of appropriateness that does justice to the Holocaust without doing damage to impressionable, young psyches. As we shall see, there are a number of strategies that have developed over the last several decades for how to portray and present the Holocaust. Ultimately we hope to learn through this inquiry just what moral and religious lessons are being taught in this particular area of children's literature. To that end, we will be keeping an eye on the connection between the solutions that authors and illustrators have come to, on the one hand, and what these authors and illustrators are actually conveying to the next generation of Jews, on the other. In short, we intend to explore the connection between the "form" of children's Holocaust books (what is being told, how it is being told, and the role illustrations play) and the content and interpretation of the events. As we proceed, we shall try to maintain a double focus on literary strategy and on the heuristic effects of those strategies.

Before proceeding, we want to point out that we will be limiting ourselves to Holocaust picture books, fiction, and some biographies for children. We have purposefully decided against looking at textbooks or history books. The reason is, first of all, that we are including a good deal of material aimed at an audience that is too young to understand what history really is. In addition, we are interested in books that relate information about the Holocaust in a more informal, personal manner. That is, readers of fiction are invited, as it were, to relate to the subject matter on a personal level rather than in an abstract, detached and academic manner. A novel or picture book puts a face on the Holocaust and allows, and maybe even forces, a child to identify with someone who had some connection with the Holocaust. In that way this fictional literature leads him or her to experience vicariously, aspects of that person's story. These books, then, are not so much intended to provide factual information about the Holocaust as to give a sense of what the Holocaust was and what it means.

We begin our study by turning to the basic issue, alluded to above, concerning whether or not young children should be exposed to the Holocaust, or, more specifically, to the more brutal aspects of the Holocaust, at all. Many librarians and other educational professionals contend that children should not read books about the Holocaust before fourth grade. They feel that below fourth grade, children have no historical perspective and should not be traumatized by reading or hearing about some of the darkest periods of modern history. Young children should be sheltered from this kind of knowledge, first because of their age and also because of their poor ability to distinguish real from make-believe. The tension between reality and appropriateness is nicely articulated by Lydia Kokkola in *Representing the Holocaust in Children's Literature*. She notes:

> In a sense, one can argue that any writing about the Holocaust for children breaks a strict taboo: that children are not to be frightened. Holocaust literature introduces the child to a world in which parents are not in control, that survival does not depend upon one's wits but upon pure luck, where evil is truly present, and worst of all, a horror story that is true. . . . Holocaust literature for children can therefore be distinguished by its combination of challenging subject matter, ethical responsibility, and its position outside the normal boundaries of children's literature. (11)

The other school of thought argues that in the post-Holocaust world, children need to be exposed to, rather than sheltered from, what happened. There are many reasons that one could put forward in favor of early exposure: in particular, that children will become aware of the Holocaust anyway through Jewish communal events. Hence, they should have some foundation for understanding it, since it is, after all, an important component of contemporary

Jewish identity. Moreover, children need to be made aware that anti-Semitism in the past and in the present continues to threaten the very survival of the Jewish people. Consequently, guided by this and other rationales, books that relate in varying degrees to the Holocaust are being written and published with the target audience being children as young as the first grade.

Needless to say, there is a broad consensus that such books for young children should not be as comprehensive or graphic as books for teenagers. Some of these books for very young children are parables about the Holocaust and so can be read differently by children and adults. But, as we will elaborate more fully below, some recent picture books for very young children are now becoming much more explicit, portraying Nazi soldiers, concentration camps, hidden children, and other traumatizing events in graphic ways that would have once been deemed unthinkable. Holocaust picture books of this sort, targeting young children, especially for children below third grade, have been published in greater number since the beginning of the 1990s.

With these thoughts in mind, we turn to the various periods of such literature and the conclusions we have drawn based on our survey of a number of representative literary works. Holocaust books for children began to appear as early as the 1950s. The plots of these first books tended to focus on evasion and escape. One of the earliest children's books about the Holocaust was written for grades three through six. *Twenty and Ten* by Claire Huchet Bishop (published in 1952) is a short book that closely resembles the mystery/adventure books commonly written for children of that age group at that time. The story is about twenty French children and their teacher, Sister Gabriel, who are sent to a refuge in the mountains during the German occupation of France. Later, Sister Gabriel agrees to take in ten Jewish children and warns her students about the importance of never telling anyone about the Jewish children. When she becomes fearful that they might be discovered, she asks the French children to look for a hiding place for these refugees. The children discover a hidden cave that proves to be the perfect solution when the German soldiers come, and thus the Jewish children successfully evade their enemy.

What is notable here is that the children are depicted as the real heroes of the story, finding a way to help each other in the face of nasty adults. There is no reference to torture or violence. The action takes place in the mountains of France, hardly a "typical" Holocaust setting. In fact, on one level this work can be seen as a typical child-oriented book of the period, with the Holocaust backdrop being only incidental. And yet there is a historical cast to the story that conventional adventure stories for children do not have—the German invasion of France. We mention this book because it was one of the earliest, and in fact one of the very few children's books of the 1950s, that even alludes to the Shoah.

This generally indirect approach of the very earliest children's literature on the Holocaust persisted into the 1960s. One popular author who wrote from a child's perspective, in this case from the point of view of a German child, was Hans Peter Richter. As a good example, we can take *I Was There* (1962), a roughly autobiographical book written in the first person and originally published in Germany. This book, written for teens, tells about three friends who join the *Hitlerjugend* (Hitler Youth Movement). The narrator and one of the other boys are enthusiastic about serving the *Führer*, but the third boy joins only due to pressure put upon him and his family. He and his family are part of a minority of German citizens who felt very uncomfortable with the political events of the time and tried, as long as possible, not to go along with the crowd. In the course of the story, the book not only informs the reader about the activities of the *Hitlerjugend* but also shows how those who disagreed with the prevailing political sentiment were shamed and humiliated. The book opens with the following powerful statement, written as the author looks back many years later on his experiences:

> I am reporting how I lived through that time and what I saw—no more. I was there. I was not merely an eyewitness. I believed—and I will never believe again. (Richter vii)

This book and others by Hans Peter Richter were translated into English and became part of the stock of children's Holocaust books available to American children in the early to mid 1960s.

Overall, however, we found that Holocaust-related children's books were few and far between in the 1950s and 1960s. This is hardly surprising for a number of reasons. For one, the Holocaust was really not discussed all that much during this time. Jews were uncomfortable talking about the Holocaust in general, all the more so to their children. In addition, the Shoah had not really become a significant part of the Jewish or secular educational agenda. What was transmitted about the Holocaust took place within Jewish families and maybe in unstructured ways in synagogues and religious schools. So a market for children's Holocaust books was largely undeveloped.

This began to change by the 1970s. At this time, the Holocaust became a more open topic of discussion in both the Jewish and the non-Jewish worlds. Many have attributed this to the trauma of the 1967 Six-Day War, but there is also a change in generation, with the Holocaust then twenty-five years in the past. Whatever the reason, the number of Holocaust books for children increased significantly, and the messages they conveyed about the Holocaust became more varied and nuanced. The subject was still handled with a certain emotional distancing, however. For example, this decade saw the publication of books such as Sonia Levitin's *Journey to America* (1970) and Judith Kerr's *When Hitler Stole Pink Rabbit* (1971). Both of these books describe the hardships of being a refugee—poverty, family separation, loneliness, and difficulty in learning a new language, for example. Like earlier books, the focus is on the ability of children and family to evade and/or escape. In these instances, however, the physical and emotional suffering that occurred comes more to the surface. But even as these and similar books are more explicit about the physical and psychological difficulties of survival, they usually end on a positive note—survival and triumph over adversity.

Another popular book of this time, but one that takes a very different angle, is *Summer of My German Soldier* by Bette Greene and Robert Hunt (1973). The story focuses on a teenager in Arkansas who experiences the Holocaust only indirectly. The heroine of the story comes into contact with the events in Europe when she meets a German soldier who is interned in a POW camp set up near her town. As she becomes friendly with the soldier, the girl from Arkansas realizes that the German soldier has a lot of the same feelings, thoughts, likes, and dislikes as the Americans that she knows. As in the stories of Hans Peter Richter, the suffering of the Holocaust is personalized and not limited only to Jews. The Holocaust here bears a more universal message.

The aim of the literature from this period, then, seems not to be so much to teach about the Holocaust from a political angle but more to show how the Holocaust and the war affected the lives of ordinary people, whether Jewish or not. These books do this by depicting events related to the Holocaust and the war in terms that teens are more likely to understand, namely, experiences of kids like themselves. In most cases the leading characters are not Jewish or at least not Jewish in any particularly overt way. The novels also emphasize putting a human face on the Holocaust. The reader of *Summer of My German Soldier* realizes that, despite the brutality of the Nazis, not all Germans should be viewed as monsters. At the same time, the book enables its young Jewish readers to understand and relate to some of the stories they might hear in synagogue or from relatives and yet not feel personally threatened. Overall, the market for Holocaust related books for children was growing, but allusions to the Holocaust still remained somewhat indirect. The anti-Jewish threat is certainly manifest, but in most instances it is kept in the background and its depiction is muted.

Another significant change occurred in the late 1970s and through the 1980s. During this decade, we witness the rapid development of new children's Holocaust fiction, some of it within the genre of "coming of age" literature. Many of these stories have to do much more explicitly with the physical and emotional challenges faced by youngsters, as they and their families struggle to survive the war. One example is Carol Matas's *Lisa's War* (1987), which depicts the experiences of a young girl who joins the resistance. More explicit in its depiction of the Holocaust's reality is Uri Orlev's *Island On Bird Street* (1984). Here we read the story of a young boy who struggles through the harsh winter of 1941–42 in the Warsaw ghetto. We also find, for the first time, children's books that deal explicitly with life in the concentration camps. A good example is Clara Asscher-Pinkhof's collection, *Star Children* (1986). Asscher-Pinkhof presents the reader with stories that describe the lives of Dutch children throughout the Holocaust, from arrest to life in camps like Westerbork to their transport and experiences in Bergen-Belsen. Another sensitive theme is explored by Ida Vos, who wrote in *Anna Is Still Here* (1986) about the trauma of a young child who is separated from her family for a number of years and then, after the war, struggles to return to a normal life. Also, significantly, books from this era tend to bring to the forefront the victimization of Jews *as Jews* at the hands of Nazis. Clearly by the 1980s, many of the earlier literary taboos on treating the Holocaust have been broken.

Curiously, just as these books were becoming both more explicit and also more focused on the Holocaust as a Jewish event, they were also tending to deal more subtly with its complexities. As one example, we can point to Doris Orgel's *The Devil in Vienna* (1978). Here is an account of the friendship between a Jewish girl and a Catholic girl in Vienna and how both are adversely affected by the Holocaust. A second example is Lois Lowry's narrative of the Danish rescue of Jews in *Number the Stars* (1989). Overall, books of this period are much more graphic and realistic reflections of the Holocaust than had previously been the case. They are also much more focused on Jewish suffering, and yet more open to introducing complexities and ambiguities.

An interesting comment on the sensitivity of the times can be found in comparing editions of *The Number on My Grandfather's Arm* by David Adler (1987). The story is about a child who notices numbers tattooed on her grandfather's arm one night when her parents are away and he is washing dinner dishes. She asks him about the tattoo, and her grandfather tells her about the persecution and humiliations that the Jews of Poland suffered and some of the horrors of the concentration camps. Though the story is fairly realistic, it is of course told by a survivor and so has, as it were, a happy ending. The story is accompanied by black-and-white photographs, which add a somber aura to the story. Yet this is also a somewhat more muted effect than might have been the case, for example, if color pictures had been employed. One of the photographs, however, shows a German soldier pointing a rifle at a mother clutching her baby. Should this have been included? Apparently the editors had a change of heart, since it was removed in the subsequent edition.

It is notable that during this period we begin to see a bifurcation of Holocaust children's literature. On the one hand, the accounts become somewhat more graphic and realistic, and on the other, many stories focus on rescue and friendship. Children in the 1980s were learning more realistically about the horrors of the Holocaust, but also about instances of resistance, friendship, and rescue. A working synthesis had evolved that allowed the Holocaust to be more or less accurately conveyed to young readers, yet without it being overly traumatic.

Children's Holocaust books really began to come of age in the 1990s. There were a number of factors that can account for this. No doubt, one was the fact that the Jewish audience had evolved by this time. Fewer and fewer Jewish children, even in Jewish day schools, were hearing of the Holocaust directly from survivors, and with the increasing numbers of children coming from families of mixed religious backgrounds, many students of Jewish heritage did not have any immediate family connection to the Holocaust. Moreover, the Holocaust by the 1990s had risen in visibility and prominence in American culture so that it had become a subject of concern to the general public. Thus, children's books began to address this much more general American audience.

A second factor was the maturation of academic studies of the Holocaust. Scholars began to focus on many more of the subtleties, complexities, and intricacies of the Shoah. This, of course, had an impact on writers and illustrators of children's Holocaust books, who were themselves exposed to a much more polychromatic view of their subject matter. They now had a greater array of themes with which to work.

Third, there were fewer and fewer Holocaust witnesses (whether survivors, refugees or liberators), and this created a sense of urgency for recording their stories and making sure, through novels and history books, that the events of the Holocaust were remembered and passed on to a new generation. Many books from the 1990s deal with more or less true personal accounts.

Finally, the Holocaust, or at least Holocaust readings (like the diary of Anne Frank), were becoming part of secular school curricula. This was itself a function of a greater openness among the general public to consider all aspects of the Holocaust—a tendency fueled to some significant degree by the impact of the TV mini-series "The Holocaust" that first aired in 1978. Not surprisingly, the introduction of the subject into general public education greatly accelerated the growing awareness of and interest in the Holocaust, not only for the Jewish but also for the non-Jewish community.

These shifts in audience, by their very nature, had a strong influence on shaping not only the strategies of the authors and illustrators, but also the content of Holocaust stories. The resulting growth in demand was answered by both an increasing number of authors and publishers entering the field and also a much broader range of topics and themes. In the 1990s, for example, the award-winning *Star of Fear, Star of Hope* by Jo Hoestlandt was published (a 1993 book written in French with an English edition published in the United States in 1995). The story is narrated by Helen, an elderly French woman (who is not Jewish), looking back on an event that occurred in her childhood. Despite the 1942 German invasion of northern France, she and her Jewish friend Lydia continued to play and go to school together. On her ninth birthday, Helen invited Lydia to sleep over at her house. But late in the evening, the "Midnight Ghost" knocked on the door (a code name for someone who came to warn Lydia to go home because of an impending roundup of Jews). When Lydia handed Helen a gift and told her she had to leave, Helen became angry at Lydia for ruining her birthday celebration and said, "You're not my friend anymore." Helen never saw Lydia again and always regretted her parting words to her friend. She continued to live with the hope that Lydia somehow survived and that perhaps some day Lydia would read this book and contact her.

Children who read this book become aware of how an incident that would have been long forgotten had it happened in ordinary times can be so painful and haunting when it happens during a time of war and persecution. They are also given a deeper sense of how the inevitable loss of the innocence and security of youth can be thrown into especially dramatic relief in the shadow of the Holocaust. The shaded illustrations by Johanna Kang, all in black, white and tones of brown, add to the somber atmosphere of this story.

Also, in the late 1990s we see more books related to the Holocaust for children below fourth or fifth grade. As noted above, this development is controversial among librarians and Jewish educators. Some of these books have been sensitive to the concerns expressed. Several, for example, deal with the

Holocaust through allusions or parables that can be understood at different levels by children and adults. In the picture book *Elisabeth* by Claire A. Nivola (1997), an elderly woman reminiscences about a beautiful doll that she had as a child. It was slightly damaged by her dog and then was lost "when the soldiers came." Many years later, she was delighted to find the doll in an antique shop in America. She recognized it because of the teeth marks that her dog had made. The technique of using vague references like "the soldiers came" is not only a way of referring to the Holocaust without directly saying so, but also ties in these experiences with other times in Jewish history, in general, when "soldiers" (that is, Romans or Crusaders or Cossacks) came.

A classic example of the "parable" style of children's books is *Terrible Things* by Eve Bunting (1989). In this book, small animals live together in a forest, all peacefully co-existing with each other. The birds and squirrels live in the trees, the rabbits and porcupines on the ground and so forth. Then one day the "Terrible Things" come. All of the animals are frightened until the "Terrible Things" say that they only want to take away animals that fly. The other animals, assuming that they are now out of danger, remain silent as the birds disappear. After the birds are gone, everyone breathes a sigh of relief. But the "Terrible Things" return and next take away all the animals with bushy tails. Again, no one speaks up for the squirrels and skunks. The "Terrible Things" return several more times, each time removing one more kind of animal until the only animals left are the rabbits. When the "Terrible Things" come once more, there is nobody left to speak up for the rabbits. This allegory, built on Pastor Martin Niemoeller's famous statement, "First they came, . . ." can be understood by young children as a not overly threatening story that still teaches the importance of supporting others in need; older readers will, of course, realize the underlying meaning of the story.

However, sometimes efforts to make vague references to the Holocaust may be open to the criticism that they leave children in need of further explanation from parents or teachers. The picture book *Don't Forget* by Patricia Lakin (1994), targeting grades one through three, arguably falls into this category. The book tries to deal with the Holocaust obliquely. Set in a post-World War II American city, the story follows Sarah, an eight year old girl, who wants to bake a birthday cake for her mother and keep it a secret. With a list of ingredients in hand, she visits several different stores and finally goes to the Singers' mom-and-pop grocery store. Sarah makes a point of not looking at the numbers tattooed on the Singers' arms, but "like a magnet" her eyes are eventually drawn to them. Sarah tells Mrs. Singer, "I tried not to stare. I know how you got them. And that they are your secret." Mrs. Singer replies that the numbers should never be a secret. "If no one knows about bad things, they can happen all over again." But the story behind the tattooed numbers is never told and, in effect, the secret that must not be forgotten is, for all intents and purposes, left unspoken in the rest of the book. The remainder of the book is devoted to telling how Mrs. Singer helps Sarah bake her cake. Although Lakin tries to couch awareness of the Holocaust within an otherwise upbeat story, she does not try to deal with the full implication of the numbers tattooed on Mr. and Mrs. Singer's arms, and so leaves this aspect of her story open-ended. This is likely intentional in light of the targeted age of her reading audience. Perhaps too, it is her aim to leave her young readers seeking more of an answer outside the pages of her book—from parents and teachers, who can best judge on an individual basis what a child can and should be told.

At the other end of the spectrum we sometimes encounter a book that might go a little too far in its efforts to bring the Holocaust to the attention of young children. In fact, the 1990s see many books aimed at children as young as first grade and which do not hesitate to make reference to Nazi soldiers, round-ups, and other potentially traumatic tragedies. These books bring starkly into question just how graphic one should be. One book that, in the view of many, goes too far in its depiction of the Holocaust is *Let the Celebrations Begin* by Margaret Wild, with illustrations by Julie Vivas (1991). It tells the story of women in a concentration camp who make toys for the camp's children. This book has a rather vivid description of the camp and the lives of the children and contains illustrations depicting starving and skeletal women with shaven heads.

Other books of this period, however, seem to find a more acceptable balance—for example, *The Butterfly* by Patricia Polacco (2000). Polacco writes about a French family that has hidden a Jewish family in a room in their basement. At night when the household is asleep, the young daughter of the Jewish family (Sevrine) secretly climbs upstairs to the bedroom of the French family's daughter (Monique) and plays with some of Monique's toys. One night Monique, who is unaware of the hidden family, wakes up and thinks at first that she has seen a ghost. After waking up a few more times, Monique learns who Sevrine is and is shocked to realize that people have been living in the basement. The two girls become friends and have many nighttime meetings. But one night, they come too close to the window and a neighbor sees them both. The girls tell Monique's mother, and the Jewish family is forced to leave, with help from Monique's family to go to another refuge. This story, in fact, is based on an event that happened to Polacco's aunt Monique, whose mother was part of the French resistance. A note at the end explains that Sevrine was the only family member to survive the escape and she and Monique remain friends to this day. Although this book deals quite openly with the rounding up of Jews, there is something of a happy ending (in that Sevrine survives), and the illustrations are much softer and less frightening than what we find, for example, in *Let the Celebration Begin*.

Another example of a book that finds a good middle ground is *The Lily Cupboard* by Shulamith Levey Oppenheim (1992). Its story takes place on a farm where a young Jewish girl has been sent by her parents to be hidden during the Holocaust. The narrative describes the child's disorientation at being separated from her home and parents. While the story itself is psychologically difficult, the illustrations are somewhat muted and make the story less traumatic than it might otherwise have been.

A different kind of approach that deserves mention is found in *Brundibar*, authored by Tony Kushner and illustrated by Maurice Sendak (2003). The book is a retelling of the opera of the same name, which was written in 1938 and then performed in the Theresienstadt Ghetto in 1943, where the actors and writers (except for the librettist) found themselves reunited. The story itself does not mention the Holocaust, and there are only slight hints of it in Sendak's illustrations. The occasional person wears a yellow star, for example, and the organ grinder wears what looks like a Nazi party (i.e., "brownshirt") uniform. Like *The Terrible Things* and other books that take a "parable" type approach, *Brundibar* offers only allusions to the Holocaust, in the text as well as in the illustrations. In fact, the original story itself has nothing overtly to do with the Holocaust at all; yet its production and history has everything to do with it.

Another approach was pioneered in *The Grey Striped Shirt* by Jacqueline Jules (1993). One day while Frannie is visiting her grandparents, she discovers an old striped shirt in a basement closet. When she asks her grandparents what it is and why it is there, they seem reluctant to talk about it. But gradually, over the course of a year, they tell Frannie bits and pieces of their story about life in Germany before the war, their expulsion to a ghetto, and finally their experiences in a concentration camp. The Holocaust accounts are interspersed with modern-day activities such as gardening and trips to the synagogue. The book transmits a good deal of information about the Holocaust, but it parcels it out gradually and intermittently, which serves to break the inherent tension of the story. Furthermore, the book enables Jewish children to understand better something about the survivor community.

We now turn for a moment to books designed for middle school children. For this age group as well, the 1990s and the current decade have brought about considerably more diversity than previous periods. This possibly is a response to the introduction of Holocaust readings, particularly the diary of Anne Frank, into school curricula. As students learned about the Holocaust in secular and religious schools, many developed a growing curiosity about these events and wanted to read books with more detail, and with personal recollections that did not soften some of the hardships that were endured. As a result, a flurry of more direct and specific Holocaust books for this age group appeared, an excellent example of which is Isaac Millman's autobiographical story, *Hidden Child* (2003). The narrative relates how, when Isaac's father and later his mother were arrested, his mother managed to bribe a prison guard to take Isaac to their landlady's house and ask her to shelter him. When she refused, the insensitive guard simply left Isaac sitting on the curb in front of the house. Deep in despair, Isaac fortunately was rescued by a Jewish neighbor who kept him until she, herself, was arrested. Throughout the war, Isaac was shuffled to a number of other homes and institutions and finally ended up in an orphanage, never to see his parents again. After the war, Isaac was adopted by a family in the United States, who cared for him until adulthood. He eventually married the daughter of the woman who saved him during the war when he was left on the street. But he continued to mourn the memory of his parents, with whom he was never reunited, while many others at the orphanage were able to find their parents again.

This book reflects a number of elements that characterize the most recent permutations in children's Holocaust literature. Most obviously, it relates a wide variety of Holocaust experiences directly, rather than by allusion. It clearly deals with disturbing facts, informing students about how families were separated, the ways in which children were saved, how luck often played an important part in whether or not an individual survived, the hardships that individuals endured, and the bittersweet endings that often occurred. The first-person account, of course, heightens the impact.

An even more striking example of the diversity of recent Holocaust literature for middle school ages is the award-winning *Hana's Suitcase* by Karen Levine (2003). It tells the true story of a young girl, Hanna Brady, who died at Auschwitz but whose suitcase disturbingly survived. The book, however, consists of two stories told in alternating segments. One is the fate of Hanna and her brother. The other interwoven story follows the teacher of a Japanese class on the Holocaust—how the children wanted to see something tangible from the Holocaust; how the teacher traveled to Poland and obtained the suitcase; and then how the students in her class wanted to know something about the person whose name was on the suitcase. This amazing story reaches its climax when it depicts how the Japanese teacher made contact with Hana's brother, who had become a plumbing supplies salesman in Toronto. It is hard to imagine that a book on the Holocaust written in the 1970s or earlier could have centered on Holocaust education in Japan or could have spanned three continents. Yet this book is innovative in another way. It not so much focuses on the Holocaust itself but more on its aftermath and in particular, contextualizes the Holocaust in the contemporary world of young readers.

Maybe the most well-known example of a Holocaust story that deals with events of that time in a fairly realistic fashion is Louise Borden's *The Journey that Saved Curious George: The True Wartime Escape of Margaret and H. A. Rey* (2005). An illustrated book about the late husband-and-wife authors of the popular "Curious George" preschool books, it describes how the Reys escaped from Paris on their bicycles with the manuscript of the first Curious George story hidden in the basket. Many school children today are likely to remember hearing the Curious George stories when they were three or four years old, and this book helps them see how the Holocaust connects to their own lives and thus makes its history much more real for them.

We should note that some books from this period deal with the Holocaust only incidentally. An unusually engaging story that nicely illustrates this is *Bridge to Freedom* by Isabel Marvin (1997). A young German soldier deserts his unit and hides in a cave in Germany. There he discovers a Jewish girl who fled Berlin and who is also hiding in the cave. The two young people do not really know what to make of each other, but as each one considers what their next course of action should be, they notice a third individual in the cave—an injured dog. After hesitantly deciding to trust each other, the soldier and the Jewish girl decide to risk their lives in order to assist the helpless dog. The soldier makes a splint for the dog's leg, and the two of them whisk the dog out of the cave and go to the girl's house. By the end of the story, the soldier has joined the Jewish family as they escape to safety in Belgium.

For older readers—that is, high school and up—the taboo against graphic depictions no longer holds, if it ever did. In high school, students begin reading adult books and books written specifically for teens. A good example of this type of literature is the collection *Salvaged Papers,* edited by Alexandra Zapruder (2002). This anthology presents selections from teenagers' diaries from different countries that describe, for example, hunger, living in the forest, betrayal by non-Jews, narrow escapes, etc. Since *Salvaged Papers* is comprised of diaries, the reader learns about the Holocaust from specific and personal accounts. A diary is neither fiction nor a "wide canvas." Rather, the reader shares the writers' day-to-day experiences along with their fear and uncertainty: what they ate (or did not eat), if their food supply was reduced because more people moved into the ghetto, how a mother worked all day and then "did sewing" at night to bring in a little extra income, if the person providing food to a family in hiding met them when he had agreed to, where they slept, how they survived the cold weather and many other anxieties, hardships, humiliations, and close calls endured day-by-day. Though the diaries do not appear in their entirety, the selections fit together to give a reasonably unvarnished sense of the daily life of young people trying to survive the Holocaust.

It is not surprising that the overwhelming majority of children's books about the Holocaust are written for students in grades four through six. Children above grade seven or eight are beginning to read regular adult literature and so do not comprise a significant market for children's books of any sort. At the other end of the age spectrum, as has been discussed, there is some understandable reluctance to write Holocaust books for children in grades three and below. In this regard, matters have persisted over the last fifty years.

Yet within this broader structure there have been changes. As a whole, books for middle school readers have become much more varied in approach. They now offer a wide range of topics and formats that meet the diverse interests of American pre-teens, Jewish and non-Jewish. In some ways, many of these books do not place their main focus on the Holocaust at all, but rather use the Holocaust as the backdrop for the presentation of universal themes of love, loss, friendship, etc. Many others, however, make it quite clear that the Holocaust is their central theme. Although books for this age-group still tend to be somewhat circumspect in describing the horrors of the Holocaust, a considerable number are much more explicit in both text and illustrations when it comes to depicting such experiences: the violence, cruelty, suffering and death that was so much a part of everyday life in the concentration camps. We have suggested above that this may be due to a couple of related factors. One is the much more explicit nature of books designed for younger children below middle school, in general. Another may be a recognition by authors and publishers of the increased violence to which American middle school children are being exposed in movies, television, and video games. It is probably a rare twelve-year-old who has not mowed down at least a couple score of fictional enemies, or in any case seen someone do so on the screen. What used to seem traumatic in the 1950s looks almost tame today. Without making a value judgment about this phenomenon, it raises the rather interesting question of whether or not it still makes sense in the twenty-first century to "water down" the Holocaust for the middle school age-group. Perhaps it is time for us to grant that, just as many books for younger children have become more vivid, so too can books for middle school students take a harder, more realistic look at life and death really during the Holocaust.

Another change is the increasing number of books on this subject for pre-middle school readers, especially for pupils in the second and even first grades, an audience that was not even on the horizon for Holocaust literature until a few years ago. Publishers, teachers, and librarians are still not in agreement about how much, if any, exposure to the Holocaust is appropriate for children this young. One could argue that many contemporary picture books and fairy tales feature stories and illustrations that would once have been considered too frightening for this age-group. Think, for example, of the very popular *Where the Wild Things Are* by Maurice Sendak where monsters are introduced in a manner that would not have been countenanced at an earlier time. We should further recall that children nowadays often hear fairy tales that have unhappy endings, such as the works collected by Hans Christian Anderson (although it has to be acknowledged that his stories were originally intended for adults). One solution, as we have seen, is to have a story and illustrations that only subtly allude to the Holocaust. The book then gently introduces the Shoah, but leaves it to the parent or teacher to decide how much to actually say. Given the trends noted above, however, it is not out of the question and perhaps even likely that, just as the Holocaust has been written about more openly for middle school audiences, so too will it become increasingly a more explicit subject for lower grades. Today, there seems to be a supposition that, rather than be sheltered, young children, especially Jewish children, are better served, better educated, if they receive some more concrete exposure to the Holocaust.

In the end, then, it appears that "Millennials" have the opportunity to learn both everything about the Holocaust; still, inevitably, they actually learn nothing; that is, they are not really able to gain an overarching, universal perspective on this transcendently horrific event. They can learn everything insofar as children's Holocaust literature has become widespread and seems to touch on every imaginable scenario and take every possible point of view. Children can read about Jews as victims, partisan resistance, the pressure on German youth, and the memories of survivors. They can further encounter the

Holocaust as the backdrop to stories about perennial themes such as growing up, loss of friends, and first love.

Yet, in the final analysis, Millennials learn nothing in the sense that there cannot really be conveyed to them a common theme, lesson, or approach to an event that by its very nature defies such simplistic characterization. Each book has its own tale to tell and its own lessons to be drawn, implicitly or explicitly. Like so much in the lives of the Millennials, the world is a marketplace in which every imaginable interest can be addressed. So no part of the Holocaust seems to be inherently privileged in the literature; no single message is being sent, and the older generations are bequeathing no universal lesson or story about the Holocaust. In fact, as we have seen, it is possible to read about the Holocaust without any explicit reference to Jews or Judaism at all; it can be depicted as another tale of human cruelty and human good, of persistence and survival against a grim background of death and destruction. If this literature is a fair reflection of Jewish popular culture in general, then the Holocaust, like every other aspect of Jewish life in the twenty-first century, has no universally agreed upon essence. This literature is also perfectly consistent with everything else we know about the context in which Millennials learn. They have lots of information, an overflow of facts, but there seems to be no clear master narrative.

There is, however, one point that this vast array of literature consistently reflects—that the stories of the Holocaust in all their shapes and forms should not be forgotten. The time is approaching when there will be no living survivors or refugees to tell first-hand about the Nazi terror. There is a broad consensus that the Holocaust should not be simply a footnote in Jewish and world history. The literature written for children of all ages, like the books and articles written for adults, is aimed at assuring that the Shoah will be remembered.

Maybe the best way to conclude our survey is to cite the closing passage of Jacqueline Jules's *The Grey Stripped Suit*.

> I still visit my grandparents whenever I can. We still walk to synagogue on Shabbat and work in the garden on Sundays. Every once in a while I go down to the cedar closet to look at the grey striped shirt. Grandpa Herman says it will belong to me someday. He wants me to show it to MY grandchildren. "You must tell them our story," he said. I promised I would. (63)

Works Cited

Adler, David. *The Number on My Grandfather's Arm*. New York: URJ, 1987.
Asscher-Pinkhof, Clara. *Star Children*. Detroit: Wayne State UP, 1986.
Bishop, Claire Huchet. *Twenty and Ten*. New York: Puffin, 1952.
Border, Louise. *The Journey that Saved Curious George: The True Wartime Escape of Margaret and H. A. Rey*. Boston: Houghton Mifflin, 2005.
Bunting, Eve. *Terrible Things*. Philadelphia: Jewish Publication Society, 1980.
Frank, Anne. *The Diary of a Young Girl*. Garden City: Doubleday & Company, 1952.
Greene, Bette and Robert Hunt. *Summer of My German*. New York: Dial, 1973.
Hoestlandt, Jo. *Star of Fear, Star of Hope*. Trans. Mark Polizzotti. New York: Walker, 1995.
Jules, Jacqueline. *The Grey Striped Shirt: How Grandma and Grandpa Survived the Holocaust*. Los Angeles: Alef Design, 1993.
Kerr, Judith. *When Hitler Stole Pink Rabbit*. New York: Dell, 1971.
Kertzer, Adrienne. "The Problem of Childhood, Children's Literature and Holocaust Representation." *Teaching the Representation of the Holocaust*. Ed. Marianne Hirsch and Irene Kacandes. New York: Modern Language Association of America, 2004. 250–62.
Kokkola, Lydia. *Representing the Holocaust in Children's Literature*. New York: Routledge, 2003.
Kushner, Tony. *Brundibar*. New York: Hyperion, 2003.
Lakin, Patricia. *Don't Forget*. New York: Tambourine, 1994.
Levine, Karen. *Hana's Suitcase*. Morton Grove, IL: Whitman, 2003.
Levitin, Sonia. *Journey to America*. New York: Atheneum, 1970.
Lowry, Lois. *Number the Stars*. Boston: Houghton Mifflin, 1989.
Marvin, Isabel. *Bridge to Freedom*. Philadelphia: Jewish Publication Society, 1991.
Matas, Carol. *Daniel's Story*. New York: Scholastic, 1993.
———. *Lisa's War*. New York: Scribner, 1987.
Millman, Isaac. *Hidden Child*. New York: Farrar, Strauss & Giroux, 2003.
Nivola, Claire A. *Elisabeth*. New York: Farrar, Straus & Giroux, 1997.
Oppenheim, Shulamith Levey. *The Lily Cupboard*. New York: HarperCollins, 1992.
Orgel, Doris. *The Devil in Vienna*. New York: Dial, 1978.
Orlev, Uri. *Island On Bird Street*. Boston: Houghton Mifflin, 1984.
Polacco, Patricia. *The Butterfly*. New York: Philomel, 2000.
Richter, Hans Peter. *I Was There*. New York: Puffin, 1962.
Vos, Ida. *Anna Is Still Here*. New York: Penguin, 1986.
Wild, Margaret. *Let the Celebrations Begin*. New York: Orchard, 1991.
Zapruder, Alexandra, ed. *Salvaged Papers: Young Writers' Diaries of the Holocaust*. New Haven: Yale UP, 2002.

The Impact of the Shoah on American Jewish-Christian Relations[1]

By Steven Leonard Jacobs

INTRODUCTION: FACT AND REALITY

That the Shoah is an historical fact with enormous implications, not only for Jewish life in the United States and in Israel but also wherever Jews reside (either by force or through choice) is self-evident. The Shoah also unarguably looms in importance due to its impact on present and future relationships among Jews and Christians, Israelis and Christians, Arabs and Jews and Israelis, Muslims and Jews and Muslims and Christians. It is also clear that, even more than six decades after the fact, we have not as yet fully plumbed the Shoah's historical data or even come close to fully weighing its significance. Indeed, this is well witnessed by the ongoing publication of books, monographs, articles and essays, documentary films and audio archives (not to mention the veritable flood of fictionalized interpretative work in all manner of genres). The horrendous years of 1933–45 continue to hold a vise-like grip on the imagination of those of us privileged to interact with the ones who survived, either by personal ingenuity, luck or accident. (Whether these survivors' memories will begin to recede from historical consciousness once the last survivor has died—even though generations yet to be born will still be able to access historical artifacts frozen in time, including video and audio testimony—remains a serious and far too little explored issue in contemporary Shoah discourse.)

One particular arena in which the Shoah continues to assert a major influence is Jewish-Christian relations, particularly in the United States. The revelations of what was done primarily to the Jews by the Nazis and their all-too-willing minions caused a dramatic self-examination on the part of *some* Christian clergy and *some* Christian intellectuals, as they simply could not escape the growing realization that two thousand years of a "teaching of contempt" and a labeling of the Jewish people as a "deicide people" had borne poisonous fruit. While Jews, too, at least in some circles, *have* wrestled with the theological implications of the Shoah, evolution in Jewish thought is far more subtle. It tends to be manifest in communal response to and strong political support for the State of Israel, observance of *Yom Ha-Shoah* (Holocaust Memorial Day) and/or active promotion of Shoah-related expressions in popular culture such as Steven Spielberg's *Schindler's List*.

Returning, however, to the impact of the Shoah on Jewish-Christian relations, one simply cannot proceed without first examining *the* document understood to have opened the doors to a true dialogical encounter between Jews and Christians: the 1965 Vatican Declaration *Nostre Aetate* ("In Our Time") that was published under the auspices of Pope John XXIII (1881–1963) and put into force by the Roman Catholic Church—and subsequently, related to pronouncements and actions. Before doing so, however, one must address serious concerns about the impact of the Shoah on Jewish-Christian relations already enumerated more than a quarter century before, as well as the unique reality of an *American* United States Holocaust Memorial Museum in Washington, DC, where no battle of the Second World War was fought, no concentration or death camp constructed and no Jews were murdered.

"NEW DEBATES ABOUT THE HOLOCAUST"

On September 4, 1980, Paula Hyman, professor of Jewish history at Columbia University, published an article in *The New York Times* entitled "New Debate on the Holocaust," giving voice to many of the same concerns presented here and surveying and quoting a range both Jewish and non-Jewish educators, thinkers, and intellectuals.

For Nobel Laureate Elie Wiesel, the very focus on the Shoah, as evidenced by the proliferation of both good and bad books, essays, monographs, television programs and films caused him to wonder whether or not any of them had a truly beneficial impact upon their audiences. One may note in this connection that the genocidal events in Rwanda and Bosnia-Herzegovina in the late 1990s largely failed to motivate and generate the kind of moral outrage and response which should have come from such increasing awareness of the

Shoah. On the other hand, the present public outcry against the ongoing genocide in the Sudan and Darfur may indicate that such awareness, however slow in coming, can develop if enough is persistently done to make people aware of such genocidal tragedies.

Rabbi Arnold Jacob Wolf of Chicago questioned the Shoah's impact upon "the image and self-image of Jews and upon Jewish-Christian relations." To be sure, the creation of and relative ease in gaining the funding for Holocaust-Studies chairs and programs in many American colleges and universities may be deemed in this context to be a positive step. On the other hand, this same focus on Holocaust in the academy has often been to the detriment of other foci in Judaic studies, and raises the concern that the only course non-Jewish students might ever take in Judaic studies would depict twentieth century Jews as simply a "victim people" without much concern for their broader cultural and religious heritage. Still as Rabbi Irving Greenberg, past chair of the United States Holocaust Memorial Council, for example, has opined, Holocaust courses and programs often effectively serve as "gateways," leading the curious Jew and non-Jew alike to further investigate the Judaic experience in an academically credible and responsible manner.

Hunter College (New York) sociology professor John Murray Cuddihy understood the Shoah as manifesting a kind of secularist triumphalism—a "chosen peopleness" in reverse—that elevates, at least in Jewish eyes, the tragedy of the Shoah above those of other victim groups. This viewpoint raises a number of closely related questions, including whether the Shoah is best viewed and taught as *sui generic* and, thus, unique (e.g., the position of Professor Steven Katz of Boston University and many others within organized American Jewish communities); or whether it is more appropriately studied comparatively (while nonetheless being recognized as having unique elements—as is the case with all genocides), if we are to learn any enduring lessons from the Shoah.

For Christian theologians, who have gone farther in rethinking the problems of their own theologies when juxtaposed with the Shoah (without self-consciously reflecting Jewish thought), there remains, even today, a broad reluctance to raise critically challenging questions, lest the taint of anti-Semitism be associated with their work. At the same time, however, these Christian theologians (e.g., Rosemary Radford Ruether, herself highly critical of Israel; the late Roy Eckardt; Franklin Littell; and others) recognize only too well that no dialogue between Jews and Christians, of whatever denominational stripe, can occur without both the Shoah and the modern State of Israel being and becoming part of the agenda of conversation.

Hyman concluded her article by noting: "The issue for many Jewish community figures is to decide how the Holocaust is to be taught and commemorated and what lessons are to be derived from it. . . . In teaching the Holocaust, some critics stress [that] the lessons of the precariousness of Jewish destiny must be balanced by the concept of mutual dependence in the cause of human survival" (Sect. 6, p. 65, col. 1). As we will see, the Washington Museum of the Holocaust (discussed below) may very well serve to address these very concerns.

THE UNITED STATES HOLOCAUST MEMORIAL MUSEUM

Now more than a decade old (it opened April, 1993), the United States Holocaust Memorial Museum in Washington, DC is one of the most popular museums in the country. Its exhibits attract numerous visitors, its seminars and lectures and research opportunities draw a wide range of scholars, academics, and others with interest in the Shoah. It is therefore arguably the flagship museum of its kind in the United States. Still, the museum has not been without controversies—ranging from leadership issues to memorializing other known genocidal tragedies, to the story of its original political creation. It is *experienced* ("seen" would seem too limiting a verb to capture the impact it has on its visitors) by more non-Jewish persons than any program or institution within organized American Jewish communities combined, and thus remains an influential factor in today's Jewish-Christian dialogical relationships.[2]

Edward T. Linenthal, professor of religion and American culture at the University of Wisconsin, Oshkosh, whose 1995 book *Preserving Memory: The Struggle to Create America's Holocaust Museum* goes a long way towards explaining the museum's apparent success, captured its very essence in an article published only six months after its official opening:

> The Holocaust is to be "inflicted" on the museum visitor as the narrative seeks to arouse empathy for victims, inform visitors about wartime America's role as both bystander and liberator, and ask visitors to ponder the power of a murderous ideology that produced those capable of implementing official mass extermination. No longer occupying American space, visitors undergo an initiatory passage through a Holocaust narrative designed, in part, to help them appreciate the virtues and frailty of American democracy and designed to instill an attitude of civic responsibility. They are to emerge from the exhibit

> "born again," chastened citizens, alert to the stirrings of genocidal possibilities in their own society and elsewhere.
>
> The exhibit is also a place where the longstanding argument about the appropriate relationship between Jewish and "other" victims is addressed. While there is only brief mention of the Armenian genocide, the exhibition at least allows the possibility of reading the Holocaust as an event linked to previous—and future—genocides. There is an unresolved tension in the exhibit's presentation of the relationship between Jewish and non-Jewish victims. The inclusion of various "others" broadens the definition of the Holocaust beyond six million Jews but maintains a careful hierarchy of victimization by locating Jewish victims at the center of the Holocaust, with others situated in relation to the Jewish center. Depending on one's perspective, the exhibit can be read as a major step toward inclusion of various victims—an expansion of the boundaries of Holocaust memory—or still too exclusive, with non-Jewish victims defined only in their relationship to Jews. (429)

Acknowledging, then, the accuracy of Linenthal's insights, the key word here is "relationship." Many of those who come away from this museum experience relate to Jews differently than they did previously. In many formally constructed dialogues between Jews and Christians, participants on both sides reference their own experiences in the museum and how those experiences have shaped the ideas, conceptions, orientations, etc., they bring to the conversation. And, while survivors are diminishing in numbers every day, the United States Holocaust Memorial Museum may very well be the single most important factor in sustaining the presence of the Shoah in any encounter between Jews and Christians as well as other non-Jews. But it is a relatively newer phenomenon than the breakthroughs three decades before, those of the Roman Catholic documents initiated by Pope John XXIII (1881–1963), which laid the solid theological groundwork for real and sustained dialogue between Jews and Roman Catholics, and, by extension, between Jews and Protestants of various denominations. We now turn to a consideration of this important document.

NOSTRE AETATE AND BEYOND

The French-Jewish historian and intellectual Jules Isaac (1877–1963) wrote his monumental *Jesus et Israel*, published in 1948, but written while he was in hiding from the Nazis, and his much slimmer volume *The Teaching of Contempt:*

Christian Roots of Anti-Semitism, published after his death, though originally written in France in 1956 under the *title Genèse de l'antisémitisme*. His initial work found its way to the attention of Pope John XXIII (1881–1963), the former Monsignor Angelo Giuseppe Roncalli, who had witnessed to some extent Nazi perfidy firsthand during his years as Apostolic Delegate in Turkey (1935–44). Invited to meet this Pope in June 1960, Isaac is said to have challenged him to respond to the Shoah as the true "Prince of the Church" that he was. How much influence that meeting had on John's convening of the Second Vatican Council in 1962 and the resultant historic declaration it produced are unclear. *Nostre Aetate* is, however, a true high-water mark in Jewish-Christian relations; its very catholicity allowing Protestants to later join in this sea-change of relationships.

Proclaimed by Pope John's successor, Pope Paul VI (1897–1978), on October 28, 1965, its full title in translation is "Declaration on the Relation of the Church to Non-Christian Religions," and it consists of five "Notes": (1) "what men have in common"—their community, origin, final goal, and quest for answers to "the unsolved riddles of the human condition"; (2) perceptions of the power of the Supreme Being by all humanity, acceptance by the Catholic Church of that which is "true and holy" in other religions, while affirming the Truth of the Christ, and an affirmative commitment to dialogue and collaboration; (3) "esteem for Moslems" and a commitment to overcome the past and work together for mutual understanding, social justice, moral welfare, peace, and freedom; (4) a spiritual bond to "Abraham's stock," the Christ's "reconciliation" of Jews and Gentiles by "His cross," the Jews' non-recognition and non-acceptance of Christ at the time of his visitation, commitment to mutual understanding, respect, and fraternal dialogue, and, then, what Jews—and others—have seen and understood as the radical break with that past:

> True, the Jewish authorities and those who followed their lead pressed for the death of Christ (John 19:6); still, what happened in His passion cannot be charged against all the Jews, without distinction, then alive, nor against the Jews of today. Although the Church is the new people of God, the Jews should not be presented as rejected or accursed by God, as if this followed from the Holy Scriptures. All should see to it, then, that in catechetical work or in the preaching of the word of God they do not teach anything that does not conform to the truth of the Gospel and the spirit of Christ.
>
> Furthermore, in her rejection of every persecution against any man, the Church, mindful of the patrimony she shares with the Jews and

moved not by political reasons but by the Gospel's spiritual love, decries hatred, persecutions, displays of anti-Semitism, directed against Jews at any time and by anyone.

And, finally, (5) reproving "any discrimination between man and man or people and people, so far as their human dignity and the rights flowing from it are concerned."

For Jews, such words found willing and heartfelt appreciation in the aftermath of the Shoah; for Jews and Catholics now found that they were able to enter—many for the first time—into sustained dialogue. Led, in part, by both national and international representative organizations and their leaders, the church rejected the lingering charge of collective deicide beyond the Roman period (and further granted that even in that time it had limited application). The church also specifically repudiated anti-Semitism in all its manifestations, thus initiating a message full of progress and promise. It would fall, however, to two other important and significant documents to "translate" these historic words into concrete actions.

On December 1, 1974, Johannes Cardinal Willebrands (1909–2006), president of the church's Commission for Religious Relations with the Jews, issued the "Guidelines and Suggestions for Implementing the Conciliar Declaration 'Nostra Aetate.'" Almost double the length of the original declaration and governed by a sense of pragmatic reality, it was divided into four parts after its "Introductory Note" and "Preamble" and prior to its "Conclusion," namely: "Dialogue," "Liturgy," "Teaching and Education," and "Joint Social Action." Summarizing and contextualizing its own text, the "Introductory Note" correctly realized these "Guidelines and Suggestions" served as "the Commission's first step toward the realization of religious relations with Judaism" and invited "our Jewish brothers" to participate in this dialogical commitment. The "Preamble" recognized not only the "persecutions and massacres of Jews" in the Europe of the Second World War and a two-thousand year past of "mutual ignorance and frequent confrontation," but, equally, understood *Nostre Aetate* to hold forth the promise of true dialogue and "better mutual understanding." It also asked Christians with the responsibility "to acquire a better knowledge of the basic components of the religious traditions of Judaism" and "to learn by what essential traits the Jews define themselves in the light of their own religious experience."

In Part I, "Dialogue," the church committed itself to a respectful relationship with its dialogue partner—in this case, the Jews—while, at the same time, it remained cognizant of its own responsibility to "preach Jesus Christ to the world." Mutual openness was encouraged by Jews and Catholics meeting and studying together the very differences that the fundamental convictions of each present, for example, as they both pursue "the struggle for peace and justice."

In Part II, "Liturgy," the church recognized the links between the two traditions and the centrality of the Bible for both. Significantly for the church, "the New Testament brings out the full meaning of the Old, while both Old and New illumine and explain each other." Priests should take particular care that text-based homilies not distort the meaning(s) of the text itself, "especially when it is a question of passages which seem to show the Jewish people as such in an unfavorable light." Catholic commissions "entrusted with the task of liturgical translation" must be particularly aware of these responsibilities.

In Part III, "Teaching and Education," several facts were brought to the attention of the church's Catholic audience: (1) the same God is the God of both the Old and New Testaments and the old and new Covenants; (2) Judaism at the time of Christ and his apostles was a "complex reality"; (3) the Old Testament and Jewish tradition should not be set against the New Testament with the former concerned only with justice, fear and legalism and the latter appealing to love of God and neighbor; (4) "Jesus was born of the Jewish people, as were his apostles and a large number of his first disciples"; (5) "what happened in his passion cannot be blamed upon all the Jews then living, without distinction, nor upon the Jews of today"; (6) "the history of Judaism did not end with the destruction of Jerusalem, but rather went on to develop a religious tradition . . . rich in religious values." The arenas where this information was to be addressed were catechisms, religious textbooks, history books, and mass media. Research into problems bearing on Judaism and Jewish-Christian relations at Catholic colleges and universities was welcomed as was collaboration with Jewish scholars.[3]

In Part IV, "Joint Social Action," the call was for collaborative work for social justice and peace locally, nationally and internationally.

The "Conclusion" reminded the reader that the local bishops would know best how to implement these "Guidelines and Suggestions," and that the commission itself was *only* established approximately five weeks prior, on October 22, 1974.

The "Guidelines and Suggestions" were followed approximately eight years later—in response to the comments of Pope John Paul II on March 6, 1982, to delegates at a conference studying the relations between the church and Judaism—with "Notes on the correct way to present the Jews and

Judaism in preaching and catechesis in the Roman Catholic Church," again by the Commission for Religious Relations with the Jews, Johannes Cardinal Willebrands, President.

Longer still than either of the first two documents, after its "Preliminary Considerations and Conclusion," it was divided into six parts: "Religious Teaching and Judaism," "Relations between the Old and New Testament," "Jewish Roots of Christianity," "The Jews in the New Testament," "The Liturgy" and "Judaism and Christianity in History." In addition to quoting relevant sections of both *Nostre Aetate* and the "Guidelines and Suggestions," the "Preliminary Considerations" emphasized Pope John Paul's commitment that such presentations be done "not only in an honest and objective manner, free from prejudices and without any offences, but also with full awareness of the heritage common" to both.

Part I, "Religious Teaching and Judaism," urged the "organic integration" of Jews and Judaism into the catechesis to better understand certain aspects of the life of the Church. It further stressed the need to balance Jewish and Catholic ideas between "the two economies of the Old and New Testament" in terms of promise and fulfillment, continuity and newness, singularity and universality, and uniqueness and exemplary nature. It further emphasized the bond between the two, rejecting anti-Semitism, but also declaring that "Church and Judaism cannot . . . be seen as two parallel ways of salvation."

Part II, "Relations between the Old and New Testament,"[4] understood the election of Israel clearly in the complete fulfillment and election of Jesus Christ in terms of announcement and promise (cf. Heb 4:1-11), recognizing, also, that there is "a Christian reading of the Old Testament which does not necessarily coincide with the Jewish reading." Significantly, the text went on to note:

> It is more clearly understood that the person of the Messiah is not only a point of division for the people of God but also a point of convergence (cf. *Sussidi per l'ecumenismo* of the diocese of Rome, n. 140). Thus it can be said that Jews and Christians meet in a comparable hope, founded on the same promise made to Abraham (cf. Gen 12:1-3; Heb 6:13-18).

In Part III, "Jewish Roots of Christianity," Jesus' Jewishness was emphasized in terms of his complex relationship to "the law" (i.e., *Halakha*, though the Hebrew word itself was not used) as well as to the Pharisees. Regarding the latter, it fully noted:

An exclusively negative picture of the Pharisees is likely to be inaccurate and unjust (cf. Guidelines, Note 1; cf. AAS, *loc. cit.*, p. 76). If in the Gospels and elsewhere in the New Testament there are all sort of unfavorable references to the Pharisees, they should be seen against the background of a complex and diversified movement.

Part IV, "The Jews in the New Testament," recognized the long and complicated editorial work and process by which the New Testament came into being, and with it a negativism with respect to "the Jews," as well as an awareness that the majority of the Jews alive during the Roman period did *not* accept Jesus as their messiah. Following the declaration, "Declaration on Religious Freedom," which was also promulgated during Vatican II, this document equally rejected coercive conversion, the very antithesis of true dialogue. On the "delicate question of responsibility for the death of Christ," it aligned itself with both *Nostre Aetate* and the "Guidelines and Suggestions," understanding that the Christ "freely underwent his passion and death," and, therefore, rejected any presentation of the Jews as "repudiated or cursed by God."

Part V, "The Liturgy," re-emphasized the liturgical bond that exists between Christianity and Judaism, the former drawing upon the latter, especially, by example, in the Passover celebration.

Part VI, "Judaism and Christianity in History," reaffirmed that the history of the Jewish people did not end in 70 CE, that the Jewish people's "permanence" is not a "living argument for Christian apologetic" but remains evidence of its chosenness. It also included, for the first time, a comment about the State of Israel: "The existence of the State of Israel and its political options should be envisaged not in a perspective which is in itself religious, but in their reference to the common principles of international law."[5]

Finally, on March 16, 1998, Cardinal Edward Idris Cassidy (1924–), now president of the Commission for Religious Relations with the Jews, published, at the express request of Pope John Paul II (1920–2005), "We Remember: A Reflection on the Shoah," the first time the Shoah and Christian-Jewish relations were fully addressed in the same document. As is well known, this pope, himself of Polish origin, had close personal friends within the Jewish community of his youth and saw Nazi crimes in his native country during his own seminary days and training for the priesthood. Longest of all these documents, it began with a Presentation by Cardinal Cassidy, including a letter from the pope, dated March 12, 1998, and was itself divided into five parts: I. "The tragedy of the Shoah and the duty of remembrance"; II. "What we must remember"; III. "Relations between Jews and Christians"; IV. "Nazi anti-Semitism and the Shoah"; and V. "Looking together to a common future." Cardinal Cassidy's "Presentation" historically contextualized the document itself, and the pope's letter of encouragement was, in part, a plea and a prayer for reconciliation and healing.

Part I of "We Remember" set its own historical context and recognized the Shoah as the Nazi regime's attempt to exterminate the Jewish people as "a major fact of the history of this [twentieth] century." For the Church, then, the duty to remember this tragedy remains "the moral imperative to ensure that never again will selfishness and hatred grow to the point of sowing such suffering and death."

Part II acknowledged the incapacity of words to truly convey the enormity of the Shoah, while its European setting "raises the question of the relation between the Nazi persecution and the attitudes down the centuries of Christians towards the Jews," characterized in Part III as a "tormented one."

In Part III, the pope himself is quoted from a 1997 address rejecting "erroneous and unjust interpretations" of the New Testament which led to mob attacks and feelings of hostility towards Jews.[6] Continuing with, perhaps, a particularly Catholic reading of European history, the document saw the end of the eighteenth century as subject to a "false and exacerbated nationalism . . . more sociological and political than religious." Equally, it saw the Nazis' use of pseudo-scientific racism coupled with extreme nationalism, which the church already condemned in 1931 and later repudiated in Pope Pius XI's (1857–1939) encyclical letter of 1937 *"Mit brennender Sorge"* ("With deep anxiety," which never explicitly mentioned either the Jews or Nazi anti-Semitism as such). Part III condemned National Socialist racial ideology as well as those who, theologically, were intent on severing connection between the Old Testament and the story of the chosen people, the Jews.

Continuing in Part IV, the church understood National Socialist ideology as fundamentally anti-Christian, and any linking of historic anti-Jewish behaviors on the part of Christians, must, therefore, be examined "on a case by case basis." While acknowledging that not all did what they could to save the Jews, and thus failed *as Christians* to behave properly and righteously, the document does address the still contentious issue of Pius XII's (1876–1958) own involvement, by citing in note 16 the thanks expressed to him by Dr. Joseph Nathan of the Italian Hebrew Commission on September 7, 1945; that of Dr. A. Leo Kubowitzki of the World Jewish Congress on September 21, 1945; and the telegram of Israeli Prime Minister Golda Meir at the pope's death in 1958.

Looking to the future in Part V, the document reiterated the church's sorrow at the failure of "her sons and daughters in every age," which it viewed as an act of repentance (Hebrew *teshuva* used in parenthesis), and it further vowed to do all within its power to see that the Shoah was never repeated. It called for a future devoid of both anti-Judaism and anti-Christianity.

GOING FORWARD IN DIALOGUE

With its foundation now firmly established—and the Shoah fully realized as the precipitating event—Roman Catholics and Jews entered a period of active and sustained dialogue that has not abated. Having opened doors to dialogue, both Catholics and Jews saw such conversations not in exclusivist terms, that is, only between themselves, but also viewed the continuing dialogue as a means of presenting opportunities for expanding conversations to various Protestant clergy and laity and Jewish denominational movements as well.[7] Thus, today, Jewish-Christian dialogues in the United States are likely to include Roman Catholics, Methodists, Presbyterians, and Lutherans (the American branches of which have formally repudiated the anti-Semitism of their founder Martin Luther), Episcopalians, some Baptists, and some few fundamentalist and/or evangelical representatives, Reform, Conservative, and Reconstructionist Jews, and some few Orthodox Jews as well. Wherever these dialogues take place throughout the United States, one can be assured that, in addition to informational discussions regarding rituals, holy day practices, and contemporary "hot button issues" (e.g., abortion and homosexuality), both the State of Israel and the Shoah are part of the conversations. By extension, the participation of non-Jews at *Yom Ha-Shoah* commemorative events has also become prominent. Whether the Shoah will be sustained in the foreseeable future and beyond as a major topic for dialogue and meaningful shared commemoration, is very much an unresolved and, thus, debated question.

AN UNSCIENTIFIC SURVEY, AND YET...

As part of this initial assessment of the impact of the Shoah on American Jewish-Christian relations—quite possibly part of a future, much larger project—a brief survey was constructed of seventeen questions in the areas of Jews and Judaism, Jewish-Christian relations, the Holocaust, and its impact and implications.[8] Several pastors of large congregations from a master list of more than forty churches in both Tuscaloosa and Huntsville, Alabama, were selected and their representatives readily agreed to be interviewed. Large church clergy were specifically chosen because their congregations would, most likely, have a large number of adult and youth education programs where the impact, if any, of the Shoah might potentially be realized. As stated in the Informed Consent Document signed by all participants:

> The study... will involve a series of interviews with working Christian clergy—from fundamentalist to moderate to liberal—as they relate their own work "in the trenches" to the realities of the Holocaust/Shoah in a post-Holocaust/Shoah world. The intent will be to address a basic issue in modern religious America: How has Christian thought and work been altered by the impact of the Holocaust/Shoah?
>
> Approximately six (6) representative clergy of the following denominations have been invited to participate: (1) Baptist, (2) Roman Catholic, (3) Episcopal, (4) Lutheran, (5) Methodist, (6) Presbyterian.

All told, eight interviews, each lasting approximately one hour in length, were conducted: three Baptist (moderate and conservative); two Presbyterian (moderate and conservative); one each, Methodist, Episcopal, and Roman Catholic. (Time constraints prevented the author from establishing a connection with a representative Lutheran clergyperson.)

Without any claim to overall scientific validity, due both to the relatively small sampling and the geographic focus on Southern clergy, nonetheless, a consistent pattern of responses revealed the following:

1. As a group, these clergy did not necessarily regard themselves as particularly knowledgeable about either Jews, Judaism or the Shoah apart from their rather formidable knowledge of "the scriptures" (Hebrew Bible/Old Testament) and personal reading. One of the seven noted that an undergraduate course in German history by a particularly outstanding professor had addressed specifically the Shoah, and, even now, resulted in his continuing interest in its story.

2. As a group, these clergy expressed, to a greater or lesser degree, familiarity with the source documents of their particular denominational communities regarding Jewish-Christian relations, but could not concretize the proposals and/or resolutions contained within these documents in specific examples within their own congregations.

3. As a group, these clergy all used stories of the Shoah as sermon illustrations to emphasize points of ethical responsibility or faith commitment (e.g., Corrie ten Boom of The Netherlands was cited more than once, as was Anne Frank, the French Huguenot village of Le Chambon, Kristallnacht, Dietrich Bonhoeffer, and *Schindler's List*). A few had even visited the United

States Holocaust Memorial Museum in Washington, DC. But none could recall preaching a specific sermon focusing directly on the Shoah and/or raising such themes as historical Christian complicity as foundational to Nazi ideology, Christian participation in the development of anti-Semitism, or the implications of the Shoah for Christian or denominational theology. Likewise, none of these clergy had themselves taught an adult or youth course in their congregations focusing directly on the Shoah, nor could they recall such courses being taught by others in their specific religious communities, nor, given the demands of their responsibilities, had they participated in organized Jewish-Christian dialogical activities.

4. Several clergy made reference to the State of Israel, the plight of the Palestinians, and the current Middle East crisis, directly relating these comments to the Shoah and expressing great concern about resolving these difficult situations. Uniformly, perhaps because the they knew their interviewer was himself Jewish, all expressed great admiration for the Jewish People—theologically as God's "chosen" or humanly as a powerful example to the world of a people able to overcome its tragic past.

5. Others topics seemingly relevant to the clergy themselves during the interviews included: the controversies surrounding Pope Pius XII's role during the Shoah as well as that of the Roman Catholic Church itself, the role of Christian churches in Germany during the Nazi period, the questionable success of the European Enlightenment, the impact of the Arab-Israeli war of 1967, and model Passover "Seder suppers" conducted in church settings.

CONCLUSION: IMPACT AND IMPLICATIONS

As the events of the Shoah and the years 1933–45 recede into history, and generations yet to be born will only be able to confront these realities from an increasing distance—without the benefit of physical contact with living witnesses—there seems to be little reason to believe that the Shoah will maintain as central a presence in the Jewish-Christian dialogical arena. To be sure, it is likely always to continue as *a* topic, especially when coupled with anti-Semitism itself and the necessity of an historical overview. Still, its impact undoubtedly will lessen in the coming years. As with any historical event, the so-called "lessons to be learned" will become increasingly problematic as the future distances us from the events themselves.

Then, too, the tendency of the American Jewish community to make the Shoah a "Jewish story," far in excess of its universal applicability to and

The Impact of the Shoah 153

for others, may very well serve as a cause for its lessening impact in Christian settings, especially where contact with Jews and knowledge about Jews and Judaism are minimal at best. One pastor in our survey suggested the need for on-line teaching resources created and made specifically available for churches, but was largely unfamiliar with what was already available "out there." Others offered no suggestions.

Equally, in a world where the so-called "war on terrorism" itself continues to occupy the media's center stage, and other genocides, both present and future, capture the attention of Americans, calling for political, economic, humanitarian and other interventions, appeals to the Shoah of the last century will not, in all likelihood, have as sustained an impact upon generations too little schooled in its realities. American non-Jewish support for the State of Israel, too, while historically connected to the revelations of the Shoah, will no longer likely be based as much upon that connection in the coming years. Indeed, Jewish organizational life in the United States, including the vast fundraising networks, will find itself no longer able as easily to draw upon either the Shoah or a future Shoah-like event to get Jews to give. Historical events will remain viable only to those for whom historical events are already meaningful; for the vast majority, the immediate worries and cares of the present impact on the future far more than events receding into the historical past.

For Jews themselves, their history is filled with dramatically horrific events—the Egyptian enslavement, the destruction of the First Temple and the Babylonian Exile, the destruction of the Second Temple and the Roman oppression, and the uneven Western migratory trek, punctuated by ghettoization, pogrom and expulsion. There have been moments of sublime exaltation as well—the theophany at Sinai after the liberation from Egyptian enslavement, the birth of the Third Jewish Commonwealth three hundred years after the arrival of the first Jews on the North American continent, and a continually rich religious, literary, and cultural heritage. For the American Jewish community, the freest and safest aggregate of Jews in all Jewish history, a hallmark characteristic of its very "at-home-ness" has been the pioneering Jewish-Christian dialogue of the post-World War II era that began in Europe but has experienced its fullest flowering here in America. There is no question that the Shoah has played an important role in the early development and sustaining of that dialogue.

Significantly enough, however, while the original Christian counterparts in that very same dialogue were, more often than not, influenced by the revelations of the Shoah, and, equally as likely, translated their encounters with

Jews into programs within their own congregations and, where possible, pulpit exchanges with local rabbis, the same cannot be said today. Though undergraduate courses in "The Holocaust" continue to be oversubscribed throughout the country, such courses have not, in the main, made their way into either Christian colleges or universities and, even less so, into denominational seminaries. Thus, those who presently occupy America's Christian pulpits and also manifest serious interest in Jews, Judaism, or the Shoah tend to do so as a result of their own personal interest, reading, travel, or attendance at film or other cultural events (e.g., live theatre, musical performances, art exhibitions, etc.).

If (and that "if" is itself worthy of a sustained conversation within the organized American Jewish community) the subject of the Shoah is important to continuing Jewish-Christian dialogical relations, then significantly more creative educational programming must be developed in concert with the various Christian denominational communities already committed to dialogue with Jews, as well as those Christian denominational communities potentially committed to this dialogue. Christian denominational colleges, universities, and seminaries that are the least-explored venues for the transmission of this specific knowledge must become the recipients of renewed contact and opportunities for such teaching, preferably in concert with other courses in Judaic studies, including courses in Israel and the Middle East. Local Jewish communities, in addition, must re-energize and re-embrace their own efforts to initiate dialogue with their neighbors, not only about Israel and the Shoah, but other arenas of Jewish knowledge as well (e.g., the literatures of Judaism, including Torah, Mishnah, Talmud, Midrash, and Responsa, Jewish political positions on contemporary "hot button" topics, etc.). In a world growing smaller communicatively while becoming fractiously divisive, continuing Jewish survival may very well become increasingly dependant upon interconnectivity with allies with whom, generations ago, such interconnection was deemed both unthinkable and unrealizable. The continuing and ongoing success of Jewish-Christian dialogue may, in fact, be the model for that survival.

Notes

1. First presented at the 38th Annual Conference of the Association for Jewish Studies, Manchester Grand Hyatt, San Diego, CA, December 17–19, 2006.
2. For a full accounting of the wide range of the programs and resources available at the United States Holocaust Memorial Museum, consult their extensive website www.ushmm.org.
3. Of particular interest to this author is the creation, wherever possible, of academic chairs in Jewish studies at such institutions, which has not yet happened, to the best of my knowledge, to any appreciable degree.
4. The document's own endnote stated the following:
   > We continue to use the expression Old Testament because it is traditional (cf. already 2 Cor 3:14) but also because "Old" does not mean "out of date" or "out-worn." In any case, it is the permanent value of the O.T. as a source of revelation that is emphasized here (cf. Dei Verbum, 3).
5. Significant, too, is the formal declaratory recognition of the State of Israel, rather than a reference to the "Holy Land" or "Land of Israel." While waffling somewhat on this modern nation-state solely as a political entity divorced from historical Jewish religious longings, its political recognition, a long-sought for goal of both world-wide Jewry and Israel herself, opened the doors to ambassadorial exchange, itself not without international significance. Religiously and theologically, by acknowledging Israel as a sovereign nation-state, in effect, the Vatican was equally refuting any notion of the Jewish people as a "failed people," alive only to give living credence to the "truth" of the Christ and Christianity.
6. Problematic for Jews and others, however, was the phrase, "I do not say on the part of the Church as such," which was understood by many as explicitly exonerating the Roman Catholic Church from any sense of institutional responsibility for the antisemitism of the past or the Shoah of the present.
7. The Mobile (AL) Jewish-Christian Dialogue, now more than twenty-five years old and initiated by the late Roman Catholic Archbishop John L. May, of Mobile and later St. Louis, MO, remains the oldest and, at times, the largest pioneering venture in such inclusive dialogical encounters in the United States.
8. The "Questions for Representative Clergy" were grouped as follows:

   I. Introductory Questions
   1. Briefly describe your denomination.
   2. Briefly describe your congregation.

   II. Jews & Judaism
   3. Aside from the Hebrew Bible (Old Testament), how knowledgeable do you consider yourself regarding Jews and Judaism?
   4. What do you consider the primary source(s) of that knowledge?
   5. Are there particular historical events and/or ideas that stick out in your mind?

III. Jewish-Christian Relations
    6. How familiar do you consider yourself with regard to the official statements of your denominational community regarding Jewish-Christian relations?
    7. How would you summarize the major (salient) points of these documents and/or resolutions?
    8. Have you implemented any or all of the concrete proposal/suggestions associated with these statements?

IV. The Holocaust
    9. How knowledgeable do you consider yourself about the Holocaust?
    10. What do you consider the primary source(s) of that knowledge?
    11. Are there particular historical events and/or ideas that stick out in your mind?

V. Impact and Implications
    12. Describe what impact, if any, the events and/or ideas associated with the Holocaust have had on your ministry work?
    13. Describe what impact, if any, the events and/or ideas associated with the Holocaust have had on your thinking about Jews and/or Judaism.
    14. Describe what impact, if any, the events and/or ideas associated with the Holocaust have had on your interaction with Jews.
    15. Describe what impact, if any, the events and/or ideas associated with the Holocaust have had on your thinking in general.

VI. Conclusion
    16. Are there other comments and/or thoughts you would like to share?
    17. Are there any recommendations and/or suggestions you would like to share?

(Special appreciation is extended to Professor Charles McLafferty, PhD, formerly of the University of Alabama at Birmingham (UAB) for vetting and arranging these questions into a more workable interview format, and to the University of Alabama Institutional Review Board, Tuscaloosa, AL, for expedited clearance to conduct the interviews themselves.)

Works Cited

Cassidy, Cardinal Edward Idris. "We Remember: A Reflection on the Shoah." 16 Mar. 1998 <www.vatican.va/roman_curia/pontifical_councils/chrstuni/documents/rc_pc_chrstuni_doc_16031998_shoah_en.html>.

Commission for Religious Relations with the Jews. "Notes on the correct way to present the Jews and Judaism in preaching and catechesis in the Roman Catholic Church." 6 Mar. 1982 <www.vatican.va/roman_curia/pontifical_councils/chrstuni/relations-jews-docs/rc_pc_chrstuni_doc_19820306_jews-judaism_en.html>.

Hyman, Paula. "New Debate on the Holocaust" *New York Times* 14 Sept. 1980.

Isaac, Jules. *Jesus et Israel*. Paris: Fasquelle, 1959 (Engl. trans. *Jesus and Israel*. New York: Holt, Rinehart and Winston, 1971).

———. *The Teaching of Contempt: Christian Roots of Anti-Semitism*. New York: McGraw-Hill Book Company, 1964.

Linenthal, Edward T. "The Boundaries of Memory: The United States Holocaust Memorial Museum." *American Quarterly* 46.3 (1994): 406–33.

———. *Preserving Memory: The Struggle to Create America's Holocaust Museum*. New York: Columbia UP, 2001.

Pope Paul VI. "Declaration on Religious Freedom: *Dignitatis Humanae*." 7 Dec. 1965 <www.vatican.va/archive/hist_councils/ii_vatican_council/documents/vat-ii_decl_19651207_dignitatis-humanae_en.html>.

Pope Paul VI. "Declaration on the Relation of the Church to Non-Christian Religions: *Nostre Aetate*." 28 Oct. 1965 <www.vatican.va/archive/hist_councils/ii_vatican_council/documents/vat-ii_decl_19651028_nostra-aetate_en.html>.

Pope Pius XI. "Lettera Enciclica *Mit brennender Sorge*." 14 Mar. 1937 <www.vatican.va/holy_father/pius_xi/encyclicals/documents/hf_p-xi_enc_14031937_mit-brennender-sorge_it.html>.

Schindler's List. Dir. Steven Spielberg. Perf. Liam Neeson, Ben Kingsley, and Ralph Fiennes. Universal, 1993.

Willebrands, Johannes Cardinal. "Guidelines and Suggestions for Implementing the Conciliar Declaration '*Nostra Aetate*'." 1 Dec. 1974 <www.vatican.va/roman_curia/pontifical_councils/chrstuni/relations-jews-docs/rc_pc_chrstuni_doc_19741201_nostra-aetate_en.html>.

Post-Shoah Theology and Jewish Biblical Interpretation In America

By Marvin A. Sweeney

PART I

The Shoah constitutes one of the greatest challenges to Jewish theology throughout the history of Judaism and Jewish thought. The destruction of some six million Jews, constituting approximately one third of the world Jewish population and the bulk of the European Jewish community, poses fundamental challenges to Jewish—and Christian—notions of divine power and righteousness that have dominated Jewish theological discussion since the conclusion of World War II.

Judaism has met such challenges before—in both ancient and more modern contexts. One may think of ancient and historical catastrophes, such as the Assyrian destruction of the northern kingdom of Israel and the deportation of much of its population in 722/721 BCE; the Babylonian destruction of Solomon's Temple in Jerusalem and the Babylonian exile of 587/586 BCE; the Roman destruction of the Second Temple in 70 CE as well as the suppression of the Bar Kochba revolt in 135 CE; and the Spanish expulsion of the Jewish people in 1492. As one advances toward modern times, other disastrous events could easily be added to this list. Despite the fundamental challenges to Jewish thought posed by each of these catastrophes, Jewish thinkers have always somehow found the means to meet those challenges by re-envisioning Judaism in such a way as to allow for the innovation necessary to adapt to the changed circumstances of life and thought in relation to the traditional structures and viewpoints of Jewish tradition. Thus, the Judean kings Hezekiah and Josiah attempted to reunite the kingdoms of Israel and Judah around the Jerusalem Temple; the exilic prophets and priesthood posited G-d's sovereignty over all the nations and rebuilt the Jerusalem Temple under Persian rule; Rabbinic Judaism emerged as the theological and social means to bind the Jewish people together during a lengthy exile; and both Kabbalah and Jewish philosophy developed as means to address questions concerning the justice and mercy of G-d.

Many interpreters point to modern Zionism and the creation of the modern state of Israel as one means to address the theological and existential questions posed by the Shoah. Although modern Zionism and Israel do constitute one basis on which to build the future of the Jewish people and Jewish thought, the failure of modern Israel to attract large segments of the western Jewish Diaspora, the originally secular nature of modern Zionism and the development of a religious embrace of Zionism primarily in Ultra-Orthodox circles raise questions as to whether modern Zionism alone can meet the philosophical challenges posed by the Shoah to the Jewish people. Moreover, beyond issues concerned with Zionism and Israel, there remain more foundational issues about G-d's relationship to his chosen people that cannot be ignored.

In this respect, a theological engagement of the Shoah and the problem of evil that it poses remains a *sine qua non* for the future of Jewish thought. Indeed, this concern remains, and will continue to remain, a central focus of Jewish theology. It is therefore not surprising that Jewish thinkers have engaged Jewish theology from the perspective of a post-Shoah world environment. For example, Ignaz Maybaum, Richard Rubenstein, Emil Fackenheim, Eliezer Berkovitz and others initially engaged the Shoah in modern Jewish thought during the 1960s and 1970s, and others, such as Zachery Braiterman, Michael Moore, Abraham Joshua Heschel, Arthur Cohen, David Blumenthal, Zev Garber and Elie Wiesel, have continued to do so through the present.[1]

However, one aspect of this theological concern with the Shoah, perhaps surprisingly, has lagged behind the general field of Jewish theology until relatively recent times: Jewish *biblical* interpretation in light of the Shoah. The slowness in the development of the biblical perspective on the Shoah is especially ironic, since the Bible gives particular attention to precisely the kind of theological question raised by the Shoah from an ancient perspective, particularly in relation to the Assyrian destruction of northern Israel and the Babylonian destruction of Jerusalem and exile of much of the surviving Judean population. The reasons for this retarded development are variable. They include the predominantly Protestant character of biblical theology and the predominantly historical character of modern Jewish biblical scholarship until recent times. But an increasing number of modern Jewish biblical scholars are now exploring the field of biblical theology, in general, and have given special note to the questions posed to biblical theology by the Shoah. Figures such as Jon Levenson, Michael Fishbane, Benjamin Sommer, Tamar Kamionkowski, and the present writer are developing models for Jewish biblical theology, including means to address the problem of evil, both human and divine, raised by the Shoah in both ancient and modern times.[2]

This essay therefore addresses the impact of the Shoah on modern Jewish biblical interpretation, with special focus on this development in America, beginning with surveys of the discussion of the Shoah, respectively in modern Jewish theology and modern Jewish biblical interpretation. It then turns to discussion of two examples of the means by which the question of the Shoah may be addressed in modern Jewish biblical interpretation: first, Moses' encounter with the biblical divinity, YHWH, in the aftermath of the Golden Calf episode in Exodus 32–34, in which Moses challenges YHWH's decision to destroy Israel in the wilderness and create a new people out of Moses' descendants, and second, Ezekiel's vision of YHWH's destruction of Jerusalem in Ezekiel 8–11, in which he portrays the destruction of the city as a divine purge of the site based on the Yom Kippur scapegoat ritual. Working with these accounts as examples, this essay argues that the Shoah has become integral to American Jewish biblical interpretation. It further contends that addressing the question of the Shoah in the Bible entails opening up a dialogue, in which modern Jews must learn both to challenge traditional modes of conceiving the Shoah while still remaining engaged with these traditions as Jewish thought evolves into the twenty-first century.

PART II

For the first two decades after World War II, Jewish theological discussion of the Shoah remained relatively under-developed, as Jews focused on establishing the modern state of Israel as a Jewish homeland and rebuilding the Diaspora in the wake of both the destruction of European Jewry and the expulsion of Middle Eastern Jews. Most religious responses to the Shoah during this period shied away from the question of divine morality and responsibility by emphasizing human action. For example, Martin Buber, heavily influenced by Hasidic perspectives, argued that human beings had turned away from an intimate relationship with G-d in an impersonal modern world and that they thereby destroyed morality; and Leo Baeck, one of the leading modern Reform theologians of the time, shifted his theological writings from questions concerning G-d to focus instead on the human dimensions of Jewish nationhood and rebirth.

After twenty years of reflection regarding the impact of the Shoah on Jewish thought, the first generation of Jewish Shoah theologians, including Ignaz Maybaum, Richard Rubenstein, Emil Fackenheim, Eliezer Berkovits and others, began to emerge in the mid-1960's in an intellectual and theological climate that saw much questioning of past traditions in both Jewish and Christian circles. This first generation of Shoah theologians laid the basic groundwork for addressing the questions of divine responsibility, power and morality in light of the Shoah. For the most part, they examined traditional understandings of divine justice and mercy and largely concluded these could no longer be maintained in the face of the communal memory of burning children. They argued that traditional notions of G-d seemed irrational in light of the enormity of the attempted genocide of the entire Jewish people.

The first major Shoah theologian was Ignaz Maybaum, an Austrian Reform Rabbi who served in Germany and then in England after the war. Hs 1965 book, *The Face of G-d after Auschwitz*, is heavily influenced by the values of classical German Reform Judaism and the European Enlightenment universalism. He denies that the Shoah was a unique event by citing the destruction of the First and Second Temples in Jewish history, which raised much the same issues. He draws upon the perspectives of the Enlightenment Jewish thinker Moses Mendelssohn to argue that the Shoah may be explained as the vicarious atonement of the victims for the sake of the world. Maybaum thereby believes that it is task of Jews to bring knowledge of G-d to the world at large. The violence of the Shoah was necessary so that Jews could speak in a language that humanity could readily understand—the language of violence and destruction, designated with the term *churban* in Hebrew. Like the destructions of the First and Second Temples, this third *churban* would mark the end of an old era and the beginning of a new one, in which the sacrifice of Jews would rouse the conscience of the Gentile world and bring it closer to G-d. In Maybaum's understanding, the Shoah marks the end of the medieval world and the beginning of the modern age, particularly since the mid-1960s saw the beginnings of the Vatican II reforms in the Roman Catholic Church, which promised a new relationship of cooperation and affirmation between Christians and Jews. Still, Maybaum's theology, however idealistic, failed to engage the fundamental questions of divine morality inherent in the Shoah: How could divine love and justice be said to be manifested in a divine decision to allow the sacrifice

European Judaism, which constituted the core of world Jewry and one third of the world's Jewish population? How could the Shoah be viewed as a punishment inflicted by G-d upon the Jewish people? What magnitude of sins would merit such indiscriminate destruction of so many of the divinely chosen people, including innocent children?

A second Shoah theologian of the first generation, Richard Rubenstein, raised precisely the questions which Maybaum had avoided. Rubenstein was a Conservative Rabbi who studied for a PhD in theology at Harvard Divinity School under Harvey Cox, a leading exponent of secularism and the death of G-d movement. Rubenstein published a revised version of his dissertation in 1966 as *After Auschwitz: Radical Theology and Contemporary Judaism* in an effort to challenge the traditional notions of divinity in Jewish thought in the aftermath of the Shoah. Rubenstein argued that Jewish theology, with its notions of an all-powerful, just and merciful G-d, as well as its notions of the "chosenness" of the Jewish people, fell in the face of the Shoah. He reasoned that, assuming that G-d was a just and moral divinity, he could only have intended the Shoah as a morally motivated punishment for Jewish sin. But such "moral" action was totally discontinuous with the experience of the Shoah. Indeed, the reality of the Shoah denied the very possibility that it could be the result of G-d's morally directed will. Such a contention would do nothing less than blaspheme against G-d, by charging Him with murderous vindictiveness, and, moreover it would further dishonor the victims of the Shoah by charging them with sin of enormous magnitude. Again the question emerges: what would justify such a punishment for an entire generation, including the one and half million children who perished in the Shoah? Consequently, Rubenstein rejected the entire structure of Jewish theology by contending that G-d must be absent and that therefore Jews cannot be considered as his uniquely chosen people. Human beings must reject theological illusions of divine power and morality since they cannot be coupled with the reality of human existence. Rubenstein's conclusion, as validated by the Shoah, left no alternative: Humans must be viewed as alone in the world and must act to create meaning and morality for themselves. For Jews, such a reality calls for a renewed emphasis on Jewish peoplehood, not as the divinely chosen people, but as a people who commit themselves to building a new Jewish society. This meant that Jews must return to national life in the land of Israel—natural life on their own soil—and must also commit to building a morally accountable society in human, rather than divine terms.

Unfortunately, Rubenstein's argument turns upon itself, for his dismissal of G-d and "chosenness" destroys the very foundation of Jewish identity.

Fundamental questions must be posed once again. Why should Jews who were not threatened in the Diaspora (i.e., American Jews) move to Israel, particularly since Israel was populated by Jews escaping European and Middle Eastern anti-Semitism? Although he argues that the notions of Jewish "chosenness" have engendered anti-Semitism among non-Jews, modern experience demonstrates that anti-Semitism persists regardless of whether Jews define themselves religiously or not, even in cultures that have little or no Jewish population.

A third Shoah theologian of the first generation, Emil Fackenheim, a German Reform Rabbi and philosopher who himself escaped the Shoah, attempted to answer both Maybaum and Rubenstein throughout a lifetime of theological scholarship focused on issues raised by the Shoah. His 1970 book, *G-d's Presence in History: Jewish Affirmations and Reflections*, attempts to steer clear of the two extremes in considering the Shoah, i.e., the absolute faith of the pious who see no special problem in the Shoah, insofar as G-d by definition must be just, and the denial of divine existence, power, or morality. Like Rubenstein, he argues that the former extreme dishonors the victims of the Shoah and that the latter extreme blasphemes against G-d. For Fackenheim, the major question is how to keep the people Israel and G-d together in the aftermath of the Shoah. He therefore refuses to vindicate G-d by claiming that the Shoah happened "because of our sins," in keeping with the traditional Jewish viewpoint, but he also argues that it is incumbent upon Jews to find the divine presence in contemporary history—even in Auschwitz—in order to build a specifically Jewish future. Such a position means that Jews cannot explain G-d's actions—or lack thereof—at Auschwitz; Jews can only affirm the divine presence. Auschwitz does not prove that G-d is dead; rather Auschwitz constitutes G-d's address to Israel. Fackenheim contends that G-d addresses Israel throughout history in the form of root experiences, such as the Exodus from Egypt and the revelation of the Torah at Mt. Sinai. These experiences provide access to G-d and build for the future; moreover, epoch-making events, such as the destructions of the First and Second Temples, challenge Israel's root experiences in order to test the resiliency of the Jewish people and prepare the way for new interpretations of those experiences. Auschwitz must be seen as another epoch-making event that gives Jews what Fackenheim considers the 614th commandment in Jewish tradition, viz., do not give Hitler a posthumous victory. For Fackenheim, the Shoah becomes a divine clarion call to renew Judaism for the future as testimony to the presence of G-d in history. The responsibility of Jews is to ensure that Judaism does not disappear and thus defeat Hitler intentions. Fackenheim's later writings focus on two concepts:

Tikkun Olam, "repairing the world," after the Shoah and the implications of the Shoah for study of the Bible. Fackenheim's work has been severely criticized for leaving open once again the question of divine morality in the face of the Jewish genocide. Does Judaism continue because G-d—or Hitler—threatens it with destruction? Does G-d feel a need to remind the world of divine power in order to be recognized? Again, the question of blasphemy would seem to become relevant to this picture of G-d and his intentions.

A fourth Shoah theologian of the first generation is Eliezer Berkovits, an Orthodox Rabbi from Transylvania who served pulpits, wrote and taught in Berlin, Australia, the United Kingdom and the United States. His 1973 study, *Faith after the Holocaust*, attempts to advance the discussion initiated by his colleagues by attempting to remove the moral character of G-d from consideration and replacing it with the question of human responsibility for confronting evil in the world. Berkovits begins by noting that the Shoah is not a unique event in Jewish history, because it is one more instance of a repetitive pattern of murder motivated by anti-Semitism. The classical response to or evaluation of such suffering and martyrdom in Jewish experience and thought is *Kiddush ha-Shem*, "sanctification of the divine Name," in which martyrdom becomes an act of ultimate trust in divine righteousness and sanctity. However, Berkovits does not conclude that the Shoah reflects an absolute injustice that is countenanced by G-d. Rather, he characterizes G-d's countenancing of such an act as a manifestation of *Hester Panim*, "the Hidden Face of G-d," known from classical Rabbinic thought, in which G-d chooses to remain hidden in order to prompt human beings to learn to accept responsibility for the world in which they live. Because human beings are partners with G-d in creation, G-d must withdraw so that humans can mature and develop morally in order to exercise their role in seeing to the welfare or completion of creation. In the manner of children, humans must learn to develop and exercise moral judgment through experiencing the consequences of their own mistakes, no matter how terrible those mistakes may be. G-d cannot therefore intervene because such intervention would undermine that learning process. Such a position sidesteps the question of divine justice and responsibility: How badly must humans behave before G-d must act to set things aright? Must humans be allowed to destroy themselves altogether to learn to serve as caretakers of creation? Nevertheless, Berkovits rightly steers the question beyond divine culpability, which humanity cannot hope to fathom, to human responsibility for the welfare of the world, which humans have the power to address.

In sum, these theologians of the first generation have set the agenda in terms of the basic theological question of the Shoah: to what extent is G-d powerful, just, merciful and culpable in a world where evil manifests itself so completely and destructively? The answers provided to this question have not been fully satisfactory, which leads to the second fundamental question posed by the first generation of Shoah theologians: to what extent must human beings take responsibility for the moral order of the world when G-d—for whatever reason—fails to act? In assessing discussion of the Shoah, Michael Morgan, a historian of philosophy and Jewish religious thought, argues that Jews cannot remain fixated only on the question of the Shoah without thinking about the future of Jewish thought and practice (211–18), and religion scholar Zachary Braiterman contends that Judaism (and, for that matter, Christianity) must begin to develop new models for understanding the interrelationship between human beings and G-d in the aftermath of the Shoah (161–78).

To a large extent, this conversation is already taking place. Like those of the first generation, other theologians have focused on G-d's inability to act or the failure of humans to understand divine action, with the consequent assertion of the need for humans to take responsibility for the welfare and future of our world. Abraham Joshua Heschel points to divine pathos in witnessing human wrongdoing and suffering, and calls upon human beings to sanctify the world in which we live (see, e.g., Heschel, *The Prophets*; and *The Sabbath: Its Meaning for Modern Man*). Arthur A. Cohen contends that G-d does not have the power to interfere in human affairs and calls upon humans to redefine our concept of G-d by recognizing that divine speech is in reality what humans have chosen to hear. David Blumenthal argues that, although G-d must be recognized as a kind of abusive parent, humans must nonetheless forgive the abuser in order to heal the self. Zev Garber points to the need to assert Jewish identity in the post-Shoah world, to challenge the anti-Semitism of the church and broader society, and to engage in dialogue with Gentiles in order to provide a moral basis for Jews and non-Jews to live and work together to advance our world (see, e.g., his volume of essays, *Shoah: The Paradigmatic Genocide: Essays in Exegesis and Eisegesis*). Elie Wiesel contends that in a world of absurdity and murder, we must battle murder by creating beauty out of nothingness and daring to challenge G-d.

Although Christian theologians initially viewed this discussion as an issue confined to Jewish theology, attitudes have begun to change. It is now more widely accepted that the negative portrayal of Jews throughout Christian tradition has sown the seeds of anti-Semitism in western culture. This has in turn prompted Christian theologians increasingly to recognize the importance of the questions raised by the Shoah, both for Christianity's relationship with Judaism and for Christianity's own understanding of G-d and moral integrity.³

PART III

Although theological discussion of the Shoah has been one of the major topics of the postwar era, its influence, as noted, has only been recently felt in the field of biblical theology. The first decades of the postwar period have seen the continued dominance of the field of biblical theology by Protestant scholars.⁴ Indeed, the most influential works of this period continue to address themes of modern Protestant concern and largely overlook and even disparage Judaism. Walther Eichrodt, for example, focuses on the question of a biblical covenant that is largely to be seen as a transition from the Mosaic covenant of the Old Testament to the "new covenant" of Christianity. He is widely and justifiably criticized for portraying Judaism's "torso-like appearance" in relation to Christianity (e.g., Levenson, "Why Jews are not Interested" 33–61). Although Gerhard von Rad refrains from denigrating Judaism, his *heilsgeschichtliche* or "sacred historical" approach to constructing Old Testament theology is designed to trace the historical path by which the Bible moved from the preliminary revelation of the Old Testament to the culminating revelation of the New Testament. Ironically, his *heilsgeschichtliche* approach does not include sustained treatment of the book of Esther or of any relationship between the "Old Testament" and Judaism. For the most part, Christian biblical theologians until very recently have tended to view the Bible's portrayal of judgment against Israel and Judah as acts of divine punishment for sin rather than recognizing in such portrayals the problems of theodicy (the compatibility of divine omnipotence and righteousness in the face of the existence of evil) that they raise.

The field of biblical theology began to change in the 1960s and 1970s, however, as previously marginalized groups, such as Roman Catholics, women, scholars from Third World nations and Jews began to play greater roles in modern biblical interpretation. In particular, Jewish biblical theologians began to emerge only in the 1970s and 1980s with the early work of Moshe Goshen-Gottstein and Mattatiahu Tsevat. Still, it has really only been in the 1990s and the 2000s that there have developed sustained efforts to address the field of Jewish biblical theology (Perdue, *Reconstructing* 183–238; Sweeney, "Emerging Field"). Significantly, much of this development has occurred in America. Although early works focused on the more general question of defining or interpreting the Jewish character of the Bible, consideration of issues raised by the Shoah—particularly the integrity of G-d and the heightened role of human beings as partners with G-d in creation—has played an increasingly larger role in the works of Jewish biblical theologians such as Jon Levenson, Michael Fishbane, Benjamin Sommer, Tamar Kamionkowski and the present writer.

Jon Levenson has advanced this discussion by bringing the concerns of Jewish biblical theology into the wider world of biblical, theological and historical scholarship. His 1987 essay "Why Jews are not Interested in Biblical Theology" was one of the first studies to consider the dominant character of biblical theology as a Protestant theological discipline and to focus on the anti-Judaic strains that have long been inherent in the field.[5] Although he largely rejects the notion of Jewish biblical theology by emphasizing that Jews tend to approach the Bible historically rather than theologically, he leaves open the possibility for such work by pointing to the Protestant interest in "repristinization," i.e., reconstructing "pristine" biblical origins, which remains a major preoccupation in the field. There is little reason why Jews cannot engage in such discussion, particularly since Jewish scholars are increasingly trained in biblical theology as well as in historical issues. By implication, this lays a foundation upon which a Jewish biblical theology can be built. After all, one must first understand the Bible in its ancient Jewish context before one can proceed to consider how it can also be relevant to a modern Jewish biblical theology.

Indeed, Levenson's own work, while emphasizing a "history of religions" approach to biblical interpretation, has important implications for the development Jewish biblical theology including questions raised by the Shoah. His early works, such as his 1975 dissertation, *Theology of the Program of Restoration of Ezekiel 40-48*, and his 1985 volume, *Sinai and Zion: An Entry into the Jewish Bible*, have focused on employing a "history of religions" approach to studying the sacred character of the restored Temple, as defined in Ezekiel's vision and to drawing the analogy between the role of the sacred Jerusalem Temple as the source of divine instruction (or Torah) and the portrayal of YHWH's revelation of Torah to Israel at Sinai.

His later works, however, have focused more specifically on questions pertinent to the Shoah, i.e., theodicy, especially in terms of divine culpability and human responsibility in reference to the biblical depiction of creation. His 1988 volume, *Creation and the Persistence of Evil*, challenges the traditional interpretation of the creation-narrative in Gen. 1:1–2:3 as an expression of *creation ex nihilo* or "creation out of nothing." Based on a close examination of the Hebrew text and a comparative study of creation traditions throughout the Bible and the ancient Near East, Levenson argues that Gen. 1:1–2:3 portrays creation as YHWH's struggle to order a preexisting world of chaos. Insofar as the Temple liturgy and the Psalms employed in that liturgy (e.g., Psalms 74; 82; see also Isaiah 51; Job 38) portray this struggle as a daily occurrence in conjunction with the Temple morning service, he maintains that YHWH's ordering of the world is a daily or ongoing event in ancient Israelite/Judean thought and that the various portrayals of YHWH's judgment against the wicked point to continuous efforts by the biblical G-d to maintain the order of creation. Human beings have a role in this struggle, as well, insofar as they are the agents or partners in the divine work of sanctifying creation.

Levenson's 1993 volume, *The Death and Resurrection of the Beloved Son: The Transformation of Child Sacrifice in Judaism and Christianity* points to the differences between Jewish and Christian readings of the Bible in relation to their respective understandings of child sacrifice (see Exod. 22:28–29, which calls on Israel to give their firstborn to YHWH). Whereas Christianity reads the narrative concerning the divine command for Abraham to sacrifice Isaac in Genesis 22, commonly referred to as the *Aqedah* (or "Binding"), as a paradigm for Jesus' vicarious sacrifice on behalf of humanity, Judaism reads the *Aqedah* as a symbol of Israel's "chosenness" and obligation to serve as YHWH's partners in sanctifying creation. Inherent in both readings is the kind of question raised by the Shoah, i.e., Christianity's assertions that, out of tragedy, the "new covenant" has supplanted the old and Judaism's experience of martyrdom at the hands of Gentiles.

Finally, Levenson's 1997 commentary on Esther challenges common Christian readings of the book as an example of Jewish vengeance against enemies by pointing instead to the fundamental issue of the "hiddenness" of G-d and the need for humans to act at a time when the Jewish community is threatened with extermination by a Gentile government. Although the Shoah is not specifically invoked in Levenson's various discussions noted above, the issues raised by the Jewish genocide stand in the background and overshadow his work. That is, the kinds of questions that Levenson raises are the kinds of questions one can hardly ignore in the aftermath of the Shoah.

Michael Fishbane's work in biblical theology emphasizes the exegetical character of Judaism's engagement with the Bible, an interpretive focus that begins within the Bible itself, where some parts of scripture serve to interpret other parts, and continues through teachings that evolve into Rabbinic and Kabbalistic traditions. His 1985 study, *Biblical Interpretation in Ancient Israel*, lays the groundwork for his conceptualization of the role of the Bible in Jewish tradition, by examining the phenomenon of inner-biblical exegesis as a model for later Rabbinic and Kabbalistic forms of biblical interpretation. He thereby takes up an aspect of biblical studies, viz., the late interpretation and expansion of the Bible that has been generally ignored and largely deemed irrelevant in Protestant biblical exegesis, insofar as it does not illuminate the original or pristine biblical tradition. Fishbane argues that both *traditum*, "tradition" or the relatively fixed biblical tradition that now appears in the written biblical text, and *tradition*, "traditioning" or the relatively fluid development of biblical interpretation in its oral and pre-canonical literary stages, as evident, for example, in the writings of the Dead Sea Scrolls from Qumran, the early rabbinical Tanaim, can also be tracked in inner-biblical exegesis.

Fishbane's 1998 study, *The Exegetical Imagination: On Jewish Thought and Theology*, points to the central role of Torah the manifest divine word, as being the center of Jewish theology while Midrash or interpretation serves the role of interpreting this central divine message. He notes that midrashic reading of Torah begins in the Bible itself, as is manifest, for example, in the writings of Jeremiah or Ezra. It also continues through the efforts of the anonymous redactors of the text beyond the confines of the Bible, for example the rabbinical Tanaim of the first century CE and their later successors. In these various levels of interpretation, one discovers how at given times the Torah was understood. The exegetical imagination in Jewish tradition therefore views interpretation as an act of *poesis* that constructs meaning on the basis of the biblical text, thereby linking interpretation into an ongoing chain of tradition analogous to divine creation, which also is viewed as an ongoing biblical event. Insofar as exegesis perpetuates and engages the ancient, even mythological levels of the Bible, it provides a basis for Jews to continue to remain connected to G-d, even in the aftermath of the destruction of the Temples in 587 BCE and again in 70 CE.

In Fishbane's 2003 study, *Biblical Myth and Rabbinic Mythmaking*, he emphasizes the role that human participation in myth and ritual plays in defining humans as agents of and partners with G-d. In creating and sanctifying the world in which they live, human beings act to maintain creation. Humanity achieves this end through active participation in exegesis and liturgy—both of which serve to actualize biblical mythology by bringing tradition into everyday life and thus giving it life. Moreover, through the practice of exegesis and liturgy, humanity may come into a dialogue with G-d, one in which even the problems of evil in the world can be engaged. Once again, while allusion to the Shoah is not explicit in Fishbane's work, it nonetheless may be seen as informing the kinds of issue he desires to address.

Fishbane's students have been especially instrumental in developing the idea of dialogue with G-d as an approach to biblical theology. Benjamin Sommer's 1998 dissertation, *A Prophet Reads Scripture: Allusion in Isaiah 40–66*, examines Second Isaiah's exegetical development of the Torah, the writings of Jeremiah, and other earlier biblical traditions in keeping with the interests of his teacher. His 1999 essay, "Revelation at Sinai in the Hebrew Bible and Jewish Theology," focuses on the role of Exodus 19, the narrative concerning revelation of Torah at Sinai, in defining the encounter between YHWH and Israel at Sinai. He further considers the role that texts such as Deuteronomy 4–5 and Exodus 24 play in elucidating that encounter. Such inner-biblical interpretation points to the role that midrashic exegesis plays in ensuring that a text like Exodus 19 is not simply an account of a historical event but is better seen as an ongoing expression of G-d's address to Israel in every generation as well as Israel's ongoing dialogue with G-d.

Marc Brettler's 1997 paper, "Biblical History and Biblical Theology," warns against analyzing biblical texts only as history or attempting to harmonize them into a single historio-critical system, thereby reducing their ability to serve as a means to address modern concerns. His paper on the Psalms, delivered at the 2003 national conference of the Society of Biblical Literature, likewise warns against harmonization and points to the means by which Psalms can provide the basis for ongoing liturgical dialogue between Israel and G-d. Tamar Kamionkowski, a student of Brettler, takes a similar approach. She argues in her 2003 SBL conference paper for a dialogical model for Jewish biblical theology that balances ancient history with modern theology She notes that interpreters must first learn to listen to the historical dimensions of biblical texts; then, working from this baseline, they can subsequently develop a means for addressing the concerns of the contemporary Jewish community. Such dialogue, as conceived by Fishbane and his students, provides a solid basis for trying to understand the nature of G-d in light of the questions raised by the Shoah. Indeed, such a model is already inherent in the book of Job, when Job demands a divine explanation for his suffering, and also in the early rabbinic story known as *Heikhalot Rabbati*, in which R. Ishmael ascends through the seven levels of heaven to ask G-d why the Temple was destroyed and why the Rabbis were martyred in the Bar Kochba Revolt against Rome in the Second Century CE. Again, these are not simply ancient questions of concern to the historian alone; rather, they have a modern relevance to Jews (and Christians alike) that is sharpened in the agenda of these scholars because these are the issues at the forefront of modern history in the aftermath of the Shoah.

My own work in Jewish biblical theology emphasizes the distinctively

Jewish character of the Hebrew Bible, a "Jewishness" closely tied to the biblical concepts of the sanctification of creation and the problem of evil in Israel's experience. My 1997 paper, "Tanakh versus the Old Testament: Concerning the Foundation for a Jewish Theology of the Bible," examines the distinctive literary structures of the Jewish *Tanakh* versus the Christian Old Testament as a basis for discerning the distinctive theological understandings of each tradition. The four part order of the Christian Old Testament emphasizes a theological progression from Israel's earliest history in the Pentateuch (the first five biblical books), through its later history in the Historical Books, through its address of non-historical questions in the Poetic and Wisdom Books, and finally through its concern with the messianic future in the Prophetic Books. In Christian interpretation, the Prophetic Books specifically point to the New Testament, which displays a similar four-part structure.[6] The three-part Jewish *Tanakh*—*Torah*, *Nevi'im* (prophets), *Ketuvim* (writings), by contrast, emphasizes a structure in which the ideal establishment of Israel is envisioned as taking a central place as the succession and culmination of creation in the Torah; that ideal is then disrupted by exile and destruction as related in the Prophets, while the Writings present both the most strident questionings of G-d's intentions (e.g., in Job, Ecclesiastes and Lamentations) as well as the projections of the restoration of that ideal (especially in the Psalms).

My 1998 paper, "Reconceiving the Paradigms of Old Testament Theology in the Post-Shoah Period," points to the need to employ historical criticism to establish the Jewish character of the Bible, as well as the need to examine—in both ancient and modern terms—the Bible's attempts to grapple with the problem of evil in the world. The prophet Amos serves as an example of the former: his message makes a prominent point of stressing his Judean identity, and this in turn drives his message of social justice concerning Israel's subjugation of his native Judah. The book of Esther serves as the example of the latter, in which the human protagonists must face and overcome a genocidal threat to the future of the Jewish people posed by an irresponsible Gentile government. This has obvious implications for addressing theodistic issues inherent in the Shoah.

My 2000 paper, "Isaiah and the Question of Theodicy," raises issues concerning YHWH's decree in Isaiah 6 that this prophet must deliver a message so offensive to the eyes and ears of his contemporaries as to ensure the people's blindness and deafness to its import. The aim of this "anti-message" is to facilitate YHWH's punishment of the people—a destruction that casts a long historical shadow on the Shoah. Also of note in this regard is Isaiah's failure

Post-Shoah Theology

to challenge YHWH's devastating and seemingly unjustifiable decree. Again, the implications for the Shoah are manifest: Can a modern Jewish community silently bend to a divine will that through the Shoah countenances the destruction of a significant portion of that same community?

My 2005 volume, *The Prophetic Literature*, which emphasizes the individual social roles of the prophets as the bases from which they develop their respective understandings of Israelite and Judean identity, explores the ways in which the prophets wrestle with G-d and tradition in addressing the problems of evil associated with exile and destruction in their own days. A forthcoming commentary on First and Second Kings, to be published in the Old Testament Library, argues that these biblical books read the history of Israel and Judah with a concern to address the question of theodicy in light of the Babylonian exile as well as earlier crises in Israelite and Judean history. Particular concerns include the condemnation of the northern Israelite kings beginning with Jeroboam ben Nebat and the charge that Manasseh's sins brought about the Babylonian Exile. It is important to note that biblical issues of this nature come to prominence in a manner that would not have been the case before the Shoah or even in its immediate aftermath. But as the historical perspective on the Shoah lengthens, so too do its issues take on dimensions that a modern generation of American Jewish biblical scholars feel the necessity to engage. We might note in passing that the discussion of the Shoah in relation to Jewish biblical theology has also had its impact on the general field of Christian Old Testament theology, as indicated by the work of Walter Brueggemann and Rolf Rentdorff, among others. But this aspect of the impact of the Shoah on the Bible is beyond the purview of this study.

PART IV

I now want to turn to two specific examples that can serve to illustrate how the Shoah can exert a powerful influence on biblical interpretation. The narrative in Exodus 32–34 concerning Israel's worship of the Golden Calf in the wilderness is commonly understood to be an ancient account from the JE pentateuchal tradition, that is, the so-called YHwistic and Elohistic editorial strands that are two of the major narrative building blocks of the Torah. This account ostensibly focuses on Israel's apostasy following the revelation at Sinai, but a closer examination of the function of the Golden Calf episode reveals a hidden agenda in relation to northern Israelite religious practice, namely to address the question of divine righteousness and power following the destruction of the majority of the Hebrew people. This is the story of the losing of the "ten lost tribes." It is their loss—which is nothing less than a genocide in an ancient context, perpetrated by Assyria, an implacable and heinous enemy no less evil than the Nazis—that is nonetheless sanctioned by divine decree. How the biblical writers, in their casting of the story of the Golden Calf, grappled with this disaster in ancient times has major implications for dealing with the Shoah today.

A second example concerns the portrayal of the destruction of Jerusalem in Ezekiel 8–11. Whereas conventional interpretation considers this narrative to be an account of YHWH's righteous judgment against sinful Jerusalem, a closer analysis of the moral problems of this text and the liturgical background of the elements of Ezekiel's vision points to another hidden agenda, namely, the attempt to justify the destruction of Jerusalem as an act of divine purification based on the priestly scapegoat sacrifice of Yom Kippur. Again, this biblical attempt to explain what would seem a divinely sanctioned but otherwise morally inexplicable event, has strong reverberations for modern Jewish theology. We will consider these narratives in succession.

The Golden Calf narrative in Exodus 32–34 is a key episode that well displays the tensions in the relationship between YHWH and Israel in the wilderness.[7] In keeping with the predominant literary-critical concern in pentateuchal studies (i.e., studies of the first five books of the Hebrew Bible, the Torah) throughout the Twentieth Century, modern scholars have tended to focus on identifying the underlying sources of the narrative in an effort to reconstruct its origins. In general, scholars consider this episode to be a combination of the J and E traditions of the Pentateuch, with some D (i.e., Deuteronomistic) material added at a later time (see, e.g., Campbell and O'Brien 146–49, 189–90, 199). Still, beyond this endeavor to reconstruct how the biblical text has come together in its canonical form, there has been little effort to grapple with the imagery of Israel's apostasy in the wilderness or with the destruction of a significant portion of the people as a consequence of that apostasy. For the most part, scholars have simply assumed that the narrative recounts a historical or quasi-historical incident from the wilderness period early in Israel's early narrative account.

Let us begin by replaying the story, itself. The narrative presupposes Moses' forty-day audience with YHWH on Mt. Sinai, in which YHWH instructs him concerning the building of the Tabernacle for holy service (Exod. 24:15–18; 25–31). It takes up the theme of the wilderness rebellion tradition by relating Israel's concern that Moses had led them into the wilderness only to abandon them. The people therefore call upon Aaron to make a G-d that will lead them out of the wilderness. Aaron, the brother of Moses, responds by fashioning the Golden Calf, which the people then worship as their own G-d. While they are still at Sinai, YHWH points out this apostasy to Moses and proposes to destroy the people and to make Moses and his direct descendents into a new nation. Moses counters YHWH by pointing out that YHWH has made a vow with the ancestors of Israel to make them into a great nation. Upon returning from Mt. Sinai with the tablets of the covenant in hand, Moses observes the people's apostasy, smashes the tablets to symbolize the broken relationship with YHWH, destroys the Golden Calf, and calls upon those who are for YHWH to come to him in order to destroy those who have sinned. The Levites respond to Moses instruction and then proceed to kill some three thousand of the people. On the next day, YHWH refuses to go in the midst of the people lest, due to his still intense anger, he destroy them. Moses therefore pitches the Tent of Meeting outside of the Israelite camp to symbolize YHWH's estrangement from the people while speaking with YHWH to determine how to proceed. Moses finally persuades YHWH to continue to lead the people; then he views YHWH's presence from the cleft of the rock on Sinai, and inscribes two new tablets with the terms of the covenant between YHWH and Israel. The account of the people's compliance with YHWH's instructions to build the Tabernacle then follows in Exodus 35–40.

A number of keys issues emerge from close analysis of this narrative. First, the narrative appears following the initial account of the revelation of Torah at Sinai in Exodus 19–24, and it includes a revised version of the laws stated in Exod. 23:10–19. The appearance of the revised laws in Exod. 34:10–26 suggests that some sort of reconceptualization of the initial laws constitutes a key concern in this narrative. In addition, the narrative appears between the account of YHWH's instructions to build the Tabernacle in Exodus 25–31 and the account of the people's compliance with YHWH's instructions in Exodus 35–40. Recent scholarship identifies the Tabernacle not simply as the holy place for the worship of YHWH in the wilderness but also as the predecessor and paradigm for the Jerusalem Temple (e.g., Levenson, *Sinai and Zion* 187–217). Insofar as YHWH's presence descends upon the Tabernacle at the end of Exodus 40, the construction of the Tabernacle becomes in part the means through which YHWH agrees to remain present in the midst of the people. The destruction of those who committed apostasy in the Golden Calf narrative is therefore crucial to the overall account of the building of the Tabernacle, viz., the people had to be purified from moral and cultic impurity before the Tabernacle could be built, thus allowing for the presence of YHWH yet again among the people.

Second, the narrative has a number of intertextual affinities with other narratives in the Pentateuch and Former Prophets (Joshua through Kings) that are particularly concerned with questions of Israel's covenantal relationship with YHWH and the portrayal of the northern kingdom of Israel as apostate against YHWH (for detailed discussion, see Sweeney, "The Wilderness Traditions" 291-99.). The most obvious parallel is the account of King Jeroboam ben Nebat's construction of the Golden Calves for the northern Israelite sanctuaries at Beth El and Dan in the aftermath of the ten northern tribes' revolt against and secession from the dynasty of David, as narrated in 1 Kings 12:25-33 (see also 1 Kings 13). In addition to the image of the Golden Calf/Calves, narrative parallels include Jeroboam's statement to the people, "Behold your G-d/G-ds, O Israel, who brought you up from the land of Egypt," in 1 Kings 12:28, which echoes Aaron's statement to Israel in Exod. 32:4, and the identification of Jeroboam's sons, Abijah and Nadab, who respectively died of disease and revolt (see 1 Kings 14:1-18; 1 Kings 14:20; 15:25-34), and Aaron's sons, Nadab and Abihu, who died for improperly offering incense before YHWH (Lev. 10:1-11). A second parallel is Elijah's experience of the presence of YHWH in a cave at Mount Horeb, the alternative name of Sinai in the Pentateuch, following his forty day flight into the wilderness at a time when the northern Israelite King Ahab and his Sidonian (and thus pagan) wife Jezebel sought to destroy all the prophets of YHWH (1 Kings 19). Whereas Moses saw YHWH's back, this narrative notes that Elijah experiences YHWH, not in fire, wind, or earthquake, but in the inner voice of YHWH speaking to him.

The third issue of particular note is the above-mentioned parallel between the renewed law code of Exod. 34:10-26 and the prior code in Exod. 23:10-19, together with the injunction against intermarrying with the Canaanite nations who would lead Israel into idolatry in Deut. 7:1-6. Indeed, the renewed covenant law code in Exod. 34:10-26 differs from Exod. 23:10-19 by emphasizing at the outset a prohibition formulated with language drawn from Deut. 7:1-6. Finally, Moses' destruction of the Golden Calf by burning it, grinding it into dust, strewing the dust on the water, and making the people drink the water in Exod. 32:20 echoes King Josiah's destruction of the idolatrous items dedicated to the Canaanite deities Baal and Asherah, which were ground to dust by the Wadi Kidron in 2 Kings 23:4-7, and the destruction of the Beth El shrine, which was also burned and ground to dust in 2 Kings 23:15. Overall, the interrelationship between Exodus 32-34 and these various texts indicates that the

Exodus 32–34 is compositionally closely related to and probably dependent upon these other narratives, insofar as it brings all of their motifs and concerns together into one narrative. It also demonstrates that Exodus 32–34 portrays Israel's sins with the Golden Calf in the wilderness in relation to the portrayal of the sins of northern Israel.

Modern biblical scholars largely interpret the Former Prophets as edited according to the particular perspective of Deuteronomy, an editorial effort primarily initiated during the time of the Judean king Josiah. Hence, it is often characterized as the Deuteronomistic Redaction or History. Insofar as the Josianic edition of the Deuteronomistic History employed this motif as a means to interpret theologically the fall of northern Israel as an act of divine punishment by YHWH,[8] it indicates a similar interest in portraying both the disruption and renewal of covenant in Exodus 32–34. In this respect, Exodus 32–34 implicitly points to apostate Israel rather than YHWH as the *true* party responsible for disaster.

Fourth is the role of the Levites in killing off the apostates in Israel and thereby in purifying the people from moral and cultic impurity. As the priestly tribe of Israel, the Levites are tasked with teaching YHWH's expectations concerning what is clean or required of the people to ensure their sanctity and what is impure or forbidden to the people (Lev. 10:10–11). Furthermore, the Levites are responsible for carrying out the ritual action necessary to maintain the relationship between YHWH and the people. When considered from a historical standpoint, this role is particularly important insofar as tradition maintains that the first born sons originally acted as priests before the Levites were designated for this role (see Numbers 3–4; 8, esp. 3:11–13; 3:40–43; 8:13–19; also note 1 Samuel 1–3, in which Samuel, first-born son of Hannah and her Ephraimite husband Elkanah, is raised to serve as a priest in the Shiloh sanctuary). It is also important historically since 1 Kings 12:31 charges that Jeroboam authorized non-Levites to serve as priests in the north; perhaps this suggests that the Levites represent a later development in Israelite or Judean religiosity. When considered from a synchronic literary standpoint, however, this narrative points to the Levites as those who would ultimately emerge as the caretakers of Israel's sanctity in the Pentateuchal narrative. Not only do they purify the people from impurity by eliminating the apostates in the Golden Calf episode, but they also emerge as the caretakers of the Tabernacle or wilderness sanctuary that will be built in Exodus 25–31 and that prefigures the Temple once the people settle into the promised land. Indeed, Num. 3:10 makes it very clear that the sons of Aaron are responsible for observing priestly duties; and outsiders, who might attempt to carry out these functions, should be put to death (see also Numbers 18).

Finally, although the people are clearly portrayed as the guilty party in this narrative, YHWH's own moral culpability also comes into question. When YHWH proposes to destroy the entire people for their apostasy in Exod. 32:9–14, Moses feels compelled to challenge YHWH and remind him of the oath he swore to the ancestors of Israel, Abraham, Isaac, and Israel (a.k.a., Jacob), that their G-d would make them into a people as numerous as the stars of the heaven and grant them the land of Israel in which to live. Although YHWH should be bound by oath to the ancestors of Israel, he is nonetheless prepared to transgress this sworn promise. Thus, Moses has to step in and stop YHWH from engaging in what would have been an immoral act. Even so, YHWH's own capacity for violence is not completely checked in this passage. The Levites are allowed to kill three thousand Israelites apostate worshippers of the Golden Calf and YHWH further unleashes a plague against Israel that selectively kills off those who are guilty of this apostasy. In sum: YHWH is vindicated in the narrative, but not without a challenge to his moral character. Ultimately, Moses' vision of YHWH's presence in Exod. 34:6–7 reaffirms the deity's mercy and capacity to provide blessing, but also emphasizes divine justice and the capacity to mete out punishment, even to the descendants of the guilty.

Based on a consideration of all these issues, it seems probable that the Golden Calf narrative in Exodus 32–34 is written as a defense of YHWH's power and righteousness in relation to the destruction of the northern kingdom of Israel in the eighth century BCE. At the outset, Exodus 32–34 is designed to articulate the need for moral and cultic purity on the part of the people of Israel when appearing before YHWH in the holy sanctuary. It further points to the role that the Levitical priests will assume in educating the people concerning their responsibilities to YHWH and in mediating the relationship between YHWH and Israel through ritual action and purification in the sanctuary. Altogether, it presumes and affirms YHWH's righteousness in the Golden Calf episode, insofar as it depicts just punishment of a people engage in apostasy. But there is also more than divine justice depicted in this narrative, since in very stark terms it further acknowledges YHWH's dangerous character. Indeed, this narrative raises questions concerning divine culpability as well, especially since it depends upon the historical experience of the destruction of northern Israel to make its case. The northern kingdom of Israel was destroyed in the late-eighth century BCE by the Assyrian empire, which sought to expand its military and economic power into western Asia. Northern Israel was an obstacle to those plans and quite possibly had broken an alliance with Assyria that originated in the early years of the Jehu dynasty that ruled Israel from 842 BCE. The Assyrians were well known to have a "take no prisoners" attitude towards those who were their enemies (see, e.g., the book of Nahum). Rather than focus on the political, economic, and military causes of northern Israel's downfall, the Former Prophets portrays Israel's destruction as the result of apostasy against YHWH from the time of King Jeroboam ben Nebat, who began his reign ca. 922 BCE (see esp. 1 Kings 12–13; 2 Kings 17). In putting forward such a portrayal, the editors of the Former Prophets try to resolve a classic problem of theodicy, by absolving YHWH of any responsibility for the disaster, and placing the blame on Israel itself for its own demise. Insofar as Exodus 32–34 draws upon this paradigm for portraying Israel as responsible for its own misfortune in the wilderness, it too must be recognized as a parallel effort to resolve the problem of theodicy by justifying the righteousness of YHWH as the perpetrator of violence against the Israelites, who deserves punishment due to the apostasy of the Golden Calf. The roles of the Tabernacle or Temple and the Levitical priesthood, then, serve respectively as symbol and agents of this biblical effort to justify the ways of G-d to man. In this manner, the Exodus 32–34 narrative—like the Former Prophets—engages in such self-condemnation and self-critique as a means to negotiate the realities of historical experience, viz., if Israel suffers, Israel and not YHWH must be held responsible, and the means to remedy that suffering is by renewed and stronger efforts of the part of the people—as mediated by the Tabernacle or Temple and the priesthood—to fulfill YHWH's expectations. In such a manner, YHWH agrees to remain present among the people and to formulate the covenant between them once again.

So in the final analysis everything would appear to balance out from a moral standpoint. G-d is successfully defended against the potential charge of unrighteous action and any potential problems of theodicy are apparently resolved. And yet . . . what is also manifest in the Golden Calf episode and the destruction of the northern kingdom of Israel that it prefigures, is an overwhelming sense of pain and even an implicit rebuke of YHWH. The fact that the genocidal actions of Assyria that cause the ten lost tribes of Israel to be lost forever must somehow be read back into the Torah indicates that this is a horrific event that just will not go away. The indication that YHWH, without being checked by Moses, would not have stopped with the deaths he initiated and perpetrated, but would have destroyed *all* the people, shows that his morally justifiable actions could—and in the case of the northern kingdom of Israel *did*—go further than what, from a human standpoint, would seem acceptable. Lurking beneath the biblical need, the moral necessity of defending YHWH, there still remains the question of the magnitude of destruction, the question of how far is too far? Of course, these questions have always been inherent in the story and the pain that motivates them has always been there to read and interpret. But our modern sensitivity to the issues raised by YHWH's actions in this episode and the deeply felt recognition of the burden of memory that these events still convey all these millennia later—there can be no question that the Shoah has made them all the more apparent to us than they ever have been before in this modern era. We reconsider these difficult, ancient questions, and relive these ancient stories because these ancient pains and ancient memories connect with our own. Indeed, they simply cannot be ignored. If we are to build a Jewish theology based somehow on biblical authority, an authority that keeps G-d in the presence of his people, then we cannot ignore the unanswered questions implicit in the Golden Calf episode nor can we simply exonerate YHWH without further coming to grips with the inherent danger of divine, unchecked power—so well documented in both ancient and modern times.

PART V

The narrative portrayal in Ezekiel 8–11 is typically treated as essentially an account by the prophet and/or his editor(s) of Ezekiel's visionary experience concerning the Babylonian destruction of Jerusalem in 587 BCE. Like the Golden Calf episode in Exodus 32–34, modern scholarship has tended to focus more on identifying the origins and authorship of the narrative rather than on examining critically the portrayal of the divine role in the destruction of an entire city and its inhabitants, including women, old people, young people, and children (see, e.g., Zimmerli 215–64). Critical examination of the synchronic literary form of the text and its contents, however, indicates the significance of the theological issues concerning the destruction of Jerusalem with which this text grapples. Ezekiel 8–11 does not simply report Ezekiel's vision. Rather, it is an interpretative depiction that emphasizes Ezekiel's identity as a Zadokite priest from the Jerusalem Temple and his concomitant need to defend YHWH's righteousness in the face of evil by contending that Jerusalem had become corrupted by the actions of its own people.

The question of the purity of the land, Temple, and people underlies the portrayal of Jerusalem's destruction in Ezekiel 8–11. These chapters introduce the long segment in Ezekiel 8–19, dated to the sixth year of Jehoiachin's exile (591 BCE), which portrays the destruction of the city and its significance. Ezekiel's portrayal of this event is central to his understanding and justification of YHWH's actions. The prophet takes the view that the Jerusalem Temple and, by extension, all creation have been corrupted by idolatry and human impurity and must be purged to allow for the reestablishment of a new Temple at the center of a renewed Israel and a renewed creation. In essence, Ezekiel 8–11 portrays the destruction of Jerusalem as a cultic action, initiated by YHWH, that is analogous to the scapegoat ritual performed by the high priest at Yom Kippur to symbolize the purging and purification of the people and land of Israel.[9] Still, one may reasonably question the validity of this analogy, since such a portrayal blames the victims for their own victimization, when, from a strictly historical perspective Jerusalem was destroyed to serve Babylonian imperial interests rather than to address any colloquial religious concerns of Judah.

Again, we can start by replaying the narrative: It begins in Ezekiel 8, as noted, in the sixth year of Jehoiachin's exile with a portrayal of Ezekiel's visionary journey to the Jerusalem Temple, led by an angelic guide. The prophet recounts that he was taken by the hair of his head from his home in Babylonia, where he was sitting with the elders of Judah and conveyed to the entrance of the Penimith Gate on the north side of the courtyard of the Jerusalem Temple. Led by his angelic guide, Ezekiel saw "the infuriating image" north of the gate of the altar. Although the text does not specify what this image might be, it is most likely a Babylonian victory stele, erected in the Temple courtyard, where it would be visible to all following the Babylonian subjugation of Jerusalem in 597 BCE. Such a stele would likely include images of Marduk and/or other Babylonian G-ds and proclaim their and the Babylonian king Nebuchadnezzar's victory over YHWH and Judah.[10]

Ezekiel was commanded to dig through the courtyard wall so that he could see the abominations practiced in the Jerusalem Temple. Such an act likely represents the siege tactics of Babylonian sappers who would dig through or under walls in order to undermine them and enable Babylonian assault troops to enter the walled city. Because the northern walls of Jerusalem were the only ones built on relatively level ground, most conquerors in antiquity attacked Jerusalem at this most vulnerable point. Upon entering the Temple, Ezekiel witnessed the detestable forms of creeping things and beasts and all the fetishes of the house of Israel on the walls of the Temple. The interior walls of the Temple were decorated with pomegranates, palm trees, lions, cherubim, etc., to represent the imagery of the Garden of Eden, but from Ezekiel's visionary perspective, such images would have represented Israel's idolatry and corruption of the House of YHWH. His vision of the seventy men led by Jaazniah ben Shaphan with their incense censers who state that "YHWH does not see" and that "YHWH has abandoned the land" (8:12) is indicative of Ezekiel's perspective as a Zadokite priest. Jaazniah ben Shaphan was a member of the rival ben Shaphan family that provided support to Jeremiah throughout this period (see Wilcoxen 151–66). Because Ezekiel was a Zadokite priest who was exiled from the Temple, it is likely that he viewed a Temple controlled by elements of a secondary priestly line as having been corrupted.

Ezekiel's vision of the women weeping for Tammuz (8:14) presupposes the worship of a key Babylonian fertility G-d who was raised from the underworld by Ishtar in the late summer to symbolize the onset of the rains at New Year's and Sukkot in the fall (Alster 828–34). Although Ezekiel identifies their actions as associated with specific worship of Tammuz, it is more likely that they were engaged in generalized mourning rituals typical of Israel and Judah in the late summer that likewise anticipated the onset of the fall rains. Ezekiel's vision of the twenty-five men with their backs to the Temple (8:16) worshipping the sun likewise illustrates his perspective, since the men would have been engaged in the typical morning service of Temple worship that would have been directed to the east at sunrise. In Ezekiel's perspective of a corrupt and idolatrous Temple, a legitimate act of Judean worship of YHWH thus becomes an idolatrous act of apostasy.

The visionary portrayal of Jerusalem's destruction begins in Ezek. 9:1–2 with the angelic guide's call for the approach of six men armed with weapons of destruction. Again, they are portrayed as approaching from the north, the direction from which ancient Jerusalem was most vulnerable to attack. Among them was a man dressed in white linen, the typical garments of a priest officiating at the Temple altar (Exod. 28:39; Lev. 6:10), with a writing case at his side to record the sacrifices. As the men approached, the presence of the throne chariot of YHWH with its four cherubim became evident as the action proceeded (Ezek. 9:3). The six men were commanded to mark the foreheads of all the men who "moan and groan because of all the abominations committed within it" (9:4), i.e., within the city of Jerusalem. Although many interpreters have struggled to discern a moral criterion in the selection of those marked for survival, the description of those to be killed in the city, viz., the "graybeard, youth and maiden, women and children" (9:6), indicates that the *men* of the city were to be spared while the old, the young, the women, and the children were all to be killed, regardless of their respective moral status (see Greenberg176-77; Zimmerli 248; Darr 1179; Odell 115-16).

With the execution of those unmarked completed in Ezekiel 10, the throne chariot of YHWH moved from the cherubim to the platform of the House of YHWH. There, YHWH commanded the man dressed in white linen to take glowing coals from among the cherubim so that he might ignite the doomed city in an act that resembles the kindling of the sacrificial altar at the Temple. Once the man in white linen had fulfilled the command, the cherubim and the throne chariot rose above the city as the Presence of YHWH prepared to depart. Because the imagery of the throne chariot is based on that of the Ark of the Covenant, which symbolizes the throne and presence of YHWH in the Jerusalem Temple, YHWH's departure signifies the final profanation of the site and perhaps even the Babylonians' removal of the Ark from the Temple in 597 BCE.

As the throne chariot departed from Jerusalem in Ezekiel 11, YHWH tells the prophet that those marked would not be killed in the city as if they were a sacrifice cooked in a pot. Rather, they were to be taken to the borders of Israel where some would be killed, apparently representing the Babylonian execution of key Judean figures at Riblah in the aftermath of the city's destruction (see 2 Kings 25:6-7, 18-21). The remnant of those not killed at the border were to be taken into Babylonian exile where they would eventually be gathered, purified with a new heart so that they could observe YHWH's Torah, and return to the land of Israel to restore and purify it from its abominations. With the vision thus completed, the throne chariot departed from Jerusalem and Ezekiel returned to his home in Babylonia to tell the exiles what he had seen.

Ezekiel's vision of the destruction of Jerusalem is quite remarkable because of its portrayal of Jerusalem's cultic impurity—even though many of the images so depicted are actually based in fact on normal Judean practice—and because of its use of sacrificial imagery to portray death and destruction in the city. The vision clearly represents Ezekiel's priestly viewpoint, viz., the city must be purged because of its impurity. Such purges are well-known throughout Judean history. Such cultic purges or purifications were carried out by King Hezekiah in 2 Kings 18:1-8 and 2 Chronicles 29-31; King Josiah in 2 Kings 23:1-25; and Judah the Maccabee in 1 Macc. 4:36-51. Each involves the sacrifice of a *ḥaṭṭā't* or "sin offering" (see Leviticus 4-5), which includes seven bulls, seven rams, seven lambs, and seven goats that symbolize the purging of the Temple from its corruption or impurity.

Although the analogy of the *ḥaṭṭā't* aids us in understanding Ezekiel's perspective, it does not fully explain the vision, particularly since the men who moan and groan over the abominations in the city are spared while all others are killed. As noted above, there is no moral distinction made between the men who survive versus the old, the young, the women, and the children who were killed. They are all treated collectively rather than on the basis of their individual moral standings. Because those who survive form the basis of the remnant that will ultimately restore the land of Israel, interpreters must look to the scapegoat offering of Leviticus 16 to understand the significance of Ezekiel's vision. The scapegoat offering calls for the presentation of two goats as *ḥaṭṭā ʾt* offerings at Yom Kippur to symbolize the purification of the nation. One goat is sacrificed as the *ḥaṭṭā ʾt* offering, but the other goat is released into the wilderness after the sins of the nation are symbolically transferred onto it by the high priest. Such a model, in which one goat is randomly sacrificed whereas another goat is randomly released to represent the restoration of the nation, underlies Ezekiel's understanding of Jerusalem's destruction and the fate of its people. Such an act is necessary in Ezekiel's view to purge Jerusalem of its impurity and to prepare for the reestablishment of a new Temple following the completion of the exile and purification of the land of Israel as depicted in Ezekiel 40–48. In this manner, Ezekiel interprets the destruction of Jerusalem and the Temple as YHWH's act of purging and purification of the corrupted city and Temple.

As is the case with the Golden Calf episode previously discussed, the underlying moral issues inherent in this prophetic vision have always been there to read and interpret. In particular, the actions of YHWH—especially his apparent indifference in regard to whom survives and who is put to death—has always been an integral part of the text as it unfolds in Ezekiel. What is striking is that, for the most part, modern biblical scholarship has never focused very much on these matters, at least in the first half of the twentieth century and earlier. Today, however, when these ancient, disastrous events are viewed in relation to the modern experience of the Shoah, they rise to a level prominence that simply will not and cannot be ignored. One senses a degree of desperation in Ezekiel's attempt to justify the ways of his deity to his community, through these events in a "priestly" interpretation that narrowly focusing on issues of purity and legitimization of cultic practice. This account becomes a classic example of an attempt to justify destruction by blaming the victims for their own victimization—an attempt that has, as we have noted, its mirror-image in some modern efforts to theologically justify the Shoah. Ezekiel is faced with a dilemma that we still face today: How to account for unjustifiable actions by an all-powerful G-d and still maintain a place for hope and community in relationship to this same G-d—theodicy ancient and modern.

PART VI

Some final thoughts: The above examples demonstrate the importance—even better, the *necessity*—of considering the modern experience of the Shoah, with its theological questions of divine power, engagement, and righteousness, when we turn to the interpretation of biblical texts. Certainly one point that the Shoah has made all too clear to the modern Jewish community is this: Any attempt to justify G-d by blaming the victims for their own suffering misses an important point concerning human and divine responsibility for the world in which we live. Moreover, in considering the significance of such a perspective, it is important to keep in mind that the questions raised about G-d in relation to the Shoah do *not* call upon us to abandon G-d—as so many have charged that G-d abandoned Jews and humanity at large as evidenced by the Shoah. Rather we should ask ourselves to what extent we need to act as partners with G-d in seeing to the order and welfare of creation to see to that such evil does not occur in human history ever again.

Notes

1. For discussion of critical reflection on the Shoah, see esp. Braiterman; Katz; and Morgan.
2. For assessments of Jewish biblical theology and Jewish biblical interpretation in America, see Perdue, *Reconstructing* 183–239; Sweeney, "Emerging Field"; and Sperling.
3. For discussion of the impact of the Shoah on Christian theology, see Williamson.
4. For discussion of the general field of biblical theology, see Hasel; and Perdue, *Collapse of History*.
5. See above. See my assessment of Levenson's work, "Why Jews are Interested in Biblical Theology."
6. The Gospels, Acts of the Apostles, Epistles, and the Book of Revelation.
7. For discussion of Exodus 32–34, see Sarna 202–22; Childs 553–624; Coats 184–91; Cassuto 407–51; and Sweeney, "The Wilderness Traditions of the Pentateuch" 291–99.
8. For discussion of the Josianic edition of the Deuteronomistic History, see Sweeney, *King Josiah of Judah* 21–177.
9. For detailed discussion of the following, see Sweeney, "The Destruction of Jerusalem" 144–55.
10. See the Egyptian examples of steles from Pharaoh Seti I at Beth Shean (*ANEP* 320–21) and Merneptah at Thebes (*ANEP* 342) as well as the Assyrian examples of Shalmaneser III (*ANEP* 351–55).

Works Cited

Alster, B. "Tammuz." *Dictionary of Deities and Demons in the Bible*. 2nd ed. Ed. Karel van der Toorn, Bob Becking, and Pieter W. van der Horst. Leiden: Brill, 1999. 828–34.

Baeck, Leo. *This People Israel: The Meaning of Jewish Existence*. New York: Holt, Rinehart, and Winston, 1965.

Berkovits, Eliezer. *Faith after the Holocaust*. New York: KTAV, 1973.

Blumenthal, David. *Facing the Abusing G-d: A Theology of Protest*. Louisville: Westminster John Knox, 1993.

Braiterman, Zachary. *G-d After Auschwitz: Tradition and Change in Post Holocaust Jewish Thought*. Princeton: Princeton UP, 1998.

Brettler, Marc. "Biblical History and Jewish Biblical Theology." *JR* 77 (1997): 563–83.

———. "Psalms and Jewish Biblical Theology." Theology of the Hebrew Scriptures Section. AAR/SBL Annual Meeting, Atlanta, GA. 23 Nov. 2003.

Brueggemann, Walter. *Theology of the Old Testament: Testimony, Dispute, Advocacy*. Minneapolis: Fortress, 1997.

Buber, Martin. *The Eclipse of G-d: Studies in the Relation between Religion and Philosophy*. New York and Evanston: Harper and Row, 1952.

Campbell, Antony F., and Mark A. O'Brien. *Sources of the Pentateuch: Texts, Introductions, Annotations*. Minneapolis: Fortress, 1993.

Cassuto, Umberto. *A Commentary on the Book of Exodus*. Jerusalem: Magnes, 1967.

Childs, Brevard S. *The Book of Exodus*. OTL. Philadelphia: Westminster, 1974.

Coats, George W. *Rebellion in the Wilderness: The Murmuring Motif in the Wilderness Traditions of the Old Testment*. Nashville: Abingdon, 1968.

Cohen, Arthur A. *The Tremendum: A Theological Interpretation of the Holocaust*. New York: Crossroad, 1988.

Eichrodt, Walther. *Theology of the Old Testament*. 2 vols. OTL. Philadelphia: Westminster, 1961–67.

Fackenheim, Emil. *G-d's Presence in History: Jewish Affirmations and Philosophical Reflections*. New York: Harper Torchbacks, 1972.

———. *The Jewish Bible after the Holocaust: A Rereading*. Bloomington and Indianapolis: Indiana UP, 1990.

———. *To Mend the World: Foundations of Post-Holocaust Jewish Thought*. New York: Schocken: 1989.

Fishbane, Michael. *Biblical Interpretation in Ancient Israel*. Oxford: Oxford UP, 1985.

———. *Biblical Myth and Rabbinic Mythmaking*. Oxford: Oxford UP, 2003.

———. *The Exegetical Imagination: On Jewish Thought and Theology*. Cambridge: Harvard UP, 1998.

Garber, Zev. *Shoah: The Paradigmatic Genocide: Essays in Exegesis and Eisegesis*. Studies in the Shoah 8. Lanham: UP of America, 1994.

Greenberg, Moshe. *Ezekiel 1-20*. AB 22. Garden City: Doubleday, 1983.

Hasel, Gerhard. *Old Testament Theology: Basic Issues in the Current Debate.* Grand Rapids: Eerdmans, 1991.

Heschel, Abraham J. *The Prophets.* New York: Harper Torchbacks, 1969.

———. *The Sabbath: Its Meaning for Modern Man.* New York: Farrar, Straus, and Young, 1951.

Kamionkowski, S. Tamar. "A Dialogic Model for Jewish Biblical Theology." Theology of the Hebrew Scriptures Section. AAR/SBL Annual Meeting, Atlanta, GA. 23 Nov. 2003.

Katz, Steven T. *Post-Holocaust Dialogues: Critical Studies in Modern Jewish Thought.* New York: New York U, 1985.

Levenson, Jon D. *Creation and the Persistence of Evil: The Jewish Drama of Divine Omnipotence.* New York: Harper and Row, 1988.

———. *The Death and Resurrection of the Beloved Son: The Transformation of Child Sacrifice in Judaism and Christianity.* New Haven: Yale UP, 1993.

———. *Esther: A Commentary.* OTL. Louisville: Westminster John Knox, 1997.

———. *Sinai and Zion: An Entry Into the Jewish Bible.* Minneapolis: Winston, 1985.

———. *Theology of the Program of Restoration in Ezekiel 40-48.* HSM 10. Missoula: Scholars, 1976.

———. "Why Jews are Not Interested in Biblical Theology." *The Hebrew Bible, the Old Testament, and Historical Criticism: Jews and Christians in Biblical Studies.* Louisville: Westminster John Knox, 1993. 33–61 (orig. pub. 1987).

Maybaum, Ignaz. *The Face of G-d after Auschwitz.* Amsterdam: Polak and Van Gennep, 1965.

Morgan, Michael L. *Beyond Auschwitz: Post-Holocaust Jewish Thought in America.* Oxford: Oxford UP, 2001.

Odell, Margaret S. *Ezekiel.* Smith and Helwys Bible Commentary. Macon, GA: Smyth and Helwys, 2005. 115–16.

Perdue, Leo G. *The Collapse of History: Reconstructing Old Testament Theology.* OBT; Minneapolis: Fortress, 1994.

———. *Reconstructing Old Testament Theology: After the Collapse of History.* OBT; Minneapolis: Fortress, 2005.

Pfisterer Darr, Katheryn. "Ezekiel." *The New Interpreter's Bible.* Ed. L. E. Keck et al. Nashville: Abingdon, 2001. 6:1179.

Pritchard, James B., ed. *Ancient Near Eastern Texts Relating to the Old Testament (ANEP).* 3rd ed. Princeton: Princeton UP.

von Rad, Gerhard. *Old Testament Theology.* 2 vols. New York: Harper and Row, 1962–65.

Rendtorff, Rolf. *The Canonical Hebrew Bible: A Theology of the Old Testament.* Leuven: Deo, 2005.

Rubenstein, Richard L. *After Auschwitz: Radical Theology and Contemporary Judaism.* Indianapolis: Bobbs-Merrill, 1966.

Sarna, Nahum. *Exodus*. JPS Torah Commentary. Philadelphia: Jewish Publication Society, 1991. 202–22.

Sommer, Benjamin. *A Prophet Reads Scripture: Allusion in Isaiah 40–66*. Stanford: Stanford UP, 1998.

———. "Revelation at Sinai in the Hebrew Bible and Jewish Theology." *JR* 79 (1999): 422–51.

Sperling, S. David, ed. *Students of the Covenant: A History of Jewish Scholarship in North America*. Atlanta: Scholars, 1992.

Sweeney, Marvin A. *1 and 2 Kings: A Commentary*. OTL. Louisville: Westminster John Knox, forthcoming.

———. "The Destruction of Jerusalem as Purification in Ezekiel 8–11." *Form and Intertextuality in Prophetic and Apocalyptic Literature*. FAT 45. Tübingen: Mohr Siebeck, 2005. 144–55.

———. "The Emerging Field of Jewish Biblical Theology." *Academic Approaches to Teaching Jewish Studies*. Ed. Z. Garber. Lanham: UP of America, 2000). 83–105.

———. "Isaiah and Theodicy after the Shoah." *Strange Fire: Reading the Bible after the Holocaust*. Ed. T. Linafelt. BibSem 71. Sheffield: Sheffield Academic, 2000. 208–19.

———. *King Josiah of Judah: The Lost Messiah of Israel*. Oxford: Oxford UP, 2001. 21–177.

———. *The Prophetic Literature*. IBT. Nashville: Abingdon, 2005.

———. "Reconceiving the Paradigms of Old Testament Theology in the Post-Shoah Period." *BibInt* 6 (1998): 142–61.

———. "Tanak versus the Old Testament: Concerning the Foundation for a Jewish Theology of the Bible." *Problems in Biblical Theology: Essays in Honor of Rolf Knierim*. Ed. H. T. C. Sun and K. L. Eades. Grand Rapids: Eerdmans, 1997. 353–72.

———. "Why Jews are Interested in Biblical Theology: A Retrospective on the Work of Jon D. Levenson." *Jewish Book Annual* 55–56 (1997–99): 134–168.

———. "The Wilderness Traditions of the Pentateuch: A Reassessment of their Function and Intent in Relation to Exodus 32–34." *Society of Biblical Literature 1989 Seminar Papers*. Ed. David J. Lull. Atlanta: Scholars, 1989. 291–99.

Wiesel, Elie. *Night*. New York: Hill and Wang, 1960.

Wilcoxen, Jay. "The Political Background of Jeremiah's Temple Sermon." *Scripture in History and Theology: Essays in Honor of J. Coert Rylaarsdam*. Ed. A. Merrill and T. Overholt. Pittsburgh: Pickwick, 1977. 151–66.

Williamson, Clark M. *A Guest in the House of Israel: Post-Holocaust Church Theology*. Louisville: Westminster John Knox, 1993.

Zimmerli, Walter. *Ezekiel 1: A Commentary on the Book of the Prophet Ezekiel Chapters 1–24*. Trans. R. E. Clements. Hermeneia. Philadelphia: Fortress, 1979.

A Citadel Fitly Constructed: Philo-Semitism and the Making of an American Holocaust Conference

By Zev Garber

MUSINGS ON PHILO-SEMITISM

Whether or not we hold that there is a direct link between the Shoah and two thousand years of Christians teaching contempt for Jews, Christian culpability in the near total destruction of European Jewry cannot be categorically denied. However, are core Christian beliefs, creed and dogma themselves anti-Semitic? It can be argued that a Christian action, initially meant to harm Jews, in the long run had beneficial results for them. For example, the ghettos of Europe were created to restrict Jews from social contact with Christians, but the forced separation from Christian society enabled Jews to develop and intensify their own value-system and beliefs while diminishing communal losses through intermarriage.

Two historical circumstances provide the criteria for European philo-Semitism: the right of existence ordered for Jews in medieval Europe and the emancipation granted Jews in nineteenth-century Europe. Pope Gregory I (590–604) ordained that Christianity had the obligation to preserve Jews from attacks. Beginning with Pope Calixtus II (1119–24) and continuing until the fifteenth century, a series of papal "bulls" (decrees) threatened Christians with excommunication if they converted Jews by force, robbed them of their possessions, exercised undue violence against them, disturbed their synagogue services, or accused them of blood libel and host desecration.

Jews were expelled from England in 1290, but in 1655 Oliver Cromwell invited a Dutch Rabbi of Portuguese descent, Menasseh ben Israel, to argue for the re-admittance of Jews into England. Likewise, ideologues of emancipation defended the Jews against medieval church stereotypes, and Jews were enfranchised during the time of the French Revolution. Arguably, the survival of European Jewry and their emancipation in nineteenth century Europe was largely due to the efforts of philo-Semites. However, there was nonetheless a hidden agenda to some philo-Semitic action.

Pope Gregory I ordained that Christians had the obligation to protect Jews from attacks, but his decree was prompted by the desire to preserve the Jewish suffering as proof of the truth of Christianity. But most medieval popes and Protestant reformers, such as Martin Luther in his early work, namely, *That Jesus Christ Was Born a Jew* (1523), wanted to convert the Jews by persuasion rather than by force. The invitation to settle or resettle Jews was not out of brotherly love but rather more to encompass and control commercial power. When advocates of the Enlightenment defended the Jews, they did not do so out of empathy for Jewish suffering but more to exploit their plight and expose the church's hatred for Jews. Similarly, the granting of civic equality to the Jews of France and elsewhere was more of an exchange than a gift—Jews were expected to give up much of their distinctiveness as a people in exchange for citizenship.

A more legitimate yardstick of philo-Semitism both in the past and now is respect—not necessarily love—for Jews, Jewishness, and Judaism. It is exemplified by Dietrich Bonhoeffer, the Lutheran pastor and theologian, who spoke out against Nazism and died at the hands of the Gestapo in 1945, but who believed in his formative years as a confessing Christian in the need for the ultimate conversion of the Jews. The heroism of Bonhoeffer was, in his view, an aspect of Christian witnessing; on the other hand, the heroism of Raoul Wallenberg and other Holocaust rescuers who acted based on more purely humanitarian motives in saving thousands of Jews from the Shoah may be considered a more idealistic philo-Semitism.

In recent decades, there has been a dramatic and positive shift in Christian perspectives on the Jews, nurtured authoritatively by ecclesiastical declarations seeking common religious ground between the church and the synagogue. Outlined by the Vatican II declaration *Nostra Aetate* (1965; "In Our Times," the statement on the relationship of the Roman Catholic Church to non-Christian religions and specifically paragraph 4 which deals with the Jews) and subsequent official Roman Catholic pronouncements on the Jewish people (e.g., "The Jewish People and their Sacred Scriptures in the Christian Bible,"

2002), the Vatican's avowed desire is to stress the importance of Jewish sources (Scriptures, rabbinics, philosophy, mysticism, Zionism) for Christianity, today as in the past. Likewise, mainstream Protestant denominations have taken a strong position against the "teaching of contempt" that Christians have projected in their depictions of the Jews. They have rejected the teachings of this nature over the past two millennia as based on errant scriptural reading (e.g., by emphasizing Jewish guilt in the Passion narrative), misguided and fallacious theology, and ignorance of the influence and impact of post-biblical Judaism on both the nascent church and the later history of Christianity. For example, note the declaration of the World Lutheran Federation: "Christians need to learn of the rich and varied history of Judaism since New Testament times, and of the Jewish people as a diverse, living community of faith today. Such an encounter with living and faithful Judaism can be profoundly enriching to Christian self-understanding" ("Guidelines for Lutheran-Jewish Relations," 1998). Also equally significant was the signing of a joint agreement between the Archbishop of Canterbury and Israel's Chief Rabbis to condemn vitriolic religious and secular anti-Semitism and to advance principles of "encounter, discussion, reflection, and reconciliation" between the Anglican Communion and the Jewish people (September 5, 2006).

To correct ethical and moral "injustices directed against the Jews at any time from any source" ("Guidelines for Catholic-Jewish Relations"), Christians have been challenged to rediscover the deep Jewish roots of their faith and to live the life of *imitatio Christi* (in imitation of Christ) without theological anti-Semitism. When relevant in Christian preaching and catechesis, the Jewish understanding of God, Torah, and Israel are to be presented without polemics, politics, or paternalism.

In comparison, Jewish reciprocal correctives about Christianity have been less forthcoming. This may be partially attributable to the residual effects of a lingering Jewish hostility toward past Christian policies against the Jews in word and deed. Moreover, many Jews have perceived that they are in a "no gain" situation in respect to Christian attitudes on basic theological matters. They have questioned, for example, whether believers in the new covenant and its Messiah, "this perfect gift from above" (as John Paul II calls it: "Pope John Paul II's Remarks"), could ever accept Israel—God's special people, "a kingdom of priests and a holy nation" (Exod. 19:6)—as religiously coequal. They have wondered whether viable common theological ground could be achieved when, unlike Christians, Jews cannot see Trinitarianism in the plain meaning of Hebrew Scriptures. In addition, there have been differences of opinion within the Jewish religious polity that impede a responsible collective response to the varied Catholic and Protestant statements about the Jews. This may explain the dearth of a communal reply to the Vatican's "Notes on the Correct Way to Present the Jews and Judaism in Preaching and Catechesis in the Roman Catholic Church" (1985), which suggests that the establishment of the State of Israel is not "in itself religious" and reports the "sad fact" that most Jews did/do not accept the salvific role of Jesus in history, while, in contrast, this is a basic tenet of classical Christianity. However, this was to change in 2000, when a cross-denominational Jewish statement (although not supported in the main by the Orthodox) *Dabru Emet* ("Speak Truth") and its accompanying book, *Christianity in Jewish Terms*, categorically delineated how contemporary Jews are encouraged to view Christianity, and, by extension, what is thought to be proper and not proper in the Christian view of Judaism. The hope is that the call to "speak truthfully" about 2,000 years of the relationship of Judaism and Christianity is now being heeded.

There is no question about the significant contribution of philo-Semitism to Jewish survival. Yet Christian theologians, ministers and other officials are not of one mind regarding how to present the intricacies of Christian accountability in teaching about how the Shoah came into being and virulently thrived in the heart of Christian Europe. Part of the problem in Christian Holocaust education concerns issues of definition. Some want to characterize the Shoah in terms of history, while others prefer to work within the context of theology. Some speak of the deliberate genocide with the focus limited to the six million Jews who were put to death, and others broaden the perspective by also including the millions of Christians who also met there end at the hands of the Nazis. Some insist on global genocide study while others maintain that this obscures the uniqueness of Hitler's "Final Solution of the Jewish Question." Consider the phrase, "Crucifixion of the Jews," used not infrequently by Christians in discussion and depiction of Christian responsibility for the Shoah; yet the battle over its intention has been as intense as the verbal assault on the word "Holocaust" (a divinely sanctioned whole-burnt offering) as the term of record for the willful murder of European Jewry.[1]

MANDATING CHRISTIAN RESPONSIBILITY IN SHOAH EDUCATION

In the mid-1960s, a number of Christian clergy, scholars and theologians—especially in America—were disturbed by the inability of the church to learn a basic lesson from the Shoah, namely, that it is not acceptable to stand idly by during the degradation of your neighbor. In particular, they were concerned about the indifference of many Catholic and Protestant leaders to—and, in some cases, active participation in— the planned assault by Arab nations on the State of Israel on the eve of the 1967 Six-Day War. Convinced that many baptized American Christians were harboring traditional teachings of alienation and hatred towards Jews and inspired by the developments of the Vatican Council II and the movement toward interfaith dialogue by member denominations of the World Council of Churches, two American, Protestant clergymen-professors, Franklin H. Littell and Hubert G. Locke, forthrightly engaged in the presentation of what they took to be a fundamental Christian issue: the collective failure of Christians to act Christ-like during the Nazi murder of the Jews and the continued indecisiveness of some Christians in the face of the assault on the Jewish state in June, 1967. In order to address these and other related issues, they convened a Scholars Conference on the "Holocaust and Church Struggle" in March, 1970 at Wayne State University in Detroit under the heading, "What Can America Learn?"[2]

The mandate of the first American Scholars Conference, as well as its immediate successors, has been clear and precise: to root out the anti-Jewish bias of *contra Judaeos* (against Jews) found at the crossroads of Christian preaching and teaching; to stress the importance of the study of Judaism on its *own* terms so that Christians are able to assess correctly the positive value of rabbinic cult, rite, and law on the nascent church and on the later history of Christianity; to confront the shameful "teaching of contempt"—traced back to pivotal New Testament passages and the comments of the early Church Fathers—that Christians have projected onto the Jews for the past two millennia across and beneath all denominational barriers; to take seriously the concept of the Jews as God's ongoing covenantal people, whom Christians in their understanding of God's Word in scriptures and tradition, are morally bound to support and protect; to rediscover the deep Jewish roots of the *corpus Christi* (Body of Christ) and live the *imitatio Christi* without anti-Semitism; and finally, to avoid Christian-centered agendas (manifest, e.g., in the argument that Christians suffered equally as did the Jews in the Shoah) as well Jewish-centered agenda (e.g., the argument that Jews are best suited to teach about the Shoah to Christians, whose primary role should be to listen passively) by learning intellectually and honestly the lessons of the Shoah in a setting that is inter-religious, international, and interdisciplinary. Overall the aim of this and successive conferences thus was to lay a solid dialogical groundwork for a citadel of understanding, fitly constructed.

Forged in the tradition of the anti-Nazi *Bekennende Kirche* (Confessing Church), and in the spirit of leading Christian thinkers, such as Dietrich Bonhoeffer, Martin Niemöller and Reinhold Niebuhr, the Scholars Conference, in the words of Hubert G. Locke, "was originally envisioned as part of a major center on the Holocaust and the German Church Struggle at Wayne State University that was to include the entire microfilmed collection of the Niemöller archives ... with some invaluable interviews with German church leaders still living in 1960s."[3] It is greatly to be regretted that Wayne State University did not complete this project, but the ongoing Scholars Conference has served as a forceful testimony that, in co-founder Locke's words, "the Shoah and the *Kirchenkampf* (Church struggle) be examined together as interwined and interrelated themes."

From the beginning, the founders (Littell and Locke) and subsequent chairpersons of the Scholars Conference (now entitled the Annual Scholars Conference on the Holocaust and the Churches) have insisted that the issue of Nazi state policy and the responsibility of the German churches, as well as the failure of churches in general to protest Nazi anti-Semitism and the Final Solution, must play a significant role in the agenda of the conference. In the sentiment of Littell and Locke, the Shoah is recognized as a critical challenge to Christianity, Christendom and Western Civilization as well as to Jewish self-definition.[4]

The highlight of the first annual conference was a remarkable interchange between Elie Wiesel and Richard L. Rubenstein—towering figures in contemporary Jewish thinking—on their theological responses to the most severe crisis faced by Jewish religious thought since the fall of the Second Temple in 70 CE, namely, the systematic annihilation of European Jewry during World War II. The kaleidoscope of information presented by Rubenstein included: 1) rethinking in light of Auschwitz the validity and credibility of a theology that claims God chose Israel and sustained her in history; 2) reinterpreting belief and tradition for an increasingly post-traditional Judaism freed from the mass of fundamental religious legalism; and 3) more generally, affirming a form of "Jewish paganism" (i.e., a Judaism stripped of it religious agenda) as the only appropriate response to the Holocaust and the birth of Israel. Wiesel's message was multi-layered and more impressionistic. He spoke of divine love and silence and the guilt and obligation of survival, all of which were interwoven with threads of midrashic teaching, Hasidic tales, Kabalistic mysticism, talmudic wisdom, and pious folklore. Theologically, his testimony was more a *Din Torah* (a disputation based on the judgment of the Torah) focused on God,

A Citadel Fitly Constructed 197

who allowed Auschwitz to occur, and with it the radical dehumanization of existence—all of which raises the possibility that the world is either not listening to or does not care about the lessons that can be learned from the Shoah. And yet... Wiesel was not ready to go so far as Rubenstein in repudiating God in light of the Shoah.[5]

A DECADE OF ANNUAL SCHOLARS CONFERENCES (1995–2005)

In the conference's formative decade, notable scholars and researchers such as Yehudah Bauer, Emil Fackenheim, Harry James Cargas, Alice L. and A. Roy Eckardt, Irving Greenberg, and Raul Hilberg presented their views. The groundwork was studiously laid for what Littell astutely called, "(t)he grandfather conference connecting the tragedy of the SHOAH [sic] and the trauma of Christendom—the oldest continuing consultation between Jews and Christians, between citizens of many countries, between representatives of several academic disciplines."[6]

For over three decades, each gathering has featured a keynote addresses, plenary sessions, and break-out working groups, covering diversified topics from hands-on pedagogy to singular themes of hard research. The following short synopsis of the meetings between 1995 and 2005, in particular, shows convincingly that the central force of the Annual Scholars Conference has remained the engagement of two seminal objectives of Holocaust Studies in America today: What can we ourselves learn? And how do we teach what we can learn about the Shoah and its lessons to others? The following chronicle is thus an attempt, however brief, to recognize and honor a uniquely American-based Jewish-Christian dialogue on the Shoah that has annually promoted and sustained communication and understanding where in the past this has been far less forthcoming.

- The Twenty-Fifth Annual Scholars Conference convened at Brigham Young University in 1995. Featured at this Silver Anniversary were the convocation speaker, Representative Tom Lantos (D-California), who is a Hungarian Shoah survivor (rescued through the efforts of Raul Wallenberg), and other witnesses, some twenty-two liberators of death camps, who bore eloquent and moving testimony that the Shoah, the paradigmatic genocide of the twentieth century, was a major historical fact that must never be discounted or ignored. By and large, papers, panels, participants, and professionals focused on that year's conference theme, "Remembrance, Repentance, Reconciliation," no doubt selected to commemorate the fiftieth anniversary of the liberation of Auschwitz, Bergen-Belsen, and the other camps.[7]

- The Twenty-Sixth Annual Scholars Conference convened in Minneapolis, Minnesota, March 3–5, 1996. Hosted by the Center for Jewish-Christian Learning of the University of St. Thomas (St. Paul and Minneapolis campuses). With support in part from the Minnesota State Legislature, it was attended by 260 scholars from fifteen countries. Addresses by Yehudah Bauer (Hebrew University of Jerusalem) on "The Trauma of the Holocaust: Some Historical Perspectives" and Deborah Lipstadt (Emory University) on "Holocaust Denial and the Media Misunderstanding the Nature of Truth" were public events that attracted many from the community.

Education issues dominated workshops and panel discussions on the first day of the conference. Sessions included educators' workshops, the status of Shoah education in the colleges and universities, using resources to teach about the Shoah and prejudice-reduction, and pedagogy. The second and third days considered a variety of Shoah topics, such as war criminals and the new anti-Semitism, post-Shoah Christian theologies, ethical responses to violence and evil, the continuing conflict generated by the Auschwitz convent controversy,[8] Christian-Jewish relations after the Shoah, and early Christian and medieval roots of Jewish persecution. Several panels were presented on the testimony of survivors, literary memoirs and responses, drama and music, art forms and public monuments, and representation in films.

New topics emerged, including, Shoah research and education in the former Soviet Union, and Israeli literature and the Shoah. Abraham Peck (National Jewish Archives, Hebrew Union College) and Gottfried Wagner (composer, writer, producer) continued their post-Shoah Jewish-German dialogue while a Jewish (Zev Garber and Steven L. Jacobs) Christian (Henry F. Knight, James F. Moore) dialogue group presented two sessions on post-Shoah theology: during the first, the participants presented their research; at the second, audience and panelists engaged in a lively discussion on views presented.[9]

The second day's lunch keynote, Ian Hancock (Romani Jewish Alliance), focused directly on the conference theme, "Confronting the Holocaust: A Mandate for the 21st Century," when he spoke on the roots of the Romani (Gypsy) genocide, which are still being largely ignored. This prompted Bauer to propose that the Scholars Conference resolve "that it is appropriate for democratic governments, religious organizations, academic and civic bodies to call upon governments and political parties in the countries mentioned to act forcefully against anti-Romani policies which, if continued, may well create another political genocide." Further resolved was a declaration against a Middle Eastern terrorist attack carried out on the eve and day of Purim, proposed by Zev Garber and individually written by him and Bauer and collated by G. Jan Colijn (Richard Stockton College of New Jersey):

> The series of terrorist outrages that hit Israel in the last few days are yet another proof that the dangers discussed at the 26th Annual Scholars' Conference on the Holocaust and the Churches are still with us. The murderers and those who send them are motivated by antisemitic and anti-democratic ideology which is directed against Israel, against any type of peace agreement in the Middle-East, and against their own Palestinian people. Scholars participating at the 26th Annual Scholars' Conference on the Holocaust and the Churches call upon the civilized world to aid those who will take action to stop the murderers from achieving their goals. We call upon people of moral conscience and good will to condemn the cowardly acts of terrorism in the streets of Jerusalem and the land of Zion. For out of Zion comes forth the Torah (Teaching): Choose life, peacemakers, not death.[10]

- The Twenty-Seventh Annual Scholars Conference on the Holocaust and the Churches convened at the Tampa Airport Marriott Hotel, March 2–4, 1997, on the theme, "Hearing the Voices: Teaching the Holocaust to Future Generations." Sponsored by the University of South Florida, in cooperation with the Tampa Bay Holocaust Memorial Museum and Educational Center and Eckerd College, it attracted participants from thirty-eight states and the District of Columbia, as well as eleven other countries. Ballroom-capacity crowds heard plenary panels reassessed the "God is Dead" theology of Richard L. Rubenstein (Michael Berenbaum, Zev Garber, John Pawlikowski, John Roth, and Rubenstein) and critiqued the German worldview of "eliminationist anti-Semitism" expressed in Daniel Goldhagen's book *Hitler's Willing Executioners* (Herbert Hirsch, Hubert Locke, Ilka Quindeau, Lars Rensmann, Roger Smith, and John Weiss). Also well received were luncheon keynote addresses by Barry S. Levey on war and public health, Eli Rosenbaum on prosecuted Nazi war crimes and the need for constant vigil (since almost nobody is totally innocent—the Swiss protected Nazi gold, for example), and a plenary address by Michael Marrus on the Vatican and the Holocaust.

Keynote Speaker Elie Wiesel questioned a variety of perspectives on the Shoah: cultural, national and religious (including why there are crosses at the

"Edith Stein Corner" at Auschwitz). His eyewitness approach carried convincingly the voices from the camps to the campus and beyond. He argued that the redemptive quality of memory, rooted in morality, does not diminish the Shoah but serves to make this imponderable event more significant and more troubling—and therefore more full of hope. It appeared that the nearly 2,000 people present at the opening convocation at the University of South Florida were in agreement.

The first day of the conference was dominated by multiple working groups designed to teach the Shoah in different settings to different audiences by different means (including, art, music and film) and philosophies. A roundtable surveyed the Holocaust teaching mandate across the United States. Concurrent sessions on other days discussed medical ethics and issues on ethical standards; Christian leadership, theology and the Shoah; historical findings, literary themes, and psychological and sociological factors in the Holocaust; survivors, deniers and testimony; and women's voices in the Shoah. Audio-visual, literary and poster sessions also took place.

The roundtable of Jews (Zev Garber, Steven L. Jacobs) and Christians (Henry F. Knight, James F. Moore) discussed the scriptures in light of the Shoah. Elizabeth Maxwell (Christian Hugenot Holocaust benefactor-scholar and wife of the international media mogul Robert Maxwell) described this as "the clearest demonstration of what an interfaith dialogue could be like; extreme courtesy reigned." The Eternal Flame Award was presented to Michael Berenbaum, president of the Survivors of the Shoah Foundation (founded by Steven Spielberg) and formerly director of the Research Institute of the United States Holocaust Memorial Museum, for his outstanding contribution to the field of Holocaust education.[11]

• Over two hundred people registered for the Twenty-Eighth Annual Scholars Conference on the Holocaust and the Churches, which was held at the University of Washington, February 28–March 3, 1998. The host committee and conference chairperson Hubert G. Locke organized and managed the event. The opening address by the Honorable David J. Scheffer, Ambassador at Large for War Crimes Issues for the United States State Department, concerned genocide and the challenges of international justice. Plenary panels on "Survivor Testimony: Its Use, Abuse and Denial" (Yaffa Eliach, Arnold Hass, Shelly Shapiro, Susan Pentlin), "The Enigma of Pius XII" (John Conway, Jacques Kornberg, John Pawlikowski with commentary by Harry James Cargas), and "Holocaust and Genocide: Current Problems and Issues" (Janice Friebaum,

Shimon Samuels, Andrew Gordon, Morton Kroll, Denise Novotny) were well attended. Keynote speaker John K. Roth (Claremont-McKenna College) raised significant points on the legacy of the Shoah on the eve of the twenty-first century, as did the conference's final speaker, Franklin H. Littell, who elaborated on early-warning signals of the Holocaust and genocide.

On the opening day, the annual seminar on reading Hebrew and Christian scriptures in light of the Shoah (Zev Garber, Steven L. Jacobs, Henry F. Knight, James F. Moore) was followed by simultaneous colloquia and section meetings on a wide variety of subjects. Session topics included arts and literature, and post-Shoah theology. Also discussed were perpetrators who planned genocide and bystanders whose indifference contributed to its reality. Sharon Gutman (from the Philadelphia Center on the Holocaust, Genocide and Human Rights) presented the Eternal Flame Award to G. Jan Colijn, Dean of General Studies at Richard Stockton College of New Jersey, for his supervision of that college's Holocaust Resource Center and its outstanding work in Holocaust education. On the same program, Garber and Richard Libowitz paid tribute to Harry James Cargas and announced their forthcoming *Festschrift* (a book honoring a respected academic) in tribute to this great Catholic Shoah scholar.

The second day saw consideration of the role of the "righteous gentiles," survivors who are living with the memory, the Anne Frank legacy, Holocaust education, Holocaust and health-care professions, the Holocaust in film and television, and film showings. A new colloquium and section made its first presentation at the conference: the Holocaust and contemporary genocides (organized and chaired by Henry Huttenbach, City University of New York) and the Holocaust and Pacific-Rim nations. Erich Geldbach (University of Bochum) addressed the controversy concerning Holocaust memory in Germany. The final sections on the third day were devoted to gender studies, anti-Semitism, history, and comparative analyses.[12]

- More than five hundred people registered for the Twenty-Ninth Annual Scholars Conference on the Holocaust and the Churches held at the Marriot Hotel Conference Center, Uniondale, New York, March 6–9, 1999, and sponsored by Nassau Community College in cooperation with Yad Vashem (the Holocaust Museum in Jerusalem) and the Philadelphia Center on the Holocaust, Genocide, and Human Rights. The primary theme was "The Burdens of History: Post-Holocaust Generations in Dialogue." In addresses, plenary panels and workshops, presenters sought ways to bridge the gaps that separate religious, national, ethnic and cultural groups in coming to terms with the Shoah, each other, and our mutual human responsibility at the close of this century of Shoah and genocide. The conference also acknowledged the efforts of Nassau Community College President Sean Fanelli and his administrative staff as well as to host co-chairpersons Sally Ann Drucker, Adam Haridopolos, Roger Tuggle, and, especially, Sharon Leder for their support and leadership in the success of the conference's first gathering to be hosted by a two-year public college.

The opening address was delivered by Gottfried Wagner (Milan, Italy), great-grandson of composer Richard Wagner, who spoke about his personal confrontation with his family's legacy of anti-Semitism associated with high culture and music. Education and methodology for teaching the Shoah at various educational levels and international settings dominated workshops and panel discussions on the first day of the conference. Luncheon keynote Vera King Farris (President, the Richard Stockton College of New Jersey) and evening keynote speaker Yaffa Eliach (Brooklyn College) stressed the importance of Holocaust education in higher education and the challenges it faces in the twenty-first century.

On the second and third days participants considered a variety of Shoah topics, such as second-generation German struggle, second-generation dialogue, second-generation and intergenerational reflection, the Holocaust and other genocides, the church role and the Holocaust, the Lutherans and the Holocaust, literary approaches, women's Holocaust history, and ethical issues and dilemmas. Several panels were presented on Holocaust deniers, survivors, interfaith dialogue, arts and aesthetics, and representation in films. The Hawthorne String Quartet of the Boston Symphony Orchestra performed their award-winning "Chamber Music from Teresienstadt" in concert. The conference concluded with an address by Robert Lifton (John Jay College, City University of New York) on "Surviving Evil: Struggling with Human Resilience," followed by concluding words from Littell.[13]

- The Thirtieth Annual Scholars Conference on the Holocaust and the Churches convened March 4–7, 2000, in Philadelphia, Pennsylvania. Sponsored by Philadelphia's (Jesuit) Saint Joseph's University—in cooperation with Yad Vashem; the United States Holocaust Memorial Museum; the Philadelphia Center on the Holocaust, Genocide and Human Rights; and the Pennsylvania Holocaust Education Task Force. It attracted over four hundred participants from across the United States and fifteen other countries. Plenary sessions included "At Century's End: Holocaust, Genocide and the Uniqueness Question"

(Yehudah Bauer via satellite from Jerusalem, Ward Churchill, Vakhan Dadrian, Paul Mojzes), "The Annual Scholars' Conference at 30: Looking Forward/Looking Back" (John Conway, Peter Hoffman, Franklin H. Littell, F. Burton Nelson, Richard Pierard, Richard L. Rubenstein), "Professional Ethics After Auschwitz" (David Lee Preston, Harry Reicher, Wolfgang Vogel, Martin Rumscheidt), "Holocaust and Genocides" (Irving Louis Horowitz, Israel Charny, Shimon Samuels, Stephen D. Smith), and "Nurses and Physicians in the Holocaust: Prisoners, Perpetrators, and Resisters" (Susan Benedict, Mary Langerwey, Cheyenne Martin).

Luncheon addresses by Steven Katz and Michael Berenbaum presented the conference theme, "The Century of Genocide." Also, co-founders Littell and Locke discussed and evaluated the important contribution made by the Annual Scholars' Conference to teaching the lessons of the Shoah in general and in Jewish-Christian settings in particular. That is to say, Jewish officialdom must let go of the notion that the Shoah is "a Jewish affair," Christians need to rethink supersessionist dogma about "the Jews" in order to proclaim an authentic Gospel-word in the post-Auschwitz world, and researching the facts and telling the true story of the Event can be effectively accomplished through interfaith dialogue.

The annual interfaith text group on reading Torah and Gospels in light of the Shoah—this year, Exodus 3 and John 8—(Steven L. Jacobs, Henry F. Knight, James F. Moore, Zev Garber) began the first day sessions. Concurrent sessions followed the first plenary meeting, and topics included education, faith, global, and literary issues and future directions. In addition to plenary sessions on the second and third days, concurrent sessions considered a variety of Holocaust topics, such as art; ethics; personalities; theology; Holocaust denial; responses from film, fiction, memoirs, and poetry; medical, psychological, and sociological studies; and teaching strategies. Timely themes included post-Shoah ethics (John K. Roth, Leonard Grob, Peter Haas, David Patterson, Didier Pollefeyt) and the language of genocide (Stephen B. Haynes, Karin Doerr and Kurt Jonassohn, Dorota Glowacka, Betty Rubenstein).

Arguably, the highlight of the conference was the awarding of a Doctor of Humane Letters (*Honoris Causa*) to Elie Wiesel in recognition of his scholarship and humanitarianism by President Nicholas S. Rashford, S.J., ScD, and faculty of Saint Joseph's University. Facing a packed audience of Christian and Jews sitting in the Chapel of St. Joseph, and standing in front of a stained glass Star of David bearing the image of a virginal Christ, Wiesel declared, "I am a Jew" and then proceeded to tell of his journey from birth in Sighet, Transylvania, to his experiences in various concentration camps to ways that his survivor's faith can help heal a post-Shoah world. Noteworthy was Wiesel's acknowledgment of real childhood fear of anti-Semitism, which restrained him from associating with Christians and entering their churches, and now his message that core negative beliefs about the Jewish People have been dramatically altered by the teachings of the church, e.g., *Nostra Aetate* (1965), recognition of the State of Israel (1993), *We Remember* (1998), and more recently, "Confession of Sins Against the People of Israel" (March 12, 2000) as well as Pope John Paul II's millennial pilgrimage to the Jewish State (March 21–26, 2000).

Clearly, the Roman Catholic *t'shuvah* (penitence)—despite political and theological flash points—toward "our dear and beloved elder brothers" (a phrase frequently uttered by Pope John Paul II in addressing Jews) is an unprecedented papal attempt to heal the cycle of pain between Christian and Jew and is one giant step forward to restore a fragile world (*tikkun 'olam*) at the start of the twenty-first century. Towards this admirable goal, the words of Elie Wiesel cited at the convocation are inspirational: "Mankind must remember that peace is not God's gift to his creatures, it is our gift to each other." In this respect, consider Pope John Paul II's words when he arrived in Israel on March 20, 2000: "The psalmist reminds us that peace is God's gift. May peace be God's gift to the land he chose as his own." Wiesel spoke from experience and survival in the valley of tears; and the pontiff, after engaging Mt. Nebo, the traditional burial spot of Moses, echoed words of Israelite belief to the strife that has long plagued the Holy Land.[14]

- The Thirty-First Annual Scholars Conference on the Holocaust and the Churches convened March 3–6, 2001, in Philadelphia, sponsored by Saint Joseph's University, in cooperation with Yad Vashem (Jerusalem) and The Philadelphia Center on the Holocaust, Genocide and Human Rights. Whether by an act of Providence ("a blizzard that fizzled") and/or because of a decision by the conference's board of directors to reconfigure the conference format (to focus on select topics and forego the traditional call for papers), the number of conference attendees was considerably lower than in previous years. Nevertheless, meaningful presentation and discussion on the general theme, "Teaching the Lessons: Identifying the Landmarks and the Landmines," were pursued in sessions on post-Shoah Midrash, post-Shoah education, the experience of ordinary people during the Shoah, the future of Holocaust denial, confronting complicity, the Holocaust and the nursing professions, genocide and the politics of prevention, remembering the women, representing the unpresentable (in arts and literature), and cutting-edge innovations in Holocaust scholarship.

Luncheon addresses were delivered by Michael Berenbaum on current controversies related to recently published Holocaust literature and attacks on Holocaust education, Carol Rittner on the Holocaust and the Christian world, and Yaffa Eliach, creator of "The Tower of Life" at the United States Holocaust Memorial Museum in Washington, DC.[15] Roundtable discussions on a variety of Shoah topics were optional with lunch. The keynote was given by Rabbi Irving Greenberg, chairman of the United States Holocaust Memorial Museum, who spoke on the ethics of power as a central post-Shoah challenge. Finally, there was an evening tribute to Eberhard Bethge, a student of Dietrich Bonhoeffer and a major player in the anti-Nazi Confessing Church (*Bekennende Kirche*).[16]

Not surprisingly, questions were raised in regard to the altered format of the Annual Scholars Conference. Some raised concern about the wisdom of invitation-only presentations, while others questioned whether it was preferable to focus on a single theme when such a subject of discourse is so easily fractured by a plurality of sub-topics. Nonetheless, there have been clear benefits to altering the format of the conference. Most notably, more time has been allotted to sustained conversation between discussants and attendees on pivotal Holocaust-issues. In this respect it needs to be recalled that a *main* concern of the conference has always been dialogue between Christians and Jews in an American context. The new format in many ways served effectively to address this goal.

- Some three hundred educators from sixteen countries registered for the Thirty-Second Annual Scholars Conference on the Holocaust and the Churches held at the Newark, New Jersey, Airport Marriott, March 2–5, 2002, on the theme, "The Genocidal Mind." Sponsored by Kean University, in cooperation with Saint Joseph's University, Richard Stockton College of New Jersey, and the Philadelphia Center on the Holocaust, Genocide, and Human Rights, the conference was ably managed by Jeffrey Glanz, conference chair, and Dennis Klein and Bernard Weinstein, program co-chairs. The well-attended plenary panels discussed "The Third Reich" (Dennis Klein, chair/commentator, Peter Hayes), "Genocide and Terrorism: The New Problematic" (Leonard Swidler, Richard L. Rubenstein, Khallid Duran), "The Holocaust, The Churches and the Contemporary Crisis in Jewish-Christian Relations" (Victoria Barnet, John Morley, Martin Rumscheidt; commentary by Henry F. Knight), "Responding to Terror and Genocide" (Ward Churchill, Paul Mojzes, Linda Melvern, Jay

Spaulding), and "Crisis of the Vocation: University Presidents Roundtable" (Vera King Farris, Robert Sheeran, Stephen Weber).

An outstanding event in the conclave was the program entitled, "A Small Light in the Darkness: Rescuers in the Holocaust," which honored the memory of Aristedes de Sousa Mendes, the Portuguese consul in Bordeaux, France, who, in defiance of his government's orders, helped saved some 30,000 Jews and others during the Shoah. Keynote speaker Mordechai Paldiel (Director of the Department for the Righteous Among the Nations at Yad Vashem) spoke on altruistic behavior of rescuers during the Shoah. Also featured was a musical piece, "Metamorphoses on Hatikvah," performed by Mathew Halper, Sharon Roffman, and Allison Brewster Franzetti. New Jersey educators Rose Thering, Joseph Prell, Paul Winkler, and the Kean University Holocaust Foundation (reflecting the role of Holocaust education in the State of New Jersey) were honored.

Education issues dominated workshops and panel discussions. Session topics included teaching through art and music, evaluating the role of seminaries in Holocaust education, teaching about the Shoah in former communist bloc countries, recognizing early warning signals, teaching prejudice-reduction, and what makes a good Holocaust resource center. Several panels were presented on the German churches and language, response by various religions, nursing during the Holocaust, and rescue and resistance.

James F. Moore, Steve L. Jacobs, Henry F. Knight, and Zev Garber conducted a pre-conference session on how to read scriptures in light of the Shoah. Inspired by the language of violence that proceeded, accompanied and followed the attack on the United States on September 11, 2001, the Midrash Group discussed the heritage of violence in the Jewish tradition. On a related matter, deeply concerned with the rising ugliness of anti-Semitism precipitated at the United Nations-sponsored world conference on racism in Durban, South Africa (September 2001), and the Nazi-like anti-Jewish rhetoric flowing from the Arab-Israeli conflict, a majority of conference participants endorsed "An Open Letter on Increasing Global Antisemitism" (drafted by James F. Moore, with a contribution from Sam Edelman):

> We, the undersigned participants of the Annual Scholars' Conference on the Holocaust and the Churches wish to express our concern about the increasing level of antisemitism around the globe and our fear that the Jewish people, wherever they are living, are again in danger. Given the frightening reality of the recent U.N. conference on racism held in Durban, South Africa, with its antisemitic agenda; the murder

of Daniel Pearl; the rise of anti-Jewish activities and propaganda in France, South America, and in the Muslim world in general; as well as the revival of Nazi-based propaganda and other anti-Jewish material, such as *The Protocols of the Learned Elders of Zion* as a means for characterizing the Arab-Israeli conflict, we believe that we are once again facing a level of anti-Jewish hatred comparable to what was experienced in Europe in the period between World War I and II. Thus, we are united in voicing our outrage at this development and our deep concern for our Jewish brothers and sisters world-wide and the immediate dangers they face.[17]

- The Thirty-Third Annual Scholars Conference on the Holocaust and the Churches convened March 1–4, 2003, in Philadelphia, Pennsylvannia. Sponsored by Philadelphia's (Jesuit) Saint Joseph's University, in cooperation with Yad Vashem (Jerusalem), Richard Stockton State College of New Jersey, the New Jersey Commission on Holocaust Education, Facing History and Ourselves National Foundation, the Philadelphia Center on the Holocaust, Genocide, and Human Rights, and the Pennsylvania Holocaust Education Task Force, it attracted 215 registrants from across the United States and eleven other countries, including Australia, Denmark, England, France, Israel, and Russia. There were four plenary sessions: "Holocaust, Genocide, and Human Rights" (Shimon Samuels), "Genocide Studies and Human Rights Education: Problems and Possibilities" (Paul Bartrop, William R. Fernekes, and Samuel Totten), "Resilience and Courage: Women, Men, and the Holocaust" (Nechama Tec), and "Forgiveness, Reconciliation, and Justice" (David Patterson, John Roth, Peter Haas, Henry F. Knight, and Leonard Grob).

    Luncheon addresses were delivered by Racelle Weiman on American Jewish responsibility or lack thereof during the Shoah, Richard L. Rubenstein on Christian ethics and myths after the Shoah, and Sibylle Sarah Niemoeller von Sell on responsibility and disobedience as exhibited by the life and teaching of her late husband, Pastor Martin Niemoeller.[18] The annual conference dinner was addressed by Knight, who gave a moving tribute to Dr. Lucja Frey Gottesman, a Polish neurologist and eminent scientist who perished at the hands of the Nazis in 1943. The Eternal Flame Award was presented to Nicholas Rashford, S. J., President of Saint Joseph's University, by conference-founder Littell, followed by an address by the Honorable Miles Lerman, Chairperson *Emeritus* of the United States Holocaust Memorial Museum.

    The conference's theme, "Ethics after Auschwitz," was addressed topically by a variety of seminars, breakout sessions, and roundtable discussions. The post-Shoah Midrash session (Steven L. Jacobs *in absentia*, Henry F. Knight, James F. Moore, Zev Garber, with response by Gary A. Philips) began the first-day sessions by referencing Matthew 23, Leviticus 10, and Malachi 2 in analyzing the topic, "National Crisis in Leadership." Concurrent sessions followed the first plenary with topics including law and human rights, German-Christian theology, new ethical imperatives, the use of art in pedagogy, Shoah education after 9/11, and the continual session on the nurses' vocation, ethics, and attributes (Evelyn R. Benson, Barbara L. Brush, Mary D. Lagerwey, Cheyenne Martin, and Susan L. Mayer). Sessions on the second and third days considered a variety of Holocaust topics, such as the profits of hate, Stalingrad and the Warsaw Ghetto, Christian theology and theologians in Nazi Europe, art and film, social structures of love and hate, issues in philosophy, responses to genocide, and teaching judgment and responsibility.[19]

• In lieu of a formal Thirty-Fourth Annual Scholars Conference, a group of thirty scholars from Canada, France, Germany, Israel, Russia, the United Kingdom and the United States met in St. Petersburg, Florida, with Elie Wiesel, Nobel Laureate, founding member and Honorary Chair of the conference, to discuss the rising wave of global anti-Semitism and terrorism. At the end of the one-day conclave, and with an eye to the 2005 conference, the participants resolved that "anti-Semitism has reached a post-Holocaust peak, demanding the urgent attention of scholars, educators, clergy, and other civic leaders, and that this crisis is of immediate concern for all faith communities."

• The Thirty-Fifth Annual Scholars Conference on the Holocaust and the Churches convened March 5–8, 2005, in Philadelphia, Pennsylvania, sponsored Saint Joseph's University. Whereas in previous decades the Annual Scholars Conference presented challenges and lessons from the Shoah primarily directed to Jews and Christians, this year's conference was broadened to include Muslim viewpoints. The Conference theme, "New Threats and Sowing Seeds of Hope: Operation Early Warning," suggested that "a new antisemitism is spreading around the world, to the point where Jewish-Christian, Jewish-Muslim, and Christian-Muslim relationships are in crisis—particularly as religious beliefs are being misused to spread hate and violence."[20]

The opening plenary session featured an address by Eternal Flame Award recipient, His Royal Highness Prince El Hassan bin Talal of Jordan (via satellite from Amman), which underscored the importance of "trialogue" in sowing seeds of hope. Other plenary sessions included, "A Commanding Voice Remembered: Emil Fackenheim" (Zev Garber, Marie L. Baird, Peter Haas, Franklin H. Littell, David Patterson, Richard Rubenstein, and Tobie Tondi),[21] "New Threats: An Inter-religious Trialogue (Erich Geldbach, Carol Ann Martinelli, Michael Pinner, Shimon Samuels, and Mahmud Aydn), "A Gathering of the Children of Abraham: Jewish-Christian-Muslim Trialogue," Public Event (Peter Batkis, Michael Berenbaum, Bob Edgar, and W. Deen Mohammed), "The Gathering Continues: Jewish-Christian-Muslim Trialogue, Part II" (Richard Rubenstein, John Schol, Alwi Shihab, and Aslam Syed), "Healers in Hell: Nurses, Physicians and Other Caregivers" (Mary Lagerway, Cheyenne Martin, Susan Mayer, Linda Shields, and Jacqueline Claude Romney), "At a Fork in the Road: Prevention or Disaster" (Ismail Bardhi, Ratomir Grozdanoski, Sanaullah Kirmani, Elise Rutagambwa, and Leonard Swidler), and "Fire in the Ashes: God, Evil, and the Holocaust" (David Patterson, Leonard Grob, Peter Hass, and Henry F. Knight) (see Patterson and Roth).

Topics at the concurrent breakout sessions dealt with the Shoah and the new anti-Semitism; Holocaust education through literature, the arts, and film; roots of genocide; seeking meaning and definition in the Shoah; Christian anti-Semitism; the role of women; and whether or not there is a redeeming voice when faced with natural evil (the Midrash Group—Zev Garber, Henry F. Knight, James F. Moore, and Steven L. Jacobs—on Job 38–41 and Matthew 27).[22] Luncheon addresses were given by Rochelle Saidel on the Jewish women of Ravensbrück concentration camp, and Yaffa Eliach on her tireless work to memorialize the nine hundred-year saga of the Lithuanian *shtetl* of Eishyshok in the State of Israel.[23] The Conference banquet remembered the Armenian Genocide of 1915 and also honored the lifetime of distinguished work of Professor Vakhan Dadrian to never forget the "first genocide" of the twentieth century.[24]

In summary, the Annual Scholars' Conference during the years 1995–2005 focused on a cross-disciplinary study of the Shoah as a field of humanistic learning, with a special interest in trends in the discipline. Sessions spanned a wide spectrum of topics and concern, from arts and literature, education, and history to dialogue, religious thought, and theology. Noteworthy was the continuing, annual face-to-face Christian-Jewish theological dialogue between Zev Garber, Henry F. Knight, Steven L. Jacobs, and James Moore on how to read scriptures in light of the Shoah. Their cutting-edge, post-Shoah Midrash sessions have been a constant of the Annual Scholars' Conference since 1993.[25]

Conference founders Littell and Locke's charge that "we yoke memory-work with our shared and interreligious commitment to enlist in the fight against the continuing anti-human curse of genocide" is clear, but do we all agree on the means through which to pursue this laudable goal? Judging from the reaction at the Twenty-Ninth Annual Scholars' Conference to John Roth's (Claremont McKenna College) "Who 'Owns' the Holocaust?" and John Pawlikowski's (Catholic Theological Union) response to him, and by the lively discussion of the plenary panel (Zev Garber, Henry F. Knight, Steven L. Jacobs, Richard Libowitz, James Moore, and Franklin H. Littell) on "The Church Struggle and the Holocaust," one must say (perhaps unsurprisingly), "not entirely." Nonetheless, conference participants have looked into the historical abyss and agree that we all have the ability and the responsibility to move forward. Learning from the Century of Shoah, we must proclaim the necessity that there be no more cases of genocide perpetrated against anyone, anywhere, anytime.

There were a number of years when horrific global events affected the intent of the Annual Scholars' Conference. For example, at the time of the 1995 conference, there was genocidal activity in Rwanda; religious and ethnic cleansing in Bosnia-Herzegovina as well as in a number of regions of the former USSR; hatred of minorities in Germany, India, Pakistan, and elsewhere; terrorist activity in Gaza, the West Bank, Tokyo, Ipil (south of Manila), Oklahoma City in the heartland of America; and other world trouble spots. Perpetrated by criminal cartels, secretive cults, nationalistic groups, liberation movements, and what have you—all inspired variously by venerated masters in the name of "supreme truth"—these acts cast a long, dark shadow on the 1995 United Nations "International Year of Tolerance." On the landscape of death, cynicism, and frustration, the Annual Scholars' Conference—mandated to teach and learn—sent forth a bold message to the world community: the world must unlearn the philosophy of "dislike of the unlike" or reap dire consequences. Indeed, this should always be the intent of responsible Shoah study and education. Moreover, knowledge of Shoah matters is mandatory to counter the revisionist claim that the Holocaust was "invented" and encourages vigilance to prevent such atrocities from ever happening again to any people, at any time, in any place.

BEGINNING OF THE END

Since 1970, the Annual Scholars' Conference has provided a forum for Jewish and Christian scholars in dialogue to ponder theistic responses to Shoah theodicy (the justification of an omnipotent and benevolent God in light of the existence of evil), to reassess post-Shoah Jewish identity, to reevaluate classical Christian theology about the Jews and the role of theological anti-Semitism, to understand why some Christians demonstrated Christian values in opposing Hitlerism and why other Christians showed indifference or participated actively in the "Final Solution," and to learn the lessons from the Shoah not only to preserve its memory but also to set in motion signals of warning to prevent genocidal activity from ever happening again. Yet this conference founded by two Christian visionaries and administered by a small band of loyalists is run on a shoestring budget and the energy of very few. By the same token, this annual conference has served well to highlight and sustain themes of major importance to our ongoing understanding of the Shoah as we leave the twentieth century and enter the twenty-first. The continuing growth and expanding work of the Annual Scholars' Conference demands a successful plan to institutionalize it in order to guarantee continual success in the years ahead.

Marcia Sachs Littell, the conference's Executive Director, notes that "the Annual Scholars Conference has been for over thirty years an on-going work in progress—growing, adapting, embracing and supporting teachers, scholars, members of the clergy and community leaders in their work and research." These are deserving words for a pioneering and leading movement in United States Holocaust Studies, but now critical issues challenge its durability. First, while the early leadership remains intact, one may now wish to consider whether the founding manifesto which spoke for a limited program in 1970 and the years that followed reflects today's wider scope of activity and diversified following?[26] Second, the Scholars' Conference faces annually a dearth of host institutions and financial support in running its meetings; can a voluntarily led and participatory group continue to sustain itself, given the plethora of Holocaust conferences now in existence or planned for the future? Third, though important and pace-setting scholarship has emerged from the annual meetings, it is unfortunate that more-than-occasionally shoddy research and faulty editing permeate the sessions and published proceedings. The absence of recognized scholars and the repetition of the same invitees to address annual meetings testify to this. What can be done?

For starters, let the leadership heed and apply well the counsel of Rabbi Tarfon: "It is not your duty to complete the work, but neither are you free to desist from it. . . ." (*M. 'Avot* 2.16). One may suggest the following steps: (1) the establishment of an advisory board with real power to decide how the organization and conferences are conducted and (2) the creation of an editorial board that acts with skill and rigor. The conference should experiment with alternate approaches and new venues. Indeed, at the Thirty-First Scholars Conference at Saint Joseph's University (March 2001), in lieu of a general call for papers, a small number of participants discussed a limited number of interrelated topics. Unfortunately, the expected in-depth examination did not prevail; seasoned scholars did not participate, and many younger scholars were not in attendance. Discouraging to be sure, but all new beginnings are difficult. Finally, the continuing growth and expanding work of the organization demand a successful plan to institutionalize it (dues-paying, shared governance, etc.) in order to guarantee future stability.

For more than a third of a century, the Annual Scholars' Conference on the Holocaust and the Churches has sponsored Christian-Jewish dialogue in the area of Shoah and genocide. It was established on the rock of ecumenism and it quickly learned that ecumenical dialogue resembles its associated activity: learning the language of ecumenism. It realized that in a mixture of Christians and Jews, achieving some fluency is manageable, but mastery is almost impossible. The goal is really the problem, that is to say, reaching the final aim by understanding and appreciating one another's goals beyond parochialism, paternalism and politics. This is the signature of the Scholars' Conference. May the need be met so that the citadel continues to be fitly constructed.[27]

Notes

1. On the meaning and use of the word Holocaust, see Garber and Zuckerman 3–30.
2. The conference was organized by Hubert Locke, director of the Office of Religious Affairs at Wayne State University (since 1958), with the backing of the school's Ecumenical Religious Center. Locke invited his friend and colleague in campus interfaith work, Franklin H. Littell, consultant for the National Conference of Christians and Jews on religion and higher education, to co-lead this conference on Shoah and church struggle. Of related interest, Littell was pivotal in establishing the National Christian Leadership Conference for Israel (NCLCI) and the Christian Study Group on Israel, both in 1970.
3. E-mail communication, 26 June 2001. For a reflection on the importance of the Wayne State conference in the chronology of Shoah education in America, see Littell 200–01. For a full conference report, see Littell and Locke.
4. In his concluding remarks at the Twenty-First Annual Scholars Conference (1991),

A Citadel Fitly Constructed 213

> Littell reflected on the important break-through of the Wayne State conference: "For the first time we brought together, in 1970, scholars, Jews and Christians, humanists and others of conscience, to concern themselves with what was after all a watershed event not only in Jewish history but in the history of Western civilization. The event was not only a crisis of faith which some Jews have gone through as a result of the Holocaust; it was also a crisis of integrity, still confronting Christianity one way or another during these years since Auschwitz. Maintaining these tensions has been the essence of our work." See Colijn and Littell, *Netherlands and Nazi Genocide* 531–32.

5. These words were the matrix around which Wiesel re-debated Rubenstein at the Twentieth Annual Scholars Conference, Vanderbilt University, March 1990.
6. From a letter mailed in 2000 to conference participants at the Thirtieth Annual Scholars Conference on the Holocaust and the Churches (St. Joseph's University, Philadelphia, PA). Littell also wrote, "For fifteen years, the Annual Scholars' Conference was the only annual Shoah conference on the American shores; however, since circa 1985, a tidal wave of like-minded conferences appeared sponsored by local or national institutions or organizations."
7. Select papers from the Twenty-Fifth Annual Scholars Conference are published in Tobler.
8. The role of language violence and religious differences emanating from the convent controversy is discussed in Garber and Zuckerman 57–78.
9. Garber, Jacobs, Knight, and Moore have been labeled the "Midrash Group" of the Scholars' Conference. The mission of the Midrash Group is to discuss ways for Christians and Jews to find meaning and direction in and from Scriptures and other sacred texts after the Shoah. For a synopsis of their work, go to the Rosenthal page at Case Western Reserve University, http://www.case.edu/artsci/rosenthal/index.html, and access Jewish-Christian Post-Shoah Midrash Group.
10. Select papers from the Twenty-Sixth Annual Scholars Conference are published in Colijn and Littell, *Confronting the Holocaust: A Mandate for the 21st Century—Part One*; and Feinstein, Schierman, and Littell, *Confronting the Holocaust; A Mandate for the 21st Century—Part Two*.
11. Proceedings of the Twenty-Seventh Annual Scholars Conference are published in Hayse, Pollefeyt, Colijn, and Littell.
12. Select papers from the Twenty-Eighth Annual Scholars Conference are published in Nefsky.
13. Select papers from the Twenty-Ninth Annual Scholars Conference are published in Leder and Teichman.
14. Proceedings of the Thirtieth Annual Scholars Conference are published in Curran, Libowitz, and Littell.
15. "The Tower of Life," a permanent exhibit at the United States Holocaust Memorial Museum, is a photographic memorial wall to the *shtetl* of Eishyshok in Lithuania.

The monumental history of Eishyshok (1065–1941) is told in Eliach's *There Once Was a World: A 900-Year Chronicle of the Shtetl of Eishyshok*.

16. Select papers from the Thirty-First Annual Scholars Conference are yet to be published.
17. Select papers are published in Klein, Libowitz, Littell, and Steeley.
18. At the Twenty-Second Annual Scholars Conference (1992), Niemoeller von Sell presented a paper, "Who Was Martin Niemoeller?" Also see Garber, "Faith from the Ashes: An Interview with Sibylle Sarah Niemoeller von Sell." Finally, for an evaluation of Martin Niemöller, the man and his work, see Garber, "Niemöller" and "Exile in the Fatherland: Martin Niemöller's Letters from Moabit Prison" 227–28, 428–29.
19. Select papers from the Thirty-Third Annual Scholars Conference are yet to be published.
20. From the front matter in the provisional program of the Thirty-Fifth Annual Scholars' Conference (2005).
21. Remarks by Garber, Haas, Littell, Patterson, and Rubenstein are based on their essays published in "Reflections on Emil L. Fackenheim," a special section of *Shofar* 22.4.
22. Papers published in *CSSR Bulletin* 35.3 52–67.
23. See N 15.
24. Select papers from the Thirty-Fifth Annual Scholars Conference are yet to be published.
25. Samples of their collaborative post-Shoah Midrashic approach are found in Moore, *Jewish-Christian Dialogue After the Shoah*; *SIDIC* 24.3–25.1 29–43; and *CSSR Bulletin* 35.3 52–67. See, also, Moore, with Garber, Jacobs, and Knight.
26. At the Twenty-Seventh Annual Scholars' Conference, longtime attendee Henry Huttenbach (City University of New York) spoke of the absence of sessions on "other genocides" and suggested that when one is scheduled, it is "a gesture of tokenism." See the remarks by Steven L. Jacobs.
27. The Thirty-Seventh Annual Scholars' Conference will convene March 11–13, 2007 [after the writing of this paper], at the Marriot Cleveland Downtown at Key Center and will be hosted by Samuel Rosenthal Center for Judaic Studies, Case Western Reserve University, under the able directorship of Professor Peter J. Haas. In my capacity as Visiting Rosenthal Professor in Holocaust and Jewish-Christian Relations (Spring 2005), Haas and I discussed the importance of interfaith dialogue between Christians and Jews, with particular emphasis on the Shoah. A tangible result of our discussions is Case's sponsorship of the Thirty-Seventh Annual Scholars Conference.

Works Cited

General Bibliography

Abbott, W. M., ed. *The Documents of Vatican II*. New York: America, 1966.

Commission for Religious Relations with the Jews. "Notes on the correct way to present the Jews and Judaism in preaching and catechesis in the Roman Catholic Church." 6 Mar. 1982 <www.vatican.va/roman_curia/pontifical_councils/chrstuni/relations-jews-docs/rc_pc_chrstuni_doc_19820306_jews-judaism_en.html>.

"Confession of Sins Against the People of Israel." 12 Mar. 2000 <www.vatican.va/news_services/liturgy/documents/ns_lit_doc_20000312_prayer-day-pardon_en.html>.

Eliach, Y. *There Once Was a World: A 900-Year Chronicle of the Shtetl Eishyshok*. Boston: Back Bay, 1998.

Evangelical Lutheran Church in America. "Guidelines for Lutheran-Jewish Relations." 16 Nov. 1998 <archive.elca.org/ecumenical/interreligious/jewish/guidelines.html>.

Frymer-Kensky et al., eds. *Christianity in Jewish Terms*. Boulder, CO: Westview, 2000.

Garber, Z. "Faith from the Ashes: An Interview with Sibylle Sarah Niemoeller von Sell." Garber and Zuckerman 167–80.

———. "Martin Niemöller" and "Exile in the Fatherland: Martin Niemöller's Letters from Moabit Prison." Ed. Thomas Riggs. *Reference Guide to Holocaust Literature*. Farmington Hills, MI: St. James, 2002. 227–28, 428–29.

Garber, Z., section ed. "Reflections on Emil L. Fackenheim." Spec. issue of *Shofar* 22.4 (2004): 107–35.

Garber, Z., and Zuckerman, B. *Double Takes: Thinking and Re-Thinking Issues of Modern Judaism in Ancient Contexts*. Lanham: UP of America, 2004.

Jacobs, Steven L. "Holocaust *and* Genocide Studies: The Future is Now." 3 Oct. 2008 <www.unr.edu/chgps/jacobs.html >.

Littell, F. H. Letter to conference participants at the Thirtieth Annual Scholars Conference on the Holocaust and the Churches. 2000.

Littell, F. H., and H. G. Locke, eds. *The German Church Struggle and the Holocaust*. Detroit: Wayne State UP, 1974.

Littell, M. S. Personal communication. 21 Mar. 2001.

Niemoeller von Sell, S. "Who Was Martin Niemoeller?" Locke and Littell 15–27.

Patterson, D., and J. Roth, eds. *Fire in the Ashes: God, Evil, and the Holocaust*. Seattle: U of Washington P, 2005.

Pontifical Biblical Commission. "The Jewish People and their Sacred Scriptures in the Christian Bible." 12 Feb. 2002 <www.vatican.va/roman_curia/congregations/cfaith/pcb_documents/rc_con_cfaith_doc_20020212_popolo-ebraico_en.html>.

"Pope John Paul II's Remarks in English at His Weekly General Audience, August 2, 1989." Catholic News Service; cited from Garber and Zuckerman 65.

Pope Paul VI. "Declaration on the Relation of the Church to Non-Christian Religions: *Nostre Aetate*." 28 Oct. 1965 <www.vatican.va/archive/hist_councils/ii_vatican_

council/documents/vat-ii_decl_19651028_nostra-aetate_en.html>.

U. S. Conference of Catholic Bishops. "Guidelines for Catholic-Jewish Relations." 1985 < http://www.usccb.org/liturgy/guidelinesjudaism.shtml >.

Select Volumes on Papers Presented at Annual Scholars Conference on the Holocaust and the Churches

Colijn, G. J., and M. S. Littell, eds., *Confronting the Holocaust: A Mandate for the 21st Century—Part One*. Lanham: UP of America, 1997.

———. *The Netherlands and Nazi Genocide*. Lewiston: Edward Mellen, 1992.

Curran, D. J., R. Libowitz, and M. S. Littell, eds. *The Century of Genocide*. Merion Station, PA: Merion Westfield, 2002.

Feinstein, S. C., K. Schierman, and M. S. Littell, eds. *Confronting the Holocaust: A Mandate for the 21st Century—Part Two*. Lanham: UP of America, 1998.

Hayse, M., D. Pollefeyt, G. J. Colijn, and M. S. Littell, eds. *Hearing the Voices: Teaching the Holocaust to Future Generations*. Merion Station, PA: Merion Westfield, 1999.

Klein, D. B., R. Libowitz, M. S. Littell, and S. B. Steeley, eds. *The Genocidal Mind: Selected Papers from the 32nd Annual Scholars Conference on the Holocaust and the Churches*. St. Paul, MN: Paragon, 2005.

Leder, S., and M. Teichman, eds. *The Burdens of History: Post-Holocaust Generations in Dialogue*. Merion Station, PA: Merion Westfield, 2000.

Locke, H. G., and M. S. Littell, eds. *Remembrance and Recollection: Essays on the Centennial Year of Martin Niemöller and Reinhold Niebuhr*. Lanham: UP of America, 1996.

Nefsky, M. F., ed. *The Pall of the Past: The Holocaust, Genocide, and the 21st Century*. Merion Station, PA: Merion Westfield, 2000.

Toblar, D. F., ed. *Remembrance, Repentance, Reconciliation: The 25th Anniversary Volume of the Annual Scholars Conference on the Holocaust and the Churches*. Lanham: UP of America, 1998.

Jewish-Christian Post-Shoah Midrash Dialogue Group

Garber, Zev. "An Interfaith Dialogue on Post-Shoah Jewish-Christian Scriptural Hermeneutics, with a Report on the Case Colloquium." *Council of Societies for the Study of Religion (CSSR) Bulletin* 34.4 (Nov. 2005): 76–79.

Garber, Z., J. Moore, S. Jacobs, and H. Knight. Articles on "Facing Texts Together: An Invitation to Midrashic Dialogue." *CSSR Bulletin* 35.3 (Sept. 2006): 52–67.

———. Articles on "Post-Shoah Dialogue: Confronting Moses and Paul in Auschwitz." *Mentalities/Mentalitiés* 21.2 (2007–08).

———. Articles on "Re-Thinking the Traditions: reading John 8 and Exodus 3 Together After the Shoah." *The Gospel of John: Conflicts and Controversies. Service International de Documentation Judéo-Chrétienne (SIDIC)* 34.3/35.1 (2001–02). 29–43.

Jewish-Christian Post-Shoah Midrash Dialogue Group. *Case Western Reserve U: Rosenthal Center.* 3 Oct. 2008 <www.case.edu/artsci/rosenthal/index.html>.

Moore, James, ed. *Jewish-Christian Dialogue After the Shoah.* Spec. issue of *Shofar* 15.1 (Fall 1996).

Moore, James, ed., with Z. Garber, S. Jacobs, H. Knight. *Post-Shoah Dialogues: Re-Thinking Our Traditions Together.* Lanham: UP of America, 2004.

Association for Jewish Studies Conference, 2006: A Response

Marc A. Krell

Editor's Note: The following is a response to papers by Zev Garber, Steven L. Jacobs, and Marvin A. Sweeney, presented at the 38th Annual Conference of the Association for Jewish Studies in San Diego, CA, December 17–19, 2006, and published in this volume.

I would first like to thank my distinguished colleagues for three interrelated papers that have highlighted the theological, cultural and political implications of the Holocaust in American life. Together, these papers reflect upon the significant progress that has been made in the United States among Jewish and Christian scholars who have brought the Holocaust to the fore of American consciousness while at the same time building upon the ashes of Auschwitz to create a new Jewish-Christian relationship based on an emerging mutual respect and acceptance of the other.

Zev Garber's paper traces the development of the Annual Scholars Conference on the Holocaust and the Churches in the United States within the larger historical context of philo-Semitism from the medieval through modern periods, demonstrating that the yardstick for philo-Semitic actions has actually been extended from mere respect to acceptance and even admiration for the eternal status of the Jews as God's chosen people. In fact, he points out that the central mandate for this ongoing conference was to "root out the anti-Jewish bias" embedded in Christian theology. Yet the Annual Scholars Conference has clearly gone beyond reformulating Christian theology and calling the German churches to account for their failure to protest Nazi anti-

Semitism. The agenda of the conference has included cultural issues such as literary, dramatic, artistic and cinematic representations of the Holocaust, as well as a political focus on war crimes, contemporary genocides and, most recently, terrorism.

Steven Jacobs's paper also deals with the development of American Jewish-Christian relations in the wake of the Holocaust on an intellectual level as well as examining its manifestations in the cultural and religious realms of American society. He first accounts for the growing pervasiveness of Holocaust Studies as a literary and cinematic genre in addition to becoming an academic discipline. He then points to the fundamental establishment of the United States Holocaust Memorial Museum, an American institution that attracts both the intellectual and cultural strata of the country. Finally, he offers an initial assessment regarding the impact of the Holocaust on Christian teaching and preaching in eight Alabama churches, concluding that, while the clergy were familiar with the Holocaust as an historical event, they had not fully probed its theological and cultural implications with their parishioners.

However, while these papers reflect the positive impact of the Holocaust upon American Jewish-Christian relations over the last half-century, they also point out the emerging pitfalls and potential obstacles still to be overcome in the future. One potential problem which surfaced in Garber's paper was that, while the principal mandate of the Annual Scholars Conference is to "root out the anti-Jewish bias" of the church, it may amount to what Martin Jaffee has described as a Christian "spiritual self-annihilation" (227–28; cf. Haynes 139). This resembles Emil Fackenheim's demand in his 1982 book To Mend the World that Christians atone for their sins against Jews by engaging in a " 'destructive recovery' of the whole Christian tradition" in order to extirpate the anti-Judaism inherent in its very makeup. As Laurie McRobert observes, the "destructive recovery" suggested by Fackenheim implies that Christians will have to "... go beyond the very roots of Christianity to a recovery of Judaism itself" (cf. McRobert 337). This has touched off a debate among Christian scholars about just how far Christians must go to reform their tradition in order to atone for the sins of anti-Judaism.

Ironically, two other interrelated issues, centering on the dynamics of power and powerlessness, have accompanied the increasing Holocaust awareness in the United States, as Jacobs has pointed out in his paper. First, some Jewish leaders like Rabbi Arnold Jacob Wolf have expressed concern that many universities are projecting an image of Jewish self-victimization to the non-Jewish community by showcasing Holocaust related courses at the expense of other Judaic Studies curricula. A similar dilemma has arisen at the United States Holocaust Memorial Museum because of its failure sufficiently to document non-Jewish victims during the Holocaust as well as account for other cultural genocides past and present. In light of the recent Holocaust revisionism by the Iranian president at his self-aggrandizing Holocaust conference, it is more important than ever to address this dilemma by including Muslims in a discussion of the Holocaust vis à vis other current genocides. As Jacobs has further noted, Edward Linenthal has argued that this reflects a "hierarchy of victimization," while other scholars such as John Murray Cuddihy and David Biale, have asserted that this type of comparative victimization illustrates a secular version of chosenness in which Jewish uniqueness and even superiority become equated with an incomparable history of suffering.

Moreover, it is problematic to view Jewish identity solely through Holocaust lenses, appealing to an essential Jewish experience of powerlessness, culminating in the Shoah. This characterization of Jewish culture ignores the ambiguous power dynamic of the Jew in relation to a Christian dominated culture in the United States, where Jews are numerically a minority, but are perceived to be part of the white patriarchal, Christian majority in the eyes of marginalized, African American, Chicano and Latino groups. It also obscures the value of Jewish culture in and of itself. Ultimately, this social ambiguity has produced a contradictory American Jewish self-consciousness, wherein Jews' identification and integration with the Christian majority directly conflicts with their equal desire to preserve their minority status in relation to a hegemonic Christian culture (Biale, Galchinsky, and Heschel 5).

In his paper, Marvin Sweeney appears to offer another way forward for Jews and Christians after the Holocaust with his portrayal of a post-Holocaust oriented biblical theology emerging in America in the 1990s and 2000s, following an initial period of dominance in the field by Protestant scholars. During this period, American Jewish scholars have begun to consider theological issues raised by the Shoah—especially those dealing with theodicy and the increasing role of humanity in relation to God as partners in the process of creation. In constructing his own seemingly antitheodic response to the Shoah, Sweeney reexamines the Golden Calf narrative in Exodus 32–34 by juxtaposing it with "intertexts" from 1 Kings and Leviticus. His aim is to raise questions of divine culpability in the context of Israelite destruction which correspond to the issue of divine vs. human responsibility for genocide during the Shoah.

In his "intertextual," biblical approach to the Holocaust, Sweeny along with other American Jewish and Christian thinkers are now moving beyond the apologetic "extratextual" approach utilized by the first phase of post-Holocaust theologians such as Richard Rubenstein, Eliezer Berkovits, Irving Greenberg and the early Emil Fackenheim, all of whom located religious meaning outside of the biblical text in the essential experience of Jewish suffering that possesses ontological significance. In his 1990 book, The Jewish Bible after the Holocaust, Fackenheim seemed to point to a more postmodern understanding of theological meaning as being produced through the intersection of Jewish and Christian discourses in an ongoing cross-cultural conversation, rather than already existing within the essential experience of one particular religious culture over against another. This is the type of biblical approach to the Holocaust that Tod Linafelt, Marvin Sweeney, Steve Jacobs and others use in Linafelt's edited volume, Strange Fire: Reading the Bible after the Holocaust. This sustained reconsideration of the Hebrew Bible in light of the Holocaust is also reflected in the work of the "Midrash Group" at the Annual Scholars Conference, consisting of Jewish scholars Zev Garber and Steve Jacobs and Christian scholars Henry Knight and James Moore.

Perhaps this new biblical approach reflects the emerging double meaning of the term "post-Holocaust" for American Jewish and liberal Protestant thinkers. On the one hand, in an effort to preserve theological meaning after the Holocaust, they have combined a radical reexamination of God's covenantal role in history, leading up to and following the Shoah with an outright condemnation of Christian theology for its failure to prevent and/or regarding its complicity in the extermination of six million Jews by the Nazis. Yet at the same time, they have begun to move beyond the apologetic discourse created in response to the Holocaust by dismantling the binary and hierarchical opposition between Judaism and Christianity. This illustrates a transition between a post-Holocaust discourse and a postmodern intertextual construction of Jewish identity in relation to Christianity that reveals the truly fragmentary yet contiguous nature of the Jewish-Christian relationship after the Shoah.

Notes

1. On the issue of "secular chosenness," see Biale 156–64, esp. 162–63. See also Cuddihy's discussion of the "metaphoricality of Jewish chosenness" Cherry 140, 142–43.
2. In their discussion of postmodern Jewish philosophy, Kepnes, Gibbs and Ochs distinguish themselves from the post-Holocaust Jewish thinkers, Rubenstein, Fackenheim and Greenberg by arguing that for postmodern Jews, there is "no one 'experience' or event which defines us. . . . be it Emancipation, Holocaust or Zionism." Moreover, they argue that unlike the post-Holocaust theologians, postmodern Jewish philosophers do not allow the Holocaust to shape their construction of Jewish theologies. See Kepnes, Ochs, and Gibbs 40–42.
3. In response to this social ambiguity, Biale raises the question as to whether or not it is appropriate for Jewish scholars to claim to represent Jewish identity objectively as a "subaltern" voice in response to a hegemonic Christian culture. Moreover, he claims that this situation has led to the emergence of a new type of "deconstructive apologetics" that is best illustrated by Jewish feminists who are engaged in a double polemic, one internally waged against the exponents of the patriarchal, rabbinic framework, and one externally enacted against those anti-Jewish feminists who attribute the origin of patriarchy to rabbinic Judaism (177, 184). On this issue, see also Heschel 103–04, 112–13, and Horowitz 119–29.
4. See my discussion of the transition between "extratextual" to "intertextual" approaches to the Holocaust among these thinkers in "Post-Holocaust vs. Postmodern: Emil Fackenheim's Evolving Dialogue with Christianity" 69–72, 89–96.
5. In *Reasoning after Revelation*, Robert Gibbs suggests that the term "post-Holocaust" does not refer to a theology in response to the Holocaust, but rather refers to Jewish scholarly work that follows the discourse of the Holocaust. However, he maintains that for him, the term "postmodern" is not historical, but rather refers to a way of thinking that could develop in many different periods of history. Moreover, Steven Kepnes asserts that the term "post-Holocaust" indicates a new beginning for postmodern Jewish thought following the failed philosophies of the modern period that ". . . married the Jewish notion of divine providence with modern progress and the modern salvific ideologies of socialism and democratic capitalism. . . ." (Kepnes, Ochs and Gibbs 40–42).
6. On the double meaning of "post-Holocaust," see my essay, " 'The Saying' vs. 'The Said': Reconstructing the Post-Holocaust Jewish-Christian Relationship Using Levinas's Theology of the Trace" 292–93.

Works Cited

Biale, David. "Between Polemics and Apologetics: Jewish Studies in the Age of Multiculturalism." Jewish Studies Quarterly 3.2 (1996): 174–84.

———. Power and Powerlessness in Jewish History. New York: Schocken, 1987.

Biale, D., M. Galchinsky, and S. Heschel, eds. Insider/Outsider: American Jews and Multiculturalism. Berkeley; University of California, 1998.

Cuddihy, John Murray. No Offense: Civil Religion and Protestant Taste. New York, Seabury, 1978).

Cherry, C. Conrad. Rev. of No Offense: Civil Religion and Protestant Taste by John Murray Cuddihy. Theology Today 36.1 (April 1979): 140, 142–143.

Fackenheim, Emil. The Jewish Bible after the Holocaust. Bloomington, IL: Indiana UP, 1990.

———. To Mend the World. New York: Schocken, 1982.

Haynes, Stephen R.. Reluctant Witnesses: Jews and the Christian Imagination. Louisville: Westminster John Knox, 1995.

Heschel, Susannah. "Jewish Studies as Counterhistory." Biale, Galchinsky, and Heschel 101–15.

Horowitz, Sara. "The Paradox of Jewish Studies in the New Academy." Biale, Galchinsky, and Heschel 116–30.

Jaffee, M. S. "The Victim-Community in Myth and History: Holocaust Ritual, the Question of Palestine, and the Rhetoric of Christian Witness," Journal of Ecumenical Studies 28.2 (Spring, 1991): 223–38.

Kepnes, Steven, Peter Ochs and Robert Gibbs, eds. Reasoning after Revelation: Dialogues in Postmodern Jewish Philosophy. Boulder: Westview, 1998.

Krell, Marc A. "Post-Holocaust vs. Postmodern: Emil Fackenheim's Evolving Dialogue with Christianity." The Journal of Jewish Thought and Philosophy 12.1 (2003): 69–96.

———. "'The Saying' vs. 'The Said': Reconstructing the Post-Holocaust Jewish-Christian Relationship Using Levinas's Theology of the Trace." Modern Judaism 26.3 (2006): 292–315.

Linafelt, Tod, ed. Strange Fire: Reading the Bible after the Holocaust. New York: New York UP, 2000.

McRobert, L. "Emil L. Fackenheim and Radical Evil: Transcendent, Unsurpassable, Absolute." Journal of the American Academy of Religion 57.2 (Summer, 1989): 325–40.

About the Contributors

LISA ANSELL is Associate Director of the Casden Institute for the Study of the Jewish Role in American Life at the University of Southern California. She received her BA in French and Near East Studies from UCLA and her MA in Middle East Studies from Harvard University. She was the Chair of the World Language Department of New Community Jewish High School for five years before coming to USC in August, 2007.

LAWRENCE BARON has held the Abraham Nasatir Chair in Modern Jewish History at San Diego State University since 1988. He received his PhD in Modern European History from the University of Wisconsin/Madison in 1974 and taught at St. Lawrence University from 1975 until 1988. He is the advisor to the MA Program in History at San Diego State University and directed the university's Jewish Studies program from 1988 until 2006. He authored *Projecting the Holocaust into the Present: The Changing Focus of Contemporary Holocaust Cinema*, and acted as the historian for Sam and Pearl Oliner's *The Altruistic Personality: Rescuers of Jews in Nazi Europe* (1988). He has over sixty articles published in various journals like *Film and History, Holocaust and Genocide Studies, The Journal of Contemporary History, The Lion and the Unicorn, Judaism*, and *Shofar*. He delivered the keynote address at Yad Vashem's first symposium on Holocaust cinema. He is the founder and president of the Western Jewish Studies Association. He currently is writing a book entitled *The Wandering View: Modern Jewish History in World Cinema*.

MICHAEL BERENBAUM is a Professor of Jewish Studies at the American Jewish University and the Executive Editor of the *Encyclopadia Judaica*, Second Edition. He was formerly President and CEO of the Survivors of the Shoah Visual History Foundation and Project Director of the creation of the United States Holocaust Memorial Museum and then Director of its Research Institute.

BETH COHEN received her PhD in Holocaust History from Clark University's Strassler Family Center for Holocaust and Genocide Studies in 2003. After completing her graduate work, she was a "Life Reborn" post-doctoral fellow at the United States Holocaust Memorial Museum, which culminated in her first book, *Case Closed: Holocaust Survivors in Postwar America*. In 2005, she relocated to Los Angeles where she teaches at local universities including UCLA, Chapman University, and California State University, Northridge. Currently she is studying child survivors' experiences in the early postwar years.

ZEV GARBER is Emeritus Professor and Chair of Jewish Studies and Philosophy at Los Angeles Valley College and has served as Visiting Professor of Religious Studies at University of California at Riverside, Visiting Rosenthal Professor of Judaic Studies at Case Western Reserve University, and as President of the National Association of Professors of Hebrew. He is the Founder and Editor-in-Chief of two academic series, Studies in Shoah (UPA) and Shofar Supplements in Jewish Studies (Purdue University Press), and serves as Co-Editor of *Shofar*. His publications include *Methodology in the Academic Teaching of Judaism, Methodology in the Academic Teaching of the Holocaust, Teaching Hebrew Language and Literature at the College Level, Shoah: the Paradigmatic Genocide, Perspectives on Zionism, Peace, In Deed: Essays in Honor of Harry James Cargas* (with Richard Libowitz), *Academic Approaches to Teaching Jewish Studies, Post-Shoah Dialogues: Rethinking Our Texts Together* (with Steven Jacobs, Henry Knight, and James Moore), *Double Takes: Thinking and Rethinking Issues of Modern Judaism in Ancient Contexts* (with Bruce Zuckerman), and *Mel Gibson's Passion: The Film, The Controversy, and Its Implications*. Finally, *Maven in Blue Jeans: A Festschrift in Honor of Zev Garber* is forthcoming from Purdue University Press in 2009.

LEE W. HAAS is a librarian who has worked in Jewish libraries for fifteen years. Currently she is the librarian at Temple Emanu El in Cleveland, Ohio. Previously, Lee was the librarian for the Jewish Federation of Nashville where she directed libraries at four synagogues and the Jewish Community Center. Lee earned a BA in anthropology from the University of Michigan, a master's degree in library science from the University of Pittsburgh, and an MA in anthropology from the University of Cincinnati.

PETER J. HAAS received his BA in Ancient Near East History from the University of Michigan in 1970 and then attended Hebrew Union College in Cincinnati, where he was ordained as a Reform rabbi in 1974. After ordination, he served as an active United States Army chaplain for three years. Upon completion of active duty, Rabbi Haas enrolled in the graduate program in religion at Brown University, earning a PhD in Jewish Studies in 1980. Joining the faculty at Vanderbilt University in 1980, he taught courses in Judaism, Jewish ethics, the Holocaust, Western religion, and the Middle East Conflict. He joined the faculty of the Department of Religious Studies at Case Western Reserve University in January, 2000, and was appointed chair of the department in 2003. He is also a visiting professor at the Spertus Institute of Jewish Studies in Chicago, Illinois. Prof. Haas has published several books and articles dealing with moral discourse and with Jewish and Christian thought after the Holocaust. He has lectured in the United States, Germany, Italy, Belgium and Israel. His most recent work is on human rights in Judaism.

STEVEN LEONARD JACOBS holds the Aaron Aronov Endowed Chair in Judaic Studies at the University of Alabama where he is also an Associate Professor of Religious Studies. He received his BA from Penn State, his BHL, MAHL, DHL, and rabbinic ordination from the Hebrew Union College-Jewish Institute of Religion. He is the author, editor, and/translator of more than sixteen books and fifty-plus articles in his primary fields of research: biblical studies (Hebrew Bible and New Testament), the Holocaust/Shoah, and historical and contemporary genocides. He is a member of numerous academic and professional organizations and currently serves as the 1st Vice President of the International Association of Genocide Scholars.

MARC A. KRELL teaches Judaic Studies at The Dr. Miriam and Sheldon G. Adelson Educational Campus in Las Vegas, Nevada. He received his PhD in The Cultural and Historical Studies of Religions at the Graduate Theological Union in Berkeley, California in 1998 after receiving an MA in Judaic Studies at the American Jewish University (formerly University of Judaism) in Los Angeles in 1991. Previously he held academic positions at the University of Arizona Center for Judaic Studies and the University of California, Riverside Department of Religious Studies. He is the author of *Intersecting Pathways: Modern Jewish Theologians in Conversation with Christianity*. His articles have appeared in such journals as *Cross Currents, Journal of Ecumenical Studies, Shofar, The Journal of Jewish Thought and Philosophy, Modern Judaism* and *Zeitschrift für Religions- und Geistesgeschichte*. He is currently preparing a new manuscript for publication entitled, "Building on the Past: Toward a Postmodern Jewish-Christian Theology after the Holocaust." His research interests include Jewish-Christian Relations, Modern Jewish Thought, Post-Holocaust Theology, and Postmodern constructions of Jewish identity.

RICHARD LIBOWITZ teaches in the Intellectual Heritage Program at Temple University and the Theology Department of Saint Joseph's University. The author/editor of nine books, including *Faith and Freedom: A Tribute to Franklin H. Littell* and *Mordecai M. Kaplan and the Development of Reconstructionism*, he has also contributed chapters and essays to many other volumes and has lectured on Holocaust-related topics throughout the United States, Israel, Germany and England. His current project is a study of Holocaust story telling in print and film.

JEREMY SCHOENBERG, when co-editing this volume, was Assistant Director of the USC Casden Institute, where he managed lectures and conferences, public relations, and campus-wide and community partnerships. He continues to work at USC, now as Executive Assistant in the Office of the Provost, where he helps manage several initiatives and projects. Holder of a Bachelor of Music degree from USC and a Master of Music degree from California State University, Northridge, both in voice performance, Mr. Schoenberg has performed throughout the Los Angeles area and toured much of the United States. For almost ten years, he has served as tenor soloist at Sinai Temple in Los Angeles, and he is currently pursuing an MBA at the USC Marshall School of Business.

MARVIN A. SWEENEY is Professor of Hebrew Bible at the Claremont School of Theology and Professor of Religion at the Claremont Graduate University. He also serves as Professor of Bible and Faculty Co-Chair at the Academy for Jewish Religion, California, and as Chief Executive Officer of the Ancient Biblical Manuscript Center for Preservation and Research. He has previously taught at the University of Miami, and has held research or visiting appointments at the Hebrew University of Jerusalem, the W. F. Albright Institute for Archaeological Research, the Lilly Theological Research Fund, the Institute for Antiquity and Christianity, and the Hebrew Union College-Jewish Institute of Religion, Los Angeles. He is the author of some ten volumes, most recently, *Reading the Hebrew Bible after the Shoah: Engaging Holocaust Theology*. He is currently writing a study focused on Jewish biblical theology.

STEVEN WINDMUELLER serves as Dean of the Los Angeles campus of Hebrew Union College-Jewish Institute of Religion. A specialist on political issues and American Jewish affairs, Dr. Windmueller holds a doctorate in International Relations from the University of Pennsylvania. Over the years his more than thirty articles and monographs have appeared in such publications as the *Los Angeles Times*, *Sh'ma* and *Moment Magazines*, the *Jerusalem Letter*, and the *Journal of Jewish Communal Service*. His Pew-funded research on the major national Jewish community relations agencies appeared in a recent publication, *Jewish Polity and American Civil Society: Communal Agencies and Religious Movements in the American Public Square*. In 2004, he produced a textbook on the practice of Jewish community relations, entitled *You Shall Not Stand Idly By*, published by the American Jewish Committee. In early 2005, Dr. Windmueller collaborated with Professor Gerald Bubis in producing the first study on the formation of the UJC (United Jewish Communities), entitled *Predictability to Chaos?? How American Jewish Leaders Reinvented their National Jewish Communal System*.

BRUCE ZUCKERMAN is the Myron and Marian Casden Director of the Casden Institute and a Professor of Religion at USC, where he teaches courses in the Hebrew Bible, the Bible in western literature, the ancient Near East, and archaeology. A specialist in photographing and reconstructing ancient texts, he is involved in numerous projects related to the Dead Sea Scrolls. On ancient topics, his major publications are *Job the Silent: A Study in Biblical Counterpoint* and *The Leningrad Codex: A Facsimile Edition*, for which he and his brother Kenneth did the principal photography. Zuckerman also has a continuing interest in modern Jewish thought, often looking at modern issues from an ancient perspective. He most recently co-authored *Double Takes: Thinking and Rethinking Issues of Modern Judaism in Ancient Contexts* with Zev Garber and contributed a chapter to Garber's book, *Mel Gibson's Passion: The Film, the Controversy, and Its Implications*.

The USC Casden Institute for the Study of the Jewish Role in American Life

The American Jewish community has played a vital role in shaping the politics, culture, commerce and multiethnic character of Southern California and the American West. Beginning in the mid-nineteenth century, when entrepreneurs like Isaias Hellman, Levi Strauss and Adolph Sutro first ventured out West, American Jews became a major force in the establishment and development of the budding Western territories. Since 1970, the number of Jews in the West has more than tripled. This dramatic demographic shift has made California—specifically, Los Angeles—home to the second largest Jewish population in the United States. Paralleling this shifting pattern of migration, Jewish voices in the West are today among the most prominent anywhere in the United States. Largely migrating from Eastern Europe, the Middle East and the East Coast of the United States, Jews have invigorated the West, where they exert a considerable presence in every sector of the economy—most notably in the media and the arts. With the emergence of Los Angeles as a world capital in entertainment and communications, the Jewish perspective and experience in the region are being amplified further. From artists and activists to scholars and professionals, Jews are significantly influencing the shape of things to come in the West and across the United States. In recognition of these important demographic and societal changes, in 1998 the University of Southern California established a scholarly institute dedicated to studying contemporary Jewish life in America with special emphasis on the western United States. The Casden Institute explores issues related to the interface between the Jewish community and the broader, multifaceted cultures that form the nation—issues of relationship as much as of Jewishness itself. It is also enhancing the educational experience for students at USC and elsewhere by exposing them to the problems—and promise—of life in Los Angeles' ethnically, socially, culturally and economically diverse community. Scholars, students and community leaders examine the ongoing contributions of American Jews in the arts, business, media, literature, education, politics, law and social relations, as well as the relationships between Jewish Americans and other groups, including African Americans,

Latinos, Asian Americans and Arab Americans. The Casden Institute's scholarly orientation and contemporary focus, combined with its location on the West Coast, set it apart from—and makes it an important complement to—the many excellent Jewish Studies programs across the nation that center on Judaism from an historical or religious perspective.

For more information about the USC Casden Institute,
visit www.usc.edu/casdeninstitute, e-mail casden@usc.edu,
or call (213) 740-3405.

www.ingramcontent.com/pod-product-compliance
Lightning Source LLC
Chambersburg PA
CBHW061956180426
43198CB00036B/1280